FORTY MINUTES
OF HELL

ALSO BY RUS BRADBURD

Paddy on the Hardwood: A Journey in Irish Hoops

FORTY MINUTES
OF HELL

THE EXTRAORDINARY LIFE OF NOLAN RICHARDSON

RUS BRADBURD

AMISTAD

An Imprint of HarperCollins*Publishers*

HarperCollins books may be purchased for educational, business, or sales promotional use. For information, please write: Special Markets Department, HarperCollins Publishers, 10 East 53rd Street, New York, NY 10022.

FIRST EDITION

Designed by Lisa Stokes

Library of Congress Cataloging-in-Publication Data
Bradburd, Rus, 1959–
    Forty minutes of hell : the extraordinary life of Nolan Richardson / Rus Bradburd. — 1st ed.
        p.   cm.
    Summary: "An exploration of the politics of race and sports in elite college basketball programs, from the Jim Crow era until today, witnessed through the life of African-American basketball coach and NCAA title winner Nolan Richardson, who took the University of Arkansas to back-to-back Final Four appearances in the 1990s"—Provided by publisher.
    ISBN 978-0-06-169046-4
    1. Richardson, Nolan. 2. Basketball coaches—United States—Biography. 3. Discrimination in sports. 4. Racism in sports. I. Title.
GV884.R525B73   2010
796.323092—dc22
[B]
                                                                            2009030440

10 11 12 13 14   OV/RRD   10 9 8 7 6 5 4 3 2 1

For Bobby Joe Hill and Ricky Cardenas
For Bob Walters and Darrell Brown
For Alma Bradburd and Yvonne Richardson

CONTENTS

FORTY MINUTES
OF HELL

SOUL ON ICE

My great-great-grandfather came over on the ship," Nolan Richardson said. "I did not come over on that ship. So I expect to be treated a little bit different."

With television cameras and tape recorders rolling, Richardson began giving the people of Arkansas and America a history lesson, although his purpose was not entirely clear. This was supposed to be another ordinary press conference—that's what most journalists had expected—and a briefing on an upcoming game was the norm. Reporters arrived Monday afternoon, February 25, 2002, figuring that Richardson might still be discouraged after Saturday's loss at Kentucky. Richardson had said that night: "If they go ahead and pay me my money, they can take the job tomorrow." Since then, there had been whispers that perhaps the coach was getting ready to retire.

That would have been big news for Razorback basketball fans. Richardson had coached Arkansas to the landmark 1994 NCAA championship. With nearly four hundred wins at Arkansas, he had earned two additional Final Four appearances, led Arkansas to thirteen NCAA Tournaments, and could brag of one of the highest winning percentages in college hoops in the 1990s. Arguably the top black coach in America, Richardson was the first black coach in the old Confederacy at a mostly white university, as well as the first to win the national championship at a Southern school.

On this Monday, however, less than a decade removed from that national title, Richardson would become the kamikaze coach.

After seventeen seasons, he was still the only black coach in any sport at the University of Arkansas, and that bothered him. "I know for a fact that I do not play on the same level as the other coaches around this school play on," he said. "I know that. You know it. And people of my color know that. And that angers me." Richardson glanced toward the door, as if all twenty white head coaches of the other Arkansas Razorback sports were lined up outside.

The journalists scratched their heads in wonder, shifted in their seats. It was a bizarre session, they thought, but not a fatal one for Richardson. The media had heard him rant, privately, about their coverage of him and his program. That kind of complaining is common among college coaches, but on this occasion, the topic veered erratically from basketball.

It was clear that Richardson wanted to talk about race.

He surveyed the media room at the Bud Walton Arena, and pointed out that everyone except him was white. "When I look at all of you people in this room," he said, "I see no one who looks like me, talks like me, or acts like me. Now why don't you recruit? Why don't the editors recruit like I'm recruiting?" The collection of media representatives swallowed hard or scribbled in their notebooks. Although he was not shouting, he used the righteous tone of an Old Testament prophet. Richardson was a bear of a man—6'3" and, at the time, close to 230 pounds—as much a linebacker as a basketball coach. He stood alone on the podium, wearing a flaming-red Arkansas pullover, and the banner behind would frame him in the same color for television viewers.

On that day, Richardson's Arkansas Razorbacks were 13-13 overall—not the kind of season that normally could be called a disaster.
Richardson said as much. "I've earned the right to have the kind of season I'm having." That was likely true. However, it was Richardson's worst
stretch since he took the job in Fayetteville. Arkansas was 5-9 in the
Southeastern Conference and had lost nine of their past twelve games.

It would be difficult to exaggerate Richardson's cachet at the
school, but the coach seemed to do just that, essentially claiming
the reason recruits—basketball and football—came to Arkansas was
because of him. "The number one thing that's talked [about] in our
deal is the fact that the greatest thing going for the University of
Arkansas is Nolan Richardson."

Richardson had kept his program, practices, and locker room
open to every reporter, but not anymore. "Do not call me ever on my
phone, none of you, at my home ever again," he added. "Those lines
are no longer open for communications with me."

Richardson must have believed his job was on the line, and yet
it seemed as though he both wanted and did not want to remain at
Arkansas. He made it clear he would not walk away; that wasn't what
he'd meant two days earlier in Kentucky. "I've dealt with it for seventeen years," he said, "and I'll deal with it for seventeen more. Because
that's my makeup. Where would I go?"

Nobody in the media had suggested he should be terminated,
but Richardson accused them of it anyway. "So maybe that's what
you want," he said. "Because you know what? Ol' granny told me,
'Nobody runs you anywhere, Nolan.' I know that. See, my great-
great-grandfather came over here on the ship. I didn't, and I don't
think you understand what I'm saying."

Then Richardson wheeled, confronted the cameras, and ended the
speech by saying, "You can run that on every TV show in America."

A question-and-answer session followed. No journalists asked
questions about race, or ships, or his grandmother. The first query:
Had he watched the tape of the Kentucky game?

"I thought it would blow over," one veteran Arkansas journalist says. "No way did I think Nolan was going to get fired. Sure, he bristled, but mostly it was surreal, bizarre."

It might have blown over but the highlights, if you can call them that, were indeed run on television shows across the country. The quotes most often broadcast were the most confusing. Why was Richardson referring to his grandmother? And what ships? He must have meant slave ships.

The highlights ran again and again.

The story grew legs: a rich and famous black man was lecturing a roomful of white media about race, reminding Arkansas, and then America, about its racist past.

Several subsequent newspaper and online accounts emphasized how obsessed Richardson had been with race throughout his career. *Sports Illustrated* called the press conference ". . . a bewildering self-immolation."

The endless cycling of the clips brought national attention to the most perplexing forty minutes in college basketball history. How could a black man who was so prosperous come across as so ungrateful?

Of all the basketball coaches who have won national championships, none had the deck stacked against him like Nolan Richardson. He grew up in the poorest neighborhood in America's most remote city; not one black man was working the sidelines in major college basketball when he began coaching high school in 1967.

Richardson was an innovator whose teams performed at a frantic and furious pace. His style of play was nicknamed "Forty Minutes of Hell."

Facing a Richardson team was physically and psychologically exhausting. He recruited players who were overlooked and had plenty to prove; then he conditioned them with a regimen of near-brutality until they were as hard and sharp as swords. During breaks in practice, between workouts, before games and at halftime, his speeches made it clear to his team that no one in the basketball hierarchy respected him—or any of them—and the only possible retribution for the snub had to be found on the basketball court. By game time they were so emotionally wired they seemed to give off sparks.

While most coaches separated their systems into offense and defense, Richardson saw the game as flowing turmoil. Substitutions came often, sometimes en masse, and the rapid rotation of players contributed to the sense that the game was descending into chaos.

His players exerted defensive pressure the entire length of the court, attacking the ball the instant it was passed into play and dogging the dribbler's every step. Traps came quickly and constantly, but rarely at a moment that could be anticipated.

If the opponent managed to split the trap or escape the press with a precise pass, the illusion of an advantage would present itself, and that momentary mirage could be their undoing because Richardson's team had badgered them into playing at a speed at which they were unaccustomed. Endurance became paramount as his platoons of substitutes weighed heavily on the backs of his opponents. His five players were locked in relentless pursuit—pursuit of the dribbler, pursuit of the pass, pursuit of the missed shot, pursuit of the coach's approval. The thronging defense further frustrated the opponent's attack when his players rotated quickly after the double-teams. If his men made a steal, it was often because a forgotten guard trailing the play refused to give up and tipped the ball from behind. They would overcome players ahead of them, overcome halftime disadvantages, overcome their (often imaginary) underdog status.

At times it appeared Richardson must have six players on the nightmarishly cramped court. After a missed shot or a steal, though, when they converted to their fast-breaking offense, the court instantly felt as wide open as a West Texas freeway.

Like his press, the half-court offense was unpredictable by design. His teams slashed, penetrated, and attacked the basket before the opponent could establish their defense. A diagram of his system on a chalkboard looked like a Jackson Pollock painting.

Purists and traditionalists found "Forty Minutes of Hell" to be a violation of everything they'd learned about the sport. It was as if Richardson's teams wanted to destroy the very decorum of the game. And that was indeed precisely what his teams wanted—to confiscate the traditional etiquette of a college basketball game and snap its neck.

Richardson was an instinctive genius who disdained basketball's textbook theories, but he was rarely credited as a brilliant teacher, and this rekindled the resentment: when he was disrespected, his players were also implicated. The only way to shed the shackles and undo the affront was to play the next game as if their very existence depended on it. In this fashion, the paradigm was endlessly renewed.

How was it possible that this pioneering coach, winner of the national championship, whose style of play had altered the way college basketball was played, was going to be most remembered for a press conference?

ONE

A BEWITCHED CROSSROAD

On March 1, 2002, Nolan Richardson was terminated by the University of Arkansas. I was finishing a graduate degree at the time, after ending my own modest career in college basketball. Burned out, I stayed away from the game. Two NCAA Tournaments had come and gone, and I had not watched a single minute. I could not, however, avert my eyes from the train wreck Nolan Richardson's career had become, and I read as much as possible about his fantastic fall. Nearly every piece said that Richardson had brought on his own firing. The coaches I talked to—the white ones, anyway—wanted to know what a guy making that kind of money had to complain about.

Richardson seemed unable to move beyond 1968, determined to fight a war most Americans believed had ended long ago.

To understand Richardson's mindset, I knew I'd have to seriously examine the two most influential people in his professional career. Both of these men were icons in the world of college athletics, but they couldn't have been more different.

One, Don Haskins, was Richardson's own basketball coach, who accidentally began the avalanche that was the desegregation of college basketball teams. The other, Frank Broyles, was Richardson's boss at the University of Arkansas.

A photograph of Nolan Richardson hung above my desk at the University of Texas–El Paso for eight years. My assistant coaching job kept me on the phone constantly, so there was plenty of time to study that photo of Richardson, with TEXAS WESTERN across his chest, soaring above some anonymous white player. Richardson was an El Paso native, who finished his playing career in 1963, the photo's caption said. I wasn't one of those people who thought basketball had much to do with a person's character, but the photo revealed something. Power, maybe. Nerve and confidence. Aggression.

UTEP (Texas Western College until 1967) had a compelling basketball history. Every wall in the basketball office was adorned with black-and-white action shots of players who had survived the decades of Don Haskins's harrowing discipline. These guys had magical names that *sounded* like they were basketball players. Willie Cager. Bobby Joe Hill and "Big Daddy" Lattin. Tiny Archibald and "Bad News" Barnes.

I had stumbled onto that job at UTEP in 1983, an entry-level graduate assistant under the Miners' coach Don Haskins. Haskins was a cult figure then because he had stunned the world of college basketball by upsetting Kentucky for the NCAA title in 1966. What got people excited wasn't simply the shock of a remote school beating a traditional power. The focus was on race. Haskins played only his black players in that final game.

No team in the Southwest Conference, where nearly all the big Texas schools competed, had ever suited up a single black player. Texas Western, however, was an independent with no conference affiliation.

The championship game had been dominated by black athletes before 1966. In 1963, Loyola beat Cincinnati for the national title. Loyola started four black players, Cincinnati three. But as chance would have it in 1966, Texas Western's Miners faced Kentucky, who had never dressed out a black player. Kentucky's entire league, the Southeast Conference, was segregated.

Given that the 1960s were an era of protest, it is tempting to interpret Haskins's move as a political statement. It wasn't. The Black Power movement of the 1960s didn't alter Haskins one bit. He was hard on his players before, during, and after, and wasn't exactly poring over the writings of Eldridge Cleaver. Haskins, who won over seven hundred games during his tenure at El Paso, was distinctly apolitical, and his only quest was to smother opponents with stifling defense. Both in interviews and during private conversation, he insisted that he merely started his best five players.

Haskins's nickname was "The Bear," and he seemed to have ridden on horseback out of the pages of a Cormac McCarthy novel. He preferred shooting pool, smoking, tavern life, and hunting quail to schmoozing with corporate types or doing television interviews. His speech was peppered with Southwestern cowboy-isms, and he rarely asked a question to which he didn't already know the answer. Making big money was of little interest to Haskins, and only once was he even offered another job.

During my eight seasons at UTEP, I became an unofficial expert in the history of the basketball team. Forty years after their historic victory, the 1966 El Paso team would become the subject of the movie *Glory Road*. At the movie's premiere, two ushers shushed me as I pointed out the numerous factual errors in the film.

In fact, the 1966 championship brought Haskins plenty of aggravation. *Sports Illustrated*, in a 1968 series called "The Black Athlete," attacked Haskins for his black players' graduation rate. Then James Michener, in his book *Sports in America*, repeated the claims: none of the black players had graduated. Both *Sports Illustrated* and Michener were off base—all but two of the entire championship team earned degrees—but Haskins's reputation suffered.

I lucked out my first year recruiting at UTEP by finding an unknown point guard out of Chicago, named Tim Hardaway. After college, Hardaway would play thirteen NBA seasons and appear in five NBA All Star games. We signed him early, and I got a reputation for being an astute judge of talent.

Hardaway's high school coach was a guy named Bob Walters. Many blacks in Chicago have ties to Mississippi's Delta; that's how the blues came to Chicago, on the backs of musicians such as Muddy Waters and Howlin' Wolf. But Walters was not from Mississippi. He was from Prescott, Arkansas. Walters had an unusually clear memory of watching the 1966 Texas Western championship and knew details about that historic match-up that only real students of the game could possibly recall.

I would smile sheepishly when people said nabbing Hardaway was a brilliant move. The talk about my shrewd evaluations was flattering; my modesty, however, was genuine. It was beginner's luck. Hardaway took just one other campus visit before signing early at UTEP, fifteen hundred miles from Chicago. I never analyzed our good fortune in landing Hardaway, or the enthusiasm Bob Walters had for UTEP.

Once an older fan, a friend of Haskins, walked in and tapped his knuckles to the photo of Richardson, who was by then a successful college coach.

"He won't shut up about racism," the man said. "Everything is black or white to Nolan Richardson."

That take on Richardson proved to be a common point of view. Even Don Haskins, the Abe Lincoln of college hoops, was occasionally perplexed when Richardson would challenge the newest SAT requirements or media coverage as racist.

I followed Richardson's coaching career closely—he was an older uncle in my new UTEP family. We met a few times, on rental car shuttles, at junior college tournaments, or at airports. In the 1985 NCAA playoffs, UTEP played his Tulsa team. But Richardson's daughter was sick, and he didn't get to the game until minutes before tip-off. We beat Tulsa that night in a fairly close game, and we got a little help from the referees since UTEP set the NCAA record for "Most Free Throws Attempted." It was not the kind of record that impresses anyone, but it was something Richardson emphasized to me when I first began interviewing him twenty years later. Fifty-five free throws UTEP shot that night, he said. He was exactly right, as it turned out, but who remembers getting screwed after two decades?

TWO

BLACK BOY

El Paso, Texas, was known as El Paso del Norte until the late 1850s. A gap between the Franklin Mountains and the Sierra de Juárez allowed travelers a convenient route to journey east to west. Because of this geographical advantage, the border town below attracted nomads and newcomers, and some boundaries blurred.

Black men could find work because four separate railroad lines ran through El Paso at the turn of the century. The railroads provided jobs as well as access. El Paso, at the edge of U.S. territory, was relatively open to working black men and even had a Negro Women's League. Plenty of social and legal pressures, however, kept the races apart, especially black men and white women. In 1893, the state of Texas enacted a law that prohibited interracial marriage.

No obvious black neighborhood existed in El Paso in the early 1900s, and there isn't one today. By the time Richardson was old enough to attend school, close to four thousand blacks lived in El Paso—a mere 3 percent of the population. Some lived near the army base, and others lived close to the border, near downtown. All black children had to attend Frederick Douglass Colored School, which opened around 1890.

In 1911, the school's principal introduced Booker T. Washington, founder of the Tuskegee Institute, to a packed house at the El Paso Theater. That day, Booker T. Washington urged blacks not to fight the forces of segregation and instead to accommodate whites based on their mutual interests—economics. This idea played well in El Paso, a town where blacks were treated a little better than in most of Texas. Around that same time, a chapter of the NAACP formed in El Paso.

The Ku Klux Klan moved into El Paso soon afterward and exerted a growing influence over city hall and El Paso's biggest newspaper.

Nolan Richardson's mother, Clareast, was just twenty-one years old when she withered away from a mysterious disease in 1944. The family was living in Los Angeles, and had little access to medical care. Clareast Richardson left behind three young kids: Shirley was five, Nolan Jr. three, Helen six months old. The Richardson kids had few options but to move in with the children's grandmother in El Paso's poorest neighborhood, the Segundo Barrio.

For years, the Segundo Barrio was the Ellis Island for many Mexican immigrants coming to the United States. Despite the constant influx of newcomers, the neighborhood had a settled and historic feel. Low-slung adobe buildings, hand-painted storefronts, blaring *norteño* music, and lively street life dominated El Paso's second ward.

Nolan's father, Nolan Richardson Sr., had a sporadic career as a prizefighter. He lived in El Paso on and off, working at a car dealership when he was in town. While he stopped by to visit his kids after their relocation, he didn't often live with the family. He battled the bottle much of his adult life.

That left the responsibility of raising Clareast's three kids to their grandmother, Rose Richardson—"Ol' Mama." Ol' Mama was from just outside of Ruston, Louisiana, but had moved to El Paso in her youth. She worked two jobs: one as a cook at Hardees, a family restaurant on Alameda Street; the other waitressing around El Paso.

Richardson's grandfather—Ol' Papa, of course—was a huge man, whose health was already declining when the grandkids moved in. He was born in 1875, ten years before Ol' Mama. He gave young Nolan the nickname "Sam." Sometimes he was "Sweet Sam" and sometimes "Sam Don't Give a Damn."

The expanded family resided in a three-room house, well before the days when air-conditioning made El Paso tolerable. The house was at 1626 Overland Street, a short walk from the downtown bridge that connected El Paso to Juárez, Mexico. Ol' Mama was a peculiarly determined and serious woman, and she made no secret of her belief that young Nolan Jr. was special. She reminded him constantly that he was going to be different from other kids, and she very much meant it. Richardson is still struck today by the bond he had with his stern, diminutive grandmother, despite the fact that the extended family was large. "I had the feeling that she loved *me* more," he says.

The gritty pocket of the Segundo Barrio where Richardson became fluent in border Spanish was called El Pujido. The area was plagued by poverty, but Richardson insists he was never hassled in the Mexican-American neighborhood, despite being the only black boy around.

Outsiders believed the El Paso neighborhood the Richardsons lived in was treacherous, but he only feared two things: Ol' Mama's disapproval, or, worse, her leaving him. His cousins would go out of town for Christmas. Not Richardson. "I'd stay around Ol' Mama because I was afraid when I came back she might be gone," he says. Richardson would sit at her feet and badger her to tell him stories.

When he was small, this meant Bible stories. "I knew the Bible better than any churchgoing friends of mine," he says.

She'd also tell Richardson about her own parents.

Ol' Mama was born in 1885; her parents had been enslaved in Louisiana. This one-person separation from that history had a profound impact on Richardson. "I grew up hearing stories about what slavery was like," he says. "Not from any *book*," he says, a refrain he'd use in his professional life, "but from my grandmother, whose very parents had lived it." A story that stuck with him was about one of the few ways a slave had to rebel: inflicting an injury on himself.

It began to register with Richardson that being black was something of consequence one day, when he was ten years old, at El Paso's Washington Park.

The El Paso summer heat can be devastating, and in the 1940s and 1950s, the only relief was at the local swimming pools. Richardson already knew he was not allowed to swim at the Segundo Barrio's Armijo Park pool: they had a no-Negroes rule. Ol' Mama figured they'd try at Washington Park, where black kids were allowed—one single afternoon a year.

The blistering sun made it almost too hot to stand in place on the cement deck that day. Not that the barefoot kids would have stood still—they sprinted before slanting a dive or cannonball into the cool, blue water.

Occasionally, a splash reached close to Richardson's sneakered feet. He kept his fingers wrapped in a fist around the fencing that kept him from the swimming pool. The yelping of the white children was joyous, but he didn't smile. He could feel the intense heat rise up from the bottom of his shoes, as if the rubber might melt and he'd be stuck watching the swimmers forever. It was over one hundred degrees, as it often was in El Paso.

The dozens of white kids didn't notice him. They shoved and

dunked each other amiably, then ran up close enough to him that it was nearly impolite of them not to say hello, or come on in, the water's fine.

Richardson knew they'd gotten the day wrong, but stood for a while anyway. It was June of 1951, but not Juneteenth, the unofficial holiday that celebrated the end of slavery in Texas. Juneteenth was the single day each year when black kids were allowed to swim. "They'd drain the pool afterward," he says, "and fill it up fresh again."

Richardson often recalls this swimming-pool story when he talks about growing up in El Paso. "Lots of people think that because Texas Western won the national championship in 1966 that El Paso was always a progressive town," he says. "But that's not true." El Paso's theaters, restaurants, and hotels were segregated as well. Mexican-Americans were welcome most places, but blacks were not.

Once-a-summer swimming in El Paso's blazing heat wasn't enough to cool him off. He found the Missouri Street Center, the only pool where black and Mexican-American kids could swim all summer. As he got older, if Richardson felt frustrated in the lagging-behind Texas town, he would head south. With the border only a baseball-throw away, he crossed into Mexico at will by the time he was a teenager. "In Juárez, I always felt freer," he says. "My Spanish was nearly as good as my English, and the folks in Mexico didn't seem the least bit concerned with a young black kid exploring the streets."

When Richardson was twelve, his father died. His grandfather, Ol' Papa, passed away soon after. With the men in his life gone, he grew even closer with Ol' Mama.

Frederick Douglass School was a small building on Eucalyptus Street that housed close to a hundred students. Because of a lack of space and teachers, every classroom served several grades, from first to twelfth. The books were ragged hand-me-downs from El Paso's white schools and included the long list of previous owners' names on the books' inside covers. Yet, by all accounts, Douglass had talented teachers and was the unifying institution for El Paso blacks. It wasn't exactly idyllic, but Douglass provided Richardson with both a sense of place and history.

The social scene for blacks in El Paso, formed at Douglass School, was limited but lively. Shiloh Baptist Church was a hub, as were places like Rusty's Playhouse, Gillespie's Steak House, and the Square Deal Barbershop.

On one scorching afternoon, when Richardson was thirteen, a teacher named Mrs. Johnnie Calvert closed the doors and windows. That got the attention of everyone in the class. "We knew that something important was up," Richardson says.

Mrs. Calvert cleared her throat and spoke softly to her subdued class. "There's going to be a big change coming to this country," she said. "Soon, Negro children and white children will be going to school together, and all of you will have a choice to make." There was a Supreme Court case, the teacher said, in which a Negro family had challenged the laws, hoping their daughter could go to the same school as the white kids. The Douglass students looked at each other but didn't speak. "You can stay at Douglass, or you can go to the school in your neighborhood," Mrs. Calvert said.

Douglass School's 1954 valedictorian, Thelma White, decided to test that Supreme Court decision. With the help of the local NAACP, she applied at Texas Western College, but was denied admission. She took Texas Western to court and won. The following year, she was admitted, along with twelve other black students. But Thelma White, put off by the snub and subsequent delays, had enrolled at nearby New Mexico State University by the time the case was decided.

George McCarty, the Texas Western basketball coach at the time, realized that the college's decision to admit blacks might be used to his advantage. He signed up a junior college player named Charlie Brown in 1956 to be the first black athlete at any mainly white school in the old Confederacy. Richardson, a high school freshman, was intrigued by the news.

El Paso during this era was torn. While the influence of the Klan had long faded, this was still Texas. The town remained segregated and blacks had to ride in the back of city buses and trolleys. Unlike most of the South, though, blacks could shop and feel welcome at premier places, such as the Popular and White House Department Store. They could even try on clothes and hats before making a purchase, something that was denied them all over the South.

The peculiar combination Richardson absorbed—the community and tradition at Douglass School, and his soulful Mexican neighborhood—gave him a unique view of the world. Richardson was the only Douglass student who lived in the Pujido section, part of the Bowie High School district. Bowie was virtually one hundred percent Mexican-American. That didn't worry Richardson. He chose Bowie and became their first black student. "All the kids I'd known forever from the barrio were going to Bowie," he says, "and I knew I'd be fine. I didn't have any kind of chip on my shoulder, because in that neighborhood, I was just Sam."

Richardson loved nearly everything about his time at Bowie. "The Mexican kids treated me so well," he says. "I was an athlete, of course, and that helped."

There were some problems before Richardson established himself as a sports hero, though. During his freshman year, he was called to the main office by an assistant principal, named, of all things, Patton. "Raymond Patton," Richardson recalls. "And he was mean."

Richardson looked down, shuffling in place as Patton chewed him out for an overdue library book. "You're not allowed back in school until this fine is paid and I see your parents," Patton said.

Richardson made the long trek home in the heat to tell Ol' Mama. She grabbed her purse, and the two walked back to Bowie to meet Patton.

"How much do you owe?" Ol' Mama asked midway to the high school.

"Six cents," Richardson said.

Ol' Mama's pace quickened. When they got to Patton's office, Ol' Mama went on the attack, insisting to Patton that the punishment didn't fit the crime. Richardson, who often stared at his shoes when confronted by authority, was quietly thrilled that Ol' Mama had straightened out the most feared faculty member in the building. He didn't expect what happened when they got outside the office.

Ol' Mama turned on Richardson and let him have it, too. "I saw you looking down at the ground in there," she said, poking him in the chest. "Don't you ever put your head down in front of anyone. You look every man in the eye, I don't care what color he is!"

Richardson offered to escort her home, but she declined, and ordered him back to class. But not until she gave him one more earful. "You don't like yourself," she said. "Don't be staring down at the floor ever again."

Richardson, who was fourteen at the time, sees this episode as a crossroads in his life. "She had given me permission to be a man," he says.

As a teenager, Nolan began to see more of El Paso. He had friends who owned *ranflas*, and they wanted to drive these jalopies to investigate more than the town's swimming pools.

"I think my first shock was trying to go to the movies, and seeing how the different theaters operated," Richardson says. "Movies were our biggest form of entertainment, but nearly all of the theaters were for whites only." At the Mission Theater, blacks could sit in the balcony. The Alcazar Theater was the only integrated movie house in El Paso until Richardson attended college, although the army base sometimes hosted integrated audiences at movies then, too. Occasionally, his Mexican-American friends had to be reminded that Richardson couldn't go everywhere they were allowed.

Mexican-Americans viewed Richardson as one of their own, and his status as an unofficial Mexican had its benefits—with perhaps one drawback. "The treatment my dad received from Mexican-Americans is very different than the way he was received by whites," his daughter Madalyn says. "Still, I don't think El Paso's Mexican people fully understood the racial discrimination he was fighting against. It was different for him as a black man. But that's because the Mexican people never assigned the color black to his skin."

During Richardson's history class his junior year at Bowie, a teacher told the students about a high school in the South where the Negro students were having problems. The National Guard had been called in to help a handful of Negro kids enroll at the all-white Central High School. Nine of them, mostly girls, came to Central, and some of those girls had been spit on, even by their classmates.

This was in Arkansas, the teacher said. Then she pulled down a tattered map and reminded the students where Arkansas was. Girls being threatened and spit upon? Richardson didn't know whether to weep or fight.

That night, he and his grandmother went across the street to a neighbor's to see Arkansas on the evening news. "All these troops were coming in, and their governor was on, too," Richardson recalls, "talking bad about President Eisenhower. Nothing like that had ever happened at Bowie. Until that day in class, there was no reason to talk about what was happening in Arkansas. Now I was frightened, scared of Arkansas, Mississippi, places like that. Ol' Mama said it was horrible there for black folks."

Fearing Ol' Mama's fierce glare, Richardson took school seriously, and developed other talents besides athletics. He played the dented trumpet issued by the school for marching band, except during football season. "The coach wouldn't let me march during the halftime shows," he says.

As a young boy, Richardson idolized Rocky Galarza, a Segundo Barrio legend with movie-star good looks. Ten years Richardson's senior, Galarza was one of the heroes on Bowie's state championship baseball team of 1949. Galarza had encouraged him to attend Bowie, emphasizing what a great leader Nemo Herrera was. Herrera coached baseball and basketball at Bowie and was regarded as the godfather of El Paso coaches.

Richardson would surpass Galarza's accomplishments, being named All-City in football, basketball, and baseball. In one basketball game, Richardson sank an incredible twenty-four baskets, missing just five shots.

The spring of Richardson's junior year in high school, the Bowie Bears baseball team won a spot in the district playoffs. A powerful left-handed hitter, Richardson batted .450 that season. He was clearly the Bears' best player, and still the only black kid on the squad. The playoff games would be held in Abilene, an eight-hour drive into the heart of Texas. This would be his first trip with a sports team, and Richardson was beside himself with excitement.

A few days before their departure, Coach Nemo Herrera surprised Richardson by showing up at Ol' Mama's shotgun house. Herrera didn't usually make house calls.

Richardson wasn't allowed to stay with his Mexican-American teammates at the hotel in Abilene, Herrera said. Playing in the games wouldn't be a problem, but the coach was going to find Richardson a family to stay with in Abilene, a Negro family.

Richardson was angry when Coach Herrera left. "To hell with Bowie baseball, then," he said to the only other set of ears in the house. Ol' Mama looked at him hard. "You're going on the trip," she said. "You let your bat do your talking for you. If you don't go, this kind of stuff is going to go on forever."

Richardson started to speak, but Ol' Mama cut him off, listing the enormous changes she'd seen in the world between 1885 and 1958. "Your children will one day get to stay in those hotels," she said.

Richardson knew what was coming next.

"If it wasn't for Jackie *Robinson*," she added, "you wouldn't be able to do this, or anything else." Ol' Mama didn't care much about sports, but she admired the baseball pioneer and would often invoke his name as if it were sacred.

When the Bowie Bears arrived in Abilene, the usually boisterous bus grew silent. The Bowie players filed off, with a nod or handshake offered to their black star, then disappeared into the hotel. Richardson, who was seated on the sidewalk side of the bus, memorized the face of the building. Then the bus driver took him to his accommodation with an elderly black couple, living, of course, on the other side of the tracks. Richardson says, "They were very kind and I had my own bed. Also, the lady's cooking was terrific."

The bus came by the next morning, this time full of Bowie players and coaches. Richardson didn't speak on the ride to the game.

Richardson clubbed two home runs that day, and the Bowie Bears won. He thought that might be the end of it—he'd let his bat do the talking for sure. Instead, he came home to another lecture from Ol'

Mama, who, as usual, was waiting on the porch for him. Somehow she'd already heard the news.

"The only way you're going to make it is to keep going," she said. If he were good enough in sports, she said, he'd get an athletics scholarship. "But you have to keep knocking on that door," she said. "And when it opens a little bit—just a crack—you knock that damn door down, you hear!"

When Richardson was sixteen, he found his own personal Jackie Robinson in Texas Western's first black player, Charlie Brown.

Charlie Brown was a twenty-six-year-old air force veteran when he arrived in El Paso on a basketball scholarship in the summer of 1956. (Jackie Robinson was a twenty-eight-year-old army veteran when he joined the Brooklyn Dodgers.) A native of Tyler, Texas, Brown had played a year of junior college ball in Amarillo.

Only 6'1", Brown paced Texas Western College in scoring and rebounding in each of his three seasons, averaging 17.4 points as well as eight rebounds per game. After he poured in 29 points against New Mexico State, their longtime coach Presley Askew—who had been the University of Arkansas coach in the early 1950s—said, "Charlie Brown is the best basketball player I have ever seen."

When Brown first arrived in El Paso, he was met by one of Texas Western's graduating guards, Alvis Glidewell. The bespectacled Glidewell was an intellectual kid who already professed a desire to coach. He carried the less-than-flattering nickname of "Tweetie Bird," but was respected by his teammates for his dedication and heady play. Glidewell and Brown became best pals. Glidewell recalls, "We tried to go to a movie at the Plaza Theater, but they wouldn't let Charlie in. But everybody liked Charlie and it wasn't just because of basketball. Charlie was the darling of the whole school."

In 1958, Glidewell began coaching at El Paso's Austin High

School, where he'd witness Richardson's final two high school seasons. "Nolan made Bowie good all by himself," he says, "and was likely the best all-around athlete we've ever seen in El Paso, and not just because of basketball. He was dominating three sports." Unbeknown to Glidewell, Richardson began keeping tabs on him as well.

Richardson began playing with Charlie Brown while he was still attending Bowie. A local basketball fan, Saul Kleinfeld, put together a traveling team to represent his company, Union Furniture, and he recruited Richardson to be their youngest member. The rest of the team consisted of players and former players from Texas Western. Kleinfeld's crew would often go deep into the interior of Mexico, and they continued to play together in the summers after Richardson had graduated from Bowie.

Texas Western's basketball coach tried to recruit Richardson to play for the Miners, but got frustrated with his indecision that spring. Richardson believed that since the Miners had no baseball team, the school was not ideal. Just before his graduation, he was offered a basketball scholarship to nearby New Mexico State University, which had both basketball and baseball. That inspired coach Nemo Herrera to honor his only black athlete. Herrera organized a collection to buy a gift for Richardson—his first suit, to be worn at commencement.

On graduation day, Richardson donned that suit, slung the cap and gown over his shoulder, ready for the ceremonies. But Ol' Mama insisted he put on the graduation gown so that everyone who saw him would understand that this was a high school graduate. Richardson complied, and they traveled on foot, Richardson complaining, Ol' Mama beaming.

The following week, Richardson changed his mind about New Mexico State, deciding that he might rather concentrate on baseball. Unsure of what to do, he asked Bert Williams for help.

Bert Williams was an El Paso city alderman who had played basketball at Texas Western after the war. He still played summer baseball, and like anyone involved in El Paso baseball, he knew Richardson. Williams phoned a friend, the coach at the University of Arizona, a baseball mecca. The Arizona coach had done his homework; he knew exactly who Richardson was, and tempted him with talk of a future in Major League baseball.

There was a hurdle, though. He had a 2.6 grade point average, and Arizona required a 3.0 for out-of-state kids. Williams, with the help of the Arizona coach, arranged for Richardson to attend Eastern Arizona Junior College for one season. Richardson didn't anticipate playing basketball, despite his admiration for Charlie Brown. "Ol' Mama wasn't the only one," he says. "By then I was totally enamored of Jackie Robinson, too."

THREE

THE KNOWN WORLD

In September of 1959, Richardson enrolled at Eastern Arizona, certain he'd be gone to Arizona on a baseball scholarship after one year. The basketball coach at Eastern Arizona learned of Richardson's background, though, and convinced him to play hoops. That was a smart move. Richardson was sensational, scoring 22 points and ten rebounds per game before the baseball season even began.

Around Christmas, Richardson married his high school sweetheart, Helen, then returned alone to Eastern Arizona. When Helen phoned to say she was pregnant, he knew that Arizona or New Mexico State could no longer be an option. He needed to go home to El Paso to be near both of their families. Harold Davis, Texas Western's basketball coach, heard rumors of Richardson's situation and offered him a full scholarship. Texas Western still didn't field a baseball team, so it seemed an abrupt end to his baseball career.

———

Richardson racked up a lot of points his first season at Texas Western. An explosive and determined wing player, he scored 21 a game as a sophomore. The team wasn't too bad that year, either, finishing 12-12. Playing for Harold Davis was a pleasure because the coach allowed Richardson to shoot whenever he got the urge.

Still, something about his time under Davis didn't sit right with Richardson.

The Miners were invited to a three-game holiday tournament at Centenary College in Shreveport, the team's first road trip. Texas Western had won their first five games in a row going into the tournament and expectations were high. Richardson was excited because Ol' Mama was from Louisiana, and he was hoping maybe some distant relatives could attend.

Harold Davis called his high-scoring wing player aside a few days before the team's scheduled departure. Davis was never threatening or aggressive with the players, and he often used his private talks to bolster their confidence, so Richardson figured it was another pep talk.

"You can't play this weekend," Davis told him.

Richardson, who'd been having a bit of trouble with an injury, yelped in protest. "My ankle's fine, coach," he said. He hopped side to side to demonstrate.

His health was not the issue. The tournament at Centenary College had a rule: no Negroes.

Richardson stayed at home, lonely and depressed, while the undefeated Texas Western team flew to Shreveport. The Miners promptly lost all three games. Richardson listened to the games on the radio, pacing back and forth and kicking his couch.

The Shreveport Tournament snub is something Richardson talks about to this day. He was fond of Davis, but was hurt and angry that the coach did not have the backbone to do what was right.

"I think that story really defined my dad," says his oldest child, Madalyn. "He always said that Harold Davis should have forfeited those games."

———

After Richardson's sophomore season in 1961, Harold Davis resigned from Texas Western. His family's oil wells out near Big Spring, Texas, had gone crazy. Money was gushing out of the ground, plenty more than the sorry salary that a Texas mining college paid its basketball coach.

One August afternoon, Richardson was standing outside the Miners Hall dorm in the shade of an overgrown cactus. A football player nudged Richardson and said, "Your new basketball coach is here." It was Davis's coaching replacement, Don Haskins, from tiny Dumas High School in the Texas panhandle.

Haskins, red-faced and cranky from his kids' crying, climbed out of the station wagon, his family's U-Haul in tow. Haskins was annoyed, because he had been straining to listen to the live radio reports as he drove into town. The world's first commercial airplane hijacking had taken place at El Paso's airport.

Richardson couldn't quite remember the new coach's name, but he stepped into the El Paso sunshine to help the man unload his station wagon.

Haskins recalled Richardson emerging from the shade: "He had muscles popping out all over and a tiny waist and just looked like an athlete. I hadn't seen anybody that looked like Nolan Richardson. I couldn't wait to get him into the gym."

Texas Western's athletics director had given Haskins the scouting report on his new team, focusing specifically on the two stars. Al Tolen, a white forward, had averaged nearly as much as Richardson. "The first one of them who got the ball shot it," Haskins said. In fact, Tolen and Richardson took more shots than the rest of the team *combined*. Everyone Haskins talked to concurred that Richardson was a terrific talent but wouldn't make an effort on defense. Haskins reckoned he understood the problem. "Nobody had ever asked him to guard anyone," he said.

When the unloading was done, Haskins got face to face with Richardson and established the terms for their next two years together.

"I heard," Haskins said, pointing a finger in Richardson's face, "that you can't guard a goddamn fencepost."

Like Richardson, Don Haskins chose to play at a college near his home. Haskins had a rocky playing career with the hyper-disciplined Henry Iba at Oklahoma A&M (later renamed Oklahoma State). He'd score a bunch of points one game, then wind up on the bench for his lack of defense or appearing too confident. Haskins even had some academic eligibility trouble, further irritating Mr. Iba.

Haskins was from Enid, where he had befriended an older boy named Herman Carr. They'd pal around or go shoot hoops. Haskins admired Carr and thought it was a shame that he was not playing college ball. Carr did not have a basketball scholarship for a reason. "Herman Carr was black," Haskins said. "Simple." Haskins and Carr would get grief wherever they went in Enid, even in the black neighborhood. "We got ran off several times," Haskins said. "He was just black and I was white and there wasn't much difference between us."

Herman Carr was at the forefront of Haskins's mind when he began interacting with Richardson and Willie Brown, the only black players at Texas Western that August. Haskins was captivated with Richardson's athletic ability, and realized that his versatility might cause him to miss court time in the off-season. "I saw him run a 9.7 hundred-yard dash at Texas Western," Haskins recalled. "He'd beat everybody without even having time to practice, and that was wearing basketball shoes."

Richardson never roomed on campus when he played for the Miners. He and Helen rented a house on Tularosa Street in central

El Paso, using the money he made at two part-time jobs to get by. It was here that Richardson's first three children were born—Madalyn, Nolan III ("Notes"), and Bradley. He was less than a mile away from his old neighborhood and felt more of a connection to the town of El Paso than to Texas Western College. Yet El Paso was still segregated by law, something that continued to irritate him.

Because of his athletic prowess, there were other El Paso businessmen who coveted Richardson for their summer baseball teams. City alderman Bert Williams, who'd helped him get to Eastern Arizona, also moonlighted as a basketball referee. That summer, after a basketball game, he convinced Richardson to join his fast-pitch softball team. After a game when Richardson batted in the winning run, Williams offered to treat him to dinner at a popular Copia Street restaurant, the Oasis. It was the summer of 1961, months before Richardson would play a game for Don Haskins.

"I can't go in there, Bert," Richardson said as they rolled into the Oasis parking lot.

"Why the hell not?" Williams said, popping the car door open. Surely they'd serve an alderman and the college's top athlete, Williams reasoned. The two men took a seat, but the waitress came over without menus or water. Williams asked for a beer, Richardson wanted a Coke. The smell of grilled hamburgers and fried potatoes floated back to their table.

"I cannot serve *him* in this restaurant," the waitress said, refusing to look at Richardson.

Williams tried to force the issue—the owner of the restaurant was Fred Hervey, who had been El Paso's mayor, and Williams mentioned that he knew him. The tables got quiet as a bitter stalemate ensued. Williams grabbed Richardson—who'd kept silent—by the elbow and led him to the door. "I'll be back," Williams warned.

Williams was so upset by the incident that he immediately began drafting legislation to officially end the segregation of El Paso hotels, restaurants, and theaters.

"The city was divided by railroad tracks," Williams recalls, "but the laws were enforced more arbitrarily for Mexican-Americans, and there were places where they could eat without trouble." The laws were nearly always enforced to keep blacks out, though.

Bert Williams became obsessed with integrating El Paso. After rallying his fellow aldermen and revising the wording, the bill was ready. The ordinance—the first of its kind, Williams says, in Texas—passed an initial vote. It would need to pass another, and get the mayor's approval to be turned into law. Both El Paso newspapers, the *Times* and the *Herald-Post*, published editorials condemning the progress. The mayor vetoed the ordinance, but Williams had enough votes to override him.

"It was just by coincidence that Nolan was there that night at the Oasis," says Williams, who was subsequently elected mayor himself. "After I witnessed the way he was treated, such a great kid and the star of the college, I knew I had to do something."

Bert Williams's heroic act made El Paso the first major city in the old Confederacy to officially desegregate. Yet Williams's courage—he ignored numerous threats and enormous pressure—was barely reported nationally and remains nearly forgotten even in El Paso. Don Haskins took notice though. The town's new progressive status would have a profound effect on Texas Western's ability to recruit black athletes. Two years after Bert Williams's legislation passed in El Paso, the United States adopted national civil rights legislation into law.

NCAA rules at the time allowed Richardson to work while he was enrolled in college. Every Wednesday he hauled heaps of wood scrap and planks around a downtown lumberyard. That wasn't as enjoyable as his Sunday job, parking cars at First Methodist Church, not too far from the college. The church was the one Haskins and his family attended, and the coach had arranged for the job. "I'd park cars for white folks coming into church," Richardson says, "and hang around until it was time to retrieve the car. Some people gave me a dollar tip, and that added up." Parking cars stands out as one of the few pleasant aspects of Richardson's time playing for Haskins.

The new coach's mannerisms were perplexing to Richardson. Haskins did not curse the players individually; instead, his invectives involved challenging the collective manhood of the entire group, or included phrases that Haskins considered derogatory. Many of these phrases simply left Richardson amused. "He'd tell us to quit our damn barbershopping," Richardson says. "He meant our gossiping."

Haskins's acerbic tone could be intimidating, yet Richardson believed the team would benefit from the discipline that had been absent under Harold Davis. "You could tell the way Coach Haskins acted—well, it *was* an act in some ways," Richardson says. "But he was different under the surface. I didn't like him much that first semester, though. He was taking away all of my shots."

In order to get his Miners to play with more patience, Haskins instituted a rule for practicing their offense. They had to pass the ball ten times before they shot. The rule didn't sit well with the team, but only Richardson openly challenged the policy.

"Sometimes when the ball came to me, I'd call out 'ten!' and shoot it," he says.

Playing for Harold Davis was more fun, but the Miners started to gain momentum, winning eight games in a row in Haskins's first season. Richardson grudgingly decided to buy into Haskins's system during the streak, recalling a favorite expression of Ol' Mama's—"A raggedy ride is better than a smooth walk." He stopped studying the stat sheet by January. "I tried not to think about my points," he says. "You could feel that the program was going to become something important."

By the end of Richardson's junior season—their first together— Haskins had molded Richardson into the Miners' best defender.

Texas Western finished Haskins's first season at 18-6. Under the new system of stubborn half-court defense and a tightly controlled passing-game offense, Richardson's offensive totals plummeted. A major college player who averages 20 points per game as a sophomore is headed toward basketball greatness and often a professional career. But Richardson went from 21 per game as a sophomore to 13.6, then finally 10.5 as a senior. In fact, in only one game in the two seasons after Haskins's arrival did Richardson again pop in 20 points, during a win against Tennessee. Any player who had his scoring average chopped in half would be sensitive about it, and Richardson was no exception. Only the fact that they were winning made it palatable.

Don Haskins was different from the previous coach in another respect, as well.

The Miners were in Abilene for a game. Haskins had Richardson and Willie Brown, as well as two other black players, Major Dennis and Bobby Joe Hill. (This was not the same Bobby Joe Hill who would star in Texas Western's upset of Kentucky in 1966, but an East Texas wing player.) The team was scheduled to stay at the same Abilene hotel that had denied Richardson a room as a Bowie player. When the Miners walked into the hotel lobby, the manager came scurrying over.

"No coloreds!" he said.

"So I told him to hell with him and his hotel," Haskins recalled. "We all stayed somewhere else."

The Miners rarely played in the South and usually traveled west for road games. But that kind of incident would recur.

"The next year," Haskins said, "we were in Salt Lake City, and the same goddamn thing happened. We got the hell out of there, too. I wasn't going to split my team up." He used the incident to motivate his team in the locker room—everyone was against the little team from El Paso, Haskins reminded the Miners again and again. He had recycled that "everyone is against us" speech since he arrived at Texas Western. The Miners beat both Utah State and Utah.

In August of 1962, Andy Stoglin enrolled at Texas Western. Stoglin was a rugged black kid from Phoenix who would become a key player for the Miners. Richardson and Stoglin weren't immediately tight, but when Richardson wound up in an El Paso hospital with a minor injury, he became friendly with Stoglin's wife, who worked as a nurse. Soon after, the two players—both married—grew close. The friendship between Stoglin and Richardson would endure for over four decades.

Stoglin was an outspoken critic of both overt and subtle racism, and Richardson admired him greatly. In fact, in the privacy of Haskins's office, Stoglin would even challenge Haskins as to why more black players weren't starting. Stoglin could hold a grudge and had little patience for the good ol' white boy system.

One day, Haskins called Stoglin into the office at Holliday Hall, the tiny gym where Texas Western played. "He pulled a drawer open, and showed me several letters saying that Texas Western was starting too many niggers," Stoglin says.

Stoglin says he perused a few of the letters, then looked up.

"Read enough?" Haskins asked him. "That's the reason I don't start you. You can handle that, but I don't want you to tell your teammates."

Stoglin remembers the incident down to the smallest detail. Haskins claimed not to recall either the letters or the talk with Stoglin.

Stoglin was a fine recruit, but Haskins would sign the best big man ever to play for the Miners the spring after Richardson's junior season.

Jim "Bad News" Barnes was raised in Arkansas but moved to Oklahoma, where he had hoped to enroll at Oklahoma State and play for Haskins's mentor, Henry Iba. Academic shortcomings forced Barnes to attend Cameron Junior College in Lawton. Haskins learned that the explosive big man still might not have the grades for OSU.

Haskins's own father was born in Arkansas, and he used that fact to try to get close with Barnes during his recruitment. Haskins spent the majority of his recruiting time and budget trying to convince Barnes to come to El Paso. In April, when he felt Barnes was stalling, Haskins played his last card. He challenged Barnes to a free-throw shooting contest. If Haskins lost, he'd leave the big man alone. If Haskins won, Texas Western got Barnes.

Barnes joined Texas Western for Richardson's final season.

Haskins shared credit for recruiting Barnes. "Nolan talked Jim into coming," he said. "I knew then Nolan would be a good recruiter." There was more than basketball on Barnes's mind. He made it clear he didn't want to live in a segregated city, but thanks to Bert Williams, that wouldn't be a problem.

Bad News Barnes was the nation's dominant big man for two years. In Richardson's senior year, the Miners qualified for the NCAA Tournament for the first time in school history, but they lost to the University of Texas in the first round.

The following year, without Richardson, the 1963–64 season, Barnes averaged a whopping 29.2 points per game. He led the Miners to their second-ever NCAA Tournament and was the first player picked in the NBA draft.

As the team's lone black player with El Paso roots, Richardson was often nominated to take visiting recruits around town. It had worked with Jim Barnes, and Haskins quickly recognized Richardson as the perfect tour guide for black prospects. Even after Richardson's playing career was over, Haskins relied on him to socialize with Texas Western's recruits, including most of the historic 1966 team.

Richardson knew El Paso still had some unofficial Jim Crow sites, and Mexico became the preferred destination.

In Juárez, black men could eat thick steaks, dance with whomever they wanted, and stay out as late as they pleased. Heroes from the 1966 team, such as Harry Flournoy, Orsten Artis, Bobby Joe Hill, and Nevil Shed all socialized in Mexico with Richardson and had a lively time. As such, Mexico as well as Bert Williams hold a place in the history of American college basketball; they were largely responsible for the recruitment and comfort of the historic Texas Western team.

———

While a professional career appeared to be a long shot, Richardson continued to train in order to improve his chances. El Paso barely had a basketball tradition, and few pickup games or playground culture existed. Finding real competition in the off-season was a challenge, so Richardson often trained at Fort Bliss, the ironically named army base. The soldiers, with their stubby beards and thick chests, were not great players, but they offered rough competition, and Richardson loved it.

Kenny John, a local high school star who was heading to UTEP, heard about the games at Fort Bliss and became a regular as well.

"Nolan had no off season," John recalls. John began challenging the older Richardson to play one on one every day, figuring that would help him improve, too. Richardson was incredibly competitive, John says. "He'd get right up next to you and head-check you."

Head-check?

As John began with the ball at the top of the key, Richardson thrust his forehead into John to control his movement. "His neck was so strong and he was so quick," John says, "that he'd stick his head into you to slow down your drive. I've never seen that, before or since. Can you imagine?"

John was no pushover—he could dunk, shoot from long range, and would soon be the starting guard at UTEP along with Nate Archibald. "If you want to understand Nolan Richardson," John says, "just visualize that head-check."

FOUR

NATIVE SON

Texas Western finally added a baseball team Richardson's senior year. He hit .421, with ten home runs. He was among the NCAA leaders in RBIs, and that single 1963 season was enough to get him noticed. The Houston Colt 45s drafted him and offered a signing bonus, but Richardson now had three children. A journey beginning in the Class C minor leagues didn't interest him.

The AFL's San Diego Chargers also drafted him in football, although Richardson had not played a minute of the sport since high school. He went to San Diego to try out but pulled a hamstring the first week and came home. Richardson lacked nearly a full semester of coursework to get his diploma from Texas Western, and he would not have returned to college quickly had the Chargers kept him. When he was waived, he opted to finish his degree at Texas Western.

He went undrafted in basketball but continued to play with a traveling team sponsored by Saul Kleinfeld, the prominent El Pasoan. Their schedule would take them into Mexico, where Richardson's fluency in Spanish came in handy. He could listen in on the opponents' strategy during free-throws and dead balls.

The trips to Mexico would provide him with an important lesson. Kleinfeld's team might have Texas Western players, including stars such as Bobby Joe Hill and David Lattin. They were far better than most college teams, and Richardson thought nobody in Mexico could possibly come close.

He was wrong. Occasionally the black stars from the best program in Texas would be frustrated by the press and fast break of the smaller—and superbly conditioned—Mexican teams. It was an epiphany of sorts for Richardson, and he kept the memory of the racehorse Mexican teams in the back of his mind.

Richardson was hired to teach and coach at Bowie High School in the fall of 1964. The principal, Frank Pollit, must have assumed Richardson's versatility in athletics meant that he was well-rounded in the classroom. Pollit assigned him a vast array of classes over the next decade, including math, English, social studies, history, and physical education. Richardson was given coaching assignments for JV and ninth-grade football, baseball, and basketball, and he stuck with these lower-level posts for three years. His total salary was $4,500 per year.

One day, Pollit asked him what sport he really wanted to build his career on.

Texas high school football, of course, was immensely popular, and the Friday night lights seduced Richardson briefly. He told Pollit that he dreamed of being a head football coach someday.

"Wrong answer," said Pollit. "It will take too long for a black man to get a chance in this town." Pollit had plans for Richardson but knew he might never be a head football coach in Texas. "There's too much of a good ol' boy system. You'll have a better chance in basketball."

Richardson felt no resentment toward his principal, a man he admired for being direct and honest. "I can take something straight up," he says, "and Pollit would tell you right to your face."

"Don't worry about your enemies," Pollit sometimes told Richardson. That echoed what Ol' Mama had told him for years. "It's the people sitting on the fence who might turn against you," she'd say. "That's who you have to be careful of."

In 1967, Richardson was drafted in a third sport. This time it was the young American Basketball Association and the Dallas Chaparrals, and they offered to match his teaching salary at Bowie. Former Kentucky star Cliff Hagan had arranged a job for Richardson at a television station. Richardson hurt his leg, however, and grew frustrated hanging around a hotel. He considered a return to El Paso.

Around this time, Richardson's nephew Butch came down with a bad cold. The boy's mother, Shirley, began to worry when Butch didn't get better. When the cold evolved into a sleepiness that wouldn't go away, the family took Butch to visit an El Paso doctor. Butch was diagnosed with acute lymphatic leukemia, ALL. After a two-month struggle, Butch died. He was seven years old. Richardson began to wonder if this was perhaps the disease that took his own mother, and he left Dallas for good, returning to El Paso in hopes of both counseling Shirley and coaching again at Bowie.

Pollit surprised Richardson upon his return, telling him he could not have his old job back. He did, however, have a new position to offer. Richardson was named varsity basketball coach at Bowie in the autumn of 1967.

Still sensitive about the way his college scoring average had taken a beating, and about the way he felt smothered by his coach, Richardson vowed one thing: he was going to be different from Don Haskins.

Ol' Mama was still prominent in Richardson's life, but her health was visibly fading. She suffered a stroke in the mid-1960s, which left her unable to walk or talk. It also forced her out of her own home. "After the stroke she would try to talk," Madalyn says, "and now I realize that she was so frustrated because her mind was still sharp."

Richardson's grandmother passed away in 1974. The family's memories of this remarkable woman are still vivid. "She was always very stern," Madalyn recalls, "and didn't tolerate a lot of nonsense from the children."

Without Ol' Mama around, the struggle to advance seemed to Richardson more severe, steeper. Head college coaching jobs were out of the question. There were no coaches of color to imitate except at historically black colleges, the closest of which was five hundred miles away. While socializing with the black college players whose teams were playing in El Paso, he began hearing talk of a coach whom he could emulate—a coach who was black and who practically invented fast-break basketball.

John McLendon was the most successful African-American coach from the 1940s through the 1960s. A pupil of basketball's inventor, James Naismith, McLendon won 264 games at historically black North Carolina College from 1940 to 1952. He was not a big or brash man, and tried to repair the racially torn world gradually. His tools were craftiness, dignity, and intelligence.

In 1944, while he was at North Carolina College, articles appeared claiming that the Duke University Medical School team, which was tearing up the intramural competition, was actually the best team in the state. McLendon requested a secret game with the Duke team, which featured a few former stars whose eligibility had expired. Duke and McLendon had an odd relationship. During his glory years at North Carolina College, which was also situated in Durham, he was invited to attend the Duke games and permitted to sit at the end of the Duke team's bench—if he'd wear a waiter's coat.

The game was illegal, and by agreeing to play it, McLendon would put everyone in danger. A challenge was issued by one of North Carolina College's players, and the game—without spectators, but with referees—was played. McLendon's team destroyed Duke by 44 points.

In his last years at North Carolina College, McLendon began petitioning the NCAA to admit the historically black colleges to compete in their national tournament. His numerous requests were denied in writing, so for years afterward the black colleges would compete in the powerful National Association of Intercollegiate Athletics (NAIA), which began including the historically black schools in their national playoffs in 1953. (Teams that were not in either the NCAA's existing University Division or College Division would compete in the NAIA, which up until the 1970s could boast of some of the best black players in America.)

When McLendon moved to Tennessee State, he won 88 percent of his games and three consecutive NAIA championships. He remains one of only four coaches to win three straight national titles. (John Wooden, Kentucky State's black coach Lucias Mitchell, and Dan McCarrell of North Park are the others.)

From 1959 until 1962, McLendon coached the integrated Cleveland Pipers of the National Industrial Basketball League—a postcollege league that was regarded as nearly as competitive as most NBA teams. In 1960, his Pipers handed the best amateur U.S. Olympic team in history—a team featuring Jerry West and Oscar Robertson—their only defeat.

In 1969, McLendon was named the first black coach in the old ABA with the Denver Rockets. He later coached at Kentucky State and then Cleveland State University, where he was the first black head coach at a predominantly white college. (Cleveland State participates in Division I today but was College Division under McLendon.) He won a total of 522 college games at a clip of 76 percent.

In both 1968 and 1972, Henry Iba invited McLendon to be an assistant coach for the Olympics. He was joined by Don Haskins on the 1972 staff.

After those stints, McLendon became America's finest basketball ambassador, traveling to nearly sixty countries to do clinics at a time when the teaching of basketball overseas was practically nonexistent. In 1979, he became the first black coach to be inducted into the Naismith Basketball Hall of Fame—although, in a disgraceful omission, he was not included as a coach, but rather, as a "contributor."

As incredible as John McLendon's success is the way he was ignored by the established white schools his entire career. He was never offered a job at a major state school and was known to only the most astute observers of basketball.

McLendon's story is part of a pattern at American colleges— reaping black talent but not black leaders. This system crushed his career, as well as those of countless other talented black coaches. Nolan Richardson, like many young black coaches in the 1960s, came to know McLendon's story well.

After a coach named Ray Mears won the NCAA's College Division title at Wittenberg College of Ohio in the early 1960s, he was named the University of Tennessee coach. Mears, who was white, was inarguably a fine coach. But McLendon had won *three* national titles in a row, right in the state of Tennessee.

It is impossible today not to look at McLendon's career and wonder what could have been. While McLendon's name is still revered, it is almost exclusively by black coaches and older players.

Richardson understood that McLendon was far from the only black coach whose talents were ignored. Each overlooked black coach was a disturbing body in the road to any young black man starting in the profession.

One of McLendon's contemporaries was the Winston-Salem State coach Clarence "Big House" Gaines. At the time of his death in 2005, Gaines was fifth on the NCAA's list of winningest coaches, with 828 career victories. All forty-seven of his seasons were at Winston-Salem State, a historically black college. His 1967 team, featuring Earl "The Pearl" Monroe, went 31-1, and won the NCAA College Division championship.

A giant of a man, Gaines is a member of eight halls of fame, including the Naismith Basketball Hall of Fame, which honored him as a coach. He and McLendon would occasionally go on recruiting trips together, promising not to lure each other's prospects. Since hotels were not always available to black men, they would often sleep in the car. Big House, of course, got the wider backseat.

Wake Forest University is in the same town as Clarence Gaines's school. During his time at Winston-Salem State, Wake Forest went through seven basketball coaches. At one point, Wake Forest struggled through thirty-three years (1962–1995) without winning a regular season or ACC Tournament title or qualifying for the NCAA tournament. Yet Clarence Gaines was never offered the Wake Forest job.

Gaines's story is not unique, either. Kentucky State coach Lucias Mitchell won three-straight NAIA national titles in 1970, 1971, and 1972, when he was still in his thirties. He was black and was never offered a job at a Division I school.

The stagnant careers of John McLendon and Big House Gaines haunted Richardson during his early years of coaching. But without the advent of videotapes or cable television, it was only through conversation that he could begin to construct a style contrasting with Don Haskins's system. Naturally, Haskins was his most prominent influence, and Richardson had a difficult time shaking off Haskins's way of thinking about the game. So Richardson's undersized all-

Mexican-American teams his first years at Bowie played patiently. The dizzying pace that would one day be a Richardson trademark was almost a decade away.

"He played a lot closer to Haskins's style those first few years than people think," recalls Alvis Glidewell, who was already making a name for himself as a shrewd coach. "He had much smaller kids than the rest of us."

Richardson was likely doing what most young coaches do—teaching the game the way they've been taught. But he was on the lookout for a specific strategy that suited him. He had no way to familiarize himself with the systems of either McLendon or Big House Gaines. Instead, Richardson first studied, then copied, Glidewell's Austin High School teams.

Glidewell says today, "We all copy off somebody. I'd seen things that John Wooden did at clinics when he was winning at UCLA, but I didn't announce it around town. Nolan certainly wasn't yet pressing the way he'd get famous for in college." Glidewell, who is unknown outside El Paso, was surprised to learn that Richardson now credits him with some of his success as a pressing college coach. "We were never close," Glidewell insists. "He never came over to practice, never let on that he was interested. But he must have been watching pretty close."

Glidewell does recall one particular bus ride to Amarillo for a tournament both their teams were competing in. "We sat together for the first time and really talked. He asked questions about our system, but he never wrote anything down, so I had no idea he was going to use it."

Richardson says, "Glidewell's teams were so disciplined that they could press after a missed shot. That really takes total control, but his guys could do it. Not many people know about him, but he should be in somebody's hall of fame."

While he was trying to find his own voice as a coach, Richardson was also struggling at home. His marriage to Helen collapsed in the mid-1960s, something he attributes today to the couple being too young to sustain the pressures of family life. After their divorce, he raised the two boys, while Helen had Madalyn. Helen became a schoolteacher, too, teaching at Bowie's rival, Jefferson High School, for decades.

Richardson was coaching three sports and teaching several subjects. He had plenty of extra duties, too, one of which was grooming the baseball field at Bowie. When the heat got the better of him on a sunny May afternoon, he recalled that his high school pal, Manuel Davila, lived across the street from the field. Richardson trudged over to beg a glass of water. That's when he met Rosario Davila, Manuel's sister, who was tending to the garden. Like anyone in the Bowie neighborhood, Rosario knew exactly who Richardson was. She also had been married but was now divorced with a daughter of her own, Sylvia. Manuel was not at home, but Richardson stuck around to talk anyway. He asked for a second glass of water.

Soon after, Richardson married Rosario—he called her Rose, which was Ol' Mama's name—and their only child, Yvonne, was born in 1972.

Richardson's first Bowie teams were good, but not exceptional. The Bears were simply too small, and the coach had to make adjustments to be competitive. They were so aggressive that local fans began calling them *Rabia*—Spanish for "rabid dogs."

Richardson's training regimens were a daily test in toughness, and his high school players named the last third of practice "Forty Minutes of Hell." Years later, the moniker would refer to his style of play in college games of that same length. His coaching philosophy was evolving, but his insistence on defensive pressure was like a mantra—"Pressure leads to poor decisions."

Despite the furious pace of Richardson's practices and his hyper-demanding style, he grew close with his players at Bowie. Years later, those players, many from broken homes, too, credit Richardson with being deeply influential as well as a close friend. Richardson's identification with and love for his scruffy underdogs from Bowie—the poorest of El Paso's poor—was authentic.

After school one afternoon in 1973, Richardson was taking a shortcut through the Bowie gym on his way home. A pickup game in progress stopped him like a forearm to the chest. He didn't recognize the gangly black youngster who was blocking shots and grabbing rebounds.

Richardson walked into the middle of the game and asked the new kid his name.

"Ralph Brewster," the boy said. He was an eighth-grader, who didn't even play competitive basketball, although he was already 6'1".

Richardson looked at Brewster's feet, which were huge. "Aren't you Joe Brewster's son?" he asked.

"My friends took off when he said that," Brewster recalls, "ran out of the gym. They thought I was in trouble. So did I. Growing up, Nolan was like God to me."

Richardson asked the younger Brewster why he wasn't playing on the junior high team.

"My father won't let me play," Brewster said.

With chores and schoolwork to tackle, not to mention Ralph's smart-aleck demeanor, sports would be a waste of time, his father felt. Joe Brewster, a Korean War hero, was a huge man—over three hundred pounds—and his word was law.

Later that evening, Richardson phoned Joe Brewster and asked for permission to coach his son.

"My Dad didn't see an athlete in me, although he liked sports," says Brewster. "I was just a gawky kid but I hated losing. Any board game, Ping-Pong, I wanted to win."

The next day Richardson went to the Brewsters' home in Segundo Barrio's Tays Housing Project and made an appeal to the father. "I've seen great players come and go," he said. "Trust me with Ralph and I'll make him something special."

Joe Brewster was surprised Richardson was interested in his sassy son. "If you think he's good," Joe Brewster said, "have at it." But Joe Brewster had one concern—his boy Ralph walking home. Although his mother was Mexican-American, and both parents were fluent, Ralph couldn't speak Spanish. Richardson would be required to drive him home every day, and the coach used the time to gain Brewster's trust.

The long hours Richardson spent coaching, driving, and telling stories to Ralph Brewster would be worth it. By the time he was a senior, Brewster would bless Richardson in a way nobody could have predicted.

Throughout the late 1960s and early 1970s, Richardson was absorbing as much as he could from the area's best coaches. Nobody was more successful than the team three hours away in Hobbs, New Mexico. If Alvis Glidewell's system was enticing to Richardson, the style of Hobbs coach Ralph Tasker must have been like cool water in the desert.

Tasker came to the oil-boom town of Hobbs shortly after World War II. He won an astounding number of games—1,122—and took home eleven state championships. Full-court pressure was his calling card.

Tasker, like Alvis Glidewell, wore glasses, and looked more like a professor than a hoops guru. Tasker preferred his team's bench to be on the baseline, to witness his press as it uncoiled like a diamondback rattlesnake. His lead defender, guarding the inbounder after made baskets, would follow the first pass and trap it; everyone else would rotate. The opponents knew when the predictable traps were coming, but it usually didn't matter. Tasker won seventy home games in a row during one stretch.

"Hobbs would come into El Paso and destroy our best teams," Richardson recalls. "They pressed every minute, but it was more extended, more exciting, than what Alvis Glidewell was doing. So I copied Tasker's system, too. Later I took it a step further by teaching my kids not to trap at the same time or place. I wanted us to be more difficult to prepare for."

Glidewell today says Richardson may have borrowed more than his full-court press. "Nolan started playing faster when he had better players. He had those two guys, Ralph Brewster and Melvin Patridge, and Nolan let them run more. But Patridge lived on our side of the freeway," Glidewell insists. "So we challenged the situation with the school district. Patridge's mother said something like 'Nolan was his uncle.' We were saying 'Richardson is recruiting,' which was illegal [for high schools], but we lost our challenge."

Today, Melvin Patridge laughs about Glidewell's old claim. "We actually are cousins, but didn't realize that until eighth grade, in 1972," he says. "We owned a home in the Bowie district, but didn't always live there." Patridge understands Glidewell's frustration. "We probably could have won state if I'd gone to Austin High School," he says.

Patridge remembers how Richardson would use his own version of shock treatment to get his Bowie Bears' attention. "He would put us on the floor with some of the UTEP players, and they'd kill us," Patridge says. "But then the high school kids we'd face, they were nothing."

Patridge recalls a trip the Bowie team made into central Texas for the state playoffs after winning the city championship. The players filed off the bus to eat a few hours before the game but sat, ignored, for half an hour. "Nolan finally got up and talked to the manager," Patridge says. Eventually the coach returned to the team and said, "Let's go." They bought hamburgers at a McDonald's and ate them in their hotel rooms.

Patridge confronted the coach the next day. "Why didn't we just stay there until we got service?" he asked.

Richardson had remembered Abilene from his high school baseball trip. "I didn't want you guys to have the humiliation that I did," he told Patridge.

"He wasn't often verbal about race at that time," Patridge says. "Nolan might say, 'Look, me being a black coach means that my players are going to have to suffer the same as I do. If a call can go either way, it's going to go against us. I have to prepare you for that.'"

The us-against-the-world mentality became a recurring theme in Richardson's pregame and postgame talks.

According to Kenny John, his former workout partner at Fort Bliss, "Nolan carried that chip on his shoulder, like he had something to prove. He could act during games like the world was against him because he was black. But that worked for him, because he'd sometimes get the calls, and his players seemed to be on a quest. I don't know if Nolan really felt that way, or if he was just trying to help his team any way he could, like all of us."

Patridge sees it differently: "The Anglo coaches could really ride the refs, but the refs would tell Nolan to shut up."

The addition of Ralph Brewster, Melvin Patridge, and high-jump hero Arthur Westbrook radically altered the Bowie team's racial makeup—and success rate. Richardson's teams were 190-80 in his ten-year career at Bowie. The trio of black players, however, would amass a sparkling record of 101-13 in his final three seasons.

Brewster grew to be 6'8" and was Richardson's first and only major college prospect. Patridge and Brewster were the two biggest and strongest kids in El Paso, and they could dominate the boards, allowing them to fast break. "We'd force the issue and push them into submission," Brewster says.

Richardson alternated deliberately between being a harsh task-master and a loving father figure with his team. Once, after a brutal Saturday practice, Richardson took Brewster to Luby's Cafeteria, where the player ate like a famished soldier. When they finished eating, the manager came over and insisted on comping Richardson's check. The manager told Richardson, loud enough for Brewster to hear, that it was an honor to have him in the restaurant.

Back in the car, Richardson turned to Brewster. "That's why I stay on you, because I want to pass that kind of respect on to you," he said. The rides home were always instructive, with Richardson lecturing or telling stories to Brewster or Patridge from behind the wheel of his dilapidated Oldsmobile.

"It was a gold 1968 Tornado," Patridge says, "and it had no shocks. The car would bounce up and down. And the needle on his speedometer would bounce up and down, too. The windshield wipers didn't work, and if it was raining, look out. Coach Richardson would have his head out the window. We were a sight."

"You could get seasick in that car," Brewster says.

Once, Patridge asked his coach why he didn't spring for a better set of wheels.

"I don't care about what people think about a car," Richardson said. "I want them to notice *me*."

Richardson would pontificate on what it took to be a player and why his two stars had to hit the books. "But he never talked about race to me, never," Brewster insists. "He talked about studying and doing well in class. I didn't experience any racism then. I thought it was something from my dad's era."

Brewster claimed an El Paso innocence that would be shattered when he went away to college—and believes the story was similar in some ways for his coach. "Bowie was special," he says, "and ironically, that's because Bowie was considered the lowest you could go. We supported each other, although it was somewhat of a bubble." Brewster believes that 1970s El Paso was far more progressive than the rest of Texas. "When I got exposed to the other Texas," he says, "I started seeing blacks being treated differently. That's what Nolan went through when he left El Paso."

Nolan Richardson's best year at Bowie was 1977, but by the end of the season, he'd made a decision. Although he longed to be a college coach, he needed a backup plan. Richardson quietly resigned, intending to go back to school for a master's degree at UTEP so he could one day become a school principal. Richardson would go out a winner at Bowie, though none of the players yet knew of this decision.

If 1977 was Richardson's best team, it may have been Don Haskins's worst. UTEP finished with a losing record for the first time in Haskins's career. Two losses to hated rival New Mexico really stung. Both schools badly wanted Ralph Brewster, who was only seventeen and didn't understand what kind of tension he was about to stir up. When Texas Tech began recruiting him, things got complicated.

In the days before nationalized scouting services and meat-market exposure camps, Brewster was initially something of a secret. Word began to seep out that there was a big kid at Bowie with a boatload of potential.

"UTEP knew about me all along," Brewster says, "and I liked UTEP. But initially I wanted to go to the University of New Mexico. The coaches offered me a new car, and a UNM coach would give me two thousand dollars in cash when he'd come see me play." This was a shock to Brewster, who was far from a worldly kid.

Brewster's indecision would drag into the spring. One April day, Brewster showed up at UTEP's new arena for a postseason pickup game. UTEP was still actively recruiting Brewster and encouraged him to come around.

"I drove up in a new 1977 Monte Carlo that UNM had arranged

for me," Brewster says. "The first person I see is [former UTEP star] Nate Archibald."

Perhaps the best point guard in the world at that time, Archibald was back in El Paso, rehabbing an injury.

"Wait a minute," Archibald said. "Where'd you get that?" Archibald was used to NBA stars driving fancy cars, but not El Paso high school kids.

"University of New Mexico," Brewster said.

"You'd better get it in your name," Archibald said, according to Brewster.

Not everyone at UTEP agreed with that assessment. When the first pickup game was over that day, Brewster noticed Richardson coming through the tunnel in the arena, motioning with his finger.

"We need to talk," Richardson said.

Archibald had told Haskins about the Monte Carlo. Haskins had phoned Richardson, who was there to put a stop to it. They marched up the tunnel to Haskins's office.

After Brewster admitted the car was a gift from UNM, Richardson spoke up. "You can't take it. People are going to see a $10,000 car being driven by a South El Paso kid?"

Brewster considered whether to pay attention to his skinny wallet or his high school coach. Then, according to Brewster, Haskins said, "I don't care whether you come to UTEP or not. But when you leave here, you take that goddamn car back."

Brewster reluctantly returned the car.

Then something happened that would change Richardson's choice and the course of his life. El Paso's remote location meant that no matter what level of success a local high school coach enjoyed, nobody outside of town noticed. The odds against Richardson advancing to be a college coach were astronomical. Don Haskins, of course, was not going anywhere, and the closest Texas colleges were the two-year schools, which were a five-hour drive away. Under normal circumstances, even they wouldn't care who was doing well in El Paso, a town where no high school coach had ever moved on to a college position.

Western Texas College was a two-year school in Snyder, Texas, nearly four hundred miles from El Paso. Many of the Texas junior colleges were remote, but few were as isolated as Snyder, which was a half-hour north of the newly built interstate. Sid Simpson, their director of athletics, felt it was time for a new direction for his basketball team. After coaching the team himself for a while, he took a chance on a hot young coach named Mike Mitchell. At just twenty-six years of age, Mitchell won the National Junior College Championship.

Simpson, an Arkansas native, found himself in a quandary when Mitchell bolted for the College of Southern Idaho after the 1977 season. Simpson wanted to keep winning, that was obvious, but Mitchell had irritated him with his harsh treatment of players.

Yet Simpson himself was halfway annoyed with the typical I'm-going-to-the-NBA mentality of junior college kids. He wanted a coach who was tough and smart, but also somebody who could emotionally connect with the kind of conscripted kids who populated the rosters of the Texas junior colleges.

When Texas Tech assistant Rob Evans walked in one April day and announced, "I've found your next coach," Simpson was intrigued and assumed Evans was referring to himself. The junior college had never had a black coach—no integrated junior college in Texas ever had—but Rob Evans was clearly head-coaching material.

Evans had played at Hobbs High School for the iconic Ralph Tasker, then starred at New Mexico State in the mid-1960s. Evans had been an assistant coach at NMSU under Lou Henson before going to Tech. He had the demeanor of an ambassador and the reputation for being honest and patient.

"Would you consider hiring a black coach?" Evans asked Simpson.

Simpson sensed it would be a great coup to land Evans. "You might be perfect, Rob," Simpson admitted.

"No, no," Evans said. "It's not me. I'm talking about an El Paso high school coach named Nolan Richardson."

Texas Tech had been hot on the trail of Ralph Brewster, and Rob Evans was leading the recruiting charge.

Around this time, near the conclusion of Brewster's senior season, Richardson had pulled his star into the office.

"You know about Texas Tech?" Richardson asked.

Of course Brewster did. He had a box of letters from Lubbock that Richardson had hand-delivered.

Richardson continued. "Rob Evans is going to offer you a full ride to Tech, and now he's interested in Melvin Patridge as well."

"That made me sit up," Brewster says, "because Melvin and I were close." Brewster began to think he'd decline the offers from UTEP and UNM.

When Tech realized Patridge was on shakier ground academically, they slowly backed off from him. Brewster's academics, on the other hand, were fine—he even had congressional approval for admission into the Air Force Academy. Richardson began hinting over the next few weeks that Tech might be the best fit.

Brewster went on his official visit to Lubbock alone, and he came back disappointed. "There was no basketball spirit," he says. "I could tell by the dirty gym that smelled like cow manure. It was a football school." Brewster decided to hold off on signing anywhere despite pressure from the three universities.

Brewster had been leaning toward taking the UNM deal. "But then Haskins came to my home, and everyone knew he never went out recruiting," Brewster says. "He met with my dad, who mentioned the UNM car."

"When you start giving kids things," Haskins said, "they start expecting that for the rest of their lives. If he wants a car so bad, here's what I'll do. I'll do it legally, but he won't be able to live on campus."

That sounded good to Brewster at first. Haskins outlined his idea. Brewster could live with his parents, then use the scholarship money normally tagged for room and board to make a modest, but legitimate, car payment.

"That got my dad's attention," Brewster says. But not his. It wouldn't be a new Monte Carlo. It wouldn't be a new anything.

When Haskins left, Ralph Brewster took a look around the little apartment. The tiny black-and-white television. The malfunctioning air-conditioning. The noisy neighbors. Keep living there? Not likely.

Richardson leveled with Brewster in the weeks after his visit to Lubbock. Brewster recalls his coach saying, "Ralph, if you go to Texas Tech, I'll get to be the coach of Western Texas College."

"They'd worked out a package deal," Brewster says today. "I was going to go wherever Nolan suggested. I had no qualms with that." And Richardson clearly favored Texas Tech.

"Some of these schools are offering Ralph the world," Joe Brewster had said to Gerald Myers, the Tech head coach, during their home visit.

"We don't do that sort of thing at Texas Tech," Gerald Myers said.

"But when I went to Lubbock," Brewster claims, "every good football player had a Thunderbird or Monte Carlo."

Still, Brewster waited. At the end of April, the Tech coaches cornered the Brewsters again in their living room for a final push. This time the Tech coaches were more direct.

According to Brewster, Rob Evans said, "If you sign, Ralph, Coach Richardson is going to be the next coach at Western Texas

College. Don't you want Nolan Richardson to be a college coach?" Package deals and quid pro quo arrangements were standard practice in college sports, but certainly new to El Paso high schools.

Brewster admitted it would be great if Richardson could be a college coach. He leaned forward on the couch, holding his head in his hands. The apartment seemed to be getting smaller by the minute.

"What if Coach Richardson told you to sign with us?" Evans asked. "Would you sign then?"

Brewster said he would.

"Just a minute," Evans said.

"They went outside and got Nolan," Brewster recalls. "He must have been waiting in the car."

Ralph Brewster signed with Texas Tech. It's possible that without Brewster, Richardson would have either been a school principal or coached his career away at Bowie—although Brewster refuses to stake that claim. "I was a talented player," he says, "although I wasn't any All-American. But sure, I went to Tech because it was good for Nolan."

In retrospect, Richardson insists Texas Tech was the right choice for Brewster, regardless of the junior college job—UNM was about to implode, and UTEP wasn't very good at the time. Neither man would have guessed then how Brewster's career at Tech would unfold.

FIVE

NOBODY KNOWS MY NAME

S nyder, a tiny oil town halfway between El Paso and Dallas, was named after a buffalo hunter, Pete Snyder, who opened a trading post in 1878. Oil was discovered in Snyder in 1948, and the population tripled. Oil derricks seem to outnumber trees.

When Western Texas College opened its doors in 1971, Snyder was home to about twelve thousand people, nearly all of them white. The towns in the Western Junior College Athletic Conference are more similar than they are unique. Odessa, the town made famous by *Friday Night Lights*, is one of those towns. So are Hobbs and Roswell, New Mexico. Throw in Texas towns like Borger, Levelland, Big Spring, Clarendon, and the more upscale Midland, and you have the nation's premier junior college conference. Former NBA stars Larry Johnson, Spud Webb, and Avery Johnson got their start in this league.

Director of Athletics Sid Simpson was quickly building a reputation as a shrewd judge of coaches, but college basketball is often about favors and paybacks. Simpson fielded phone calls from all over about the coaching job. "Bobby Knight even called," Simpson says, "but I figured, what did Bobby Knight know about Snyder? Rob Evans knew our league, had been around it all his life. I trusted him."

Even employees of the junior college had suggestions for Simpson. One man had gotten wind of the fact that Sid Simpson was considering hiring a black coach and wanted to recommend his own coaching pal, but he must have sensed Simpson was leaning toward Nolan Richardson.

"You're going to be sorry if you hire that nigger," the school employee said.

"I didn't worry about any of that," Simpson says. "I wanted a guy who cared about Western Texas College."

Simpson drove to El Paso to interview Richardson and his family over dinner at a steak house, where a procession of people came over to greet Richardson throughout the meal. Whites. Mexicans. Blacks. "It was people of all ages, too," Simpson recalls, "and you could tell they held him in the highest esteem. I could see he could get along with all kinds of people."

Simpson knew coaching could tear up families and render the coach ineffective, so he closely considered Richardson's immediate circle. "I instantly liked Rosario," he says. "She was supportive and captivated by Nolan, but was clearly a strong woman."

One other thing stuck in Simpson's head. Simpson was charmed by their daughter, Yvonne, who was then six years old. "She was the cutest kid," he says, "smart as could be. You could have a conversation with her just like she was an adult. The way Nolan interacted with his wife and child, well, that had a lot to do with why I was impressed with him."

Simpson drove back to Snyder with the radio off. There had never been a black coach at any integrated junior college in Texas, school employees kept reminding him. The next morning Simpson told his president that he wanted to hire Nolan Richardson.

The school's president, Dr. Robert Clinton, ran the proposal by the school's board, but there was plenty of unease. Dr. Clinton wasn't opposed to the idea of hiring a black coach, but knew it was a gamble in Snyder. The business of Rosario, his Mexican-American wife, and their child, had to be considered—an interracial couple and a biracial child in Snyder, Texas? Simpson told Dr. Clinton, "If somebody sees Nolan walking with his wife, it's going to look different."

Simpson asked for a single year for Richardson to prove himself.

Dr. Clinton told Simpson it would be his decision, but added a warning. "If this Nolan Richardson is not what you say he is," Dr. Clinton said, "and we don't win, it's going to reflect on you. You'll have to get a couple one-way bus tickets out of town."

Simpson says, "Dr. Clinton wasn't all that prejudiced, he was just being practical. There was going to be pressure on us both, Nolan and myself."

Nolan Richardson signed on for $19,000 a season, a raise of $2,000. It was 1977, and a historic hire. (Richardson was not, however, the first black coach at a majority-white college in Texas. Bob "Snake" Legrand was named the head coach at the University of Texas–Arlington in 1977, just before Richardson went to Snyder. There were less than a half-dozen black major college coaches in America at the time.)

"Snyder is redneck central," Don Haskins said. "It was about as tough a place for Nolan Richardson to start out as you could imagine. Sid Simpson was gutsy to take a chance on him."

Richardson's first junior college team featured eight El Paso kids whom he'd rounded up and brought along. "They looked like a team from the United Nations," Simpson laughs. "They were white, brown, and black, and all sizes."

Perhaps feeling a little unmoored being away from El Paso, Richardson reached back to his roots, but not to Don Haskins.

Richardson wanted to speed the game up and needed reminders of Alvis Glidewell's system—he'd used parts of it for a few years, but now he wanted more. By November, Richardson had implemented as much of Glidewell's system as he could recall.

Dwight Williams, his new fireplug guard who had played high school ball for Glidewell, would be Richardson's bridge back to El Paso. At Richardson's insistence, Williams sought out Glidewell at Christmas break that first year, with specific instructions: collect the rules, cues, options, and rotations of the full-court pressure.

By January, Richardson's first team had implemented Glidewell's presses, and they tore through the competition during the conference season.

The team adjusted to "redneck central" as quickly as their coach had. Players who are winning make peace with their surroundings, and Dwight Williams was no different. "Snyder had one stoplight, a typical little Texas town, but it was a wonderful place because it was all centered around the college," he says. "Race didn't come into play until my sophomore year, although it was always in our minds."

Sid Simpson was more than just the athletics director. He coached the women's team, too, but he made sure to watch nearly every Richardson-run practice and game. "Nolan would just have his team jump in the other team's face the second they got off the bus," Simpson says. "They'd spread the court with their defense, and run, run, run. There was playing time for everyone. I'd been trying to press and do some of the things that Nolan was doing, but it was funny—when I told my team to do it, they wouldn't respond to me, although I was often saying nearly the same thing Nolan was."

Simpson had neglected to reveal one of the oddities of the job in Snyder during the interview process. The college was outside of town, and it was too far to walk. That was fine with Richardson— nothing to distract his players from school and basketball. But the cafeteria was closed on the weekends. That meant the players would have to cram into a few cars to buy fast food with the minimal meal allowance Simpson could supply.

Richardson realized the athletics department wasn't as frugal as he and Rosario were. He suggested to Simpson that they use the money to buy groceries instead.

"Who is going to cook?" Simpson asked.

"Rose and I will," Richardson said. Rosario had run a barbecue stand and Mexican restaurant in El Paso and could do wonders with a low budget.

The next Saturday morning, shopping for groceries for team meals, Rose noticed the manager taking meat off the shelf and putting it into a large cart. She asked him what he was doing.

"These are pull-backs," he told Rose. "They're still good, but we can't sell them after a certain date."

From that day forward, the Western Texas College team feasted on pull-backs, and the regular weekend meals helped the ballplayers to bond. Richardson delivered the meals to the dorms personally, with Yvonne dragging a basket of her own. It was one thing when the brash new coach hollered at you and ran you to exhaustion for three hours. But when the coach, his wife, and daughter donned aprons, chopped onions, and then hauled out enormous baskets of home cooking every Saturday and Sunday?

"The meals were outstanding!" Dwight Williams says. "Mrs. Richardson used to run the kitchen in The King's X, which is famous for Mexican food in El Paso. Coach would be staggering under the weight of the baskets, and he'd hand-deliver it to our rooms."

"It was a family atmosphere like I've never seen before or since," Simpson says. "Nolan could make a purse out of a sow's ear."

Yvonne would roam from room to room, goofing with the players, pretending to be a waitress taking food orders. Her sense of fun rubbed off on her father. "Coach Richardson can be a very mischievous guy," Dwight Williams says, "and Yvonne brought that out in him. She personified the best parts of Rose and Nolan. Yvonne got her father's fearlessness and her mother's endurance."

Since the family was away from El Paso and their families, Yvonne and her father had time and space to grow close in a way Richardson had not been able to with his first three children. He had been busier and less patient with them; then the divorce complicated things. His youngest daughter understood him, he felt. They were closely matched, personality-wise.

She knew how to push his buttons, as well, especially if she needed his attention. "I want an interview!" she would say.

Richardson, who had mainly lived in El Paso, could immediately sense a different racial mindset in Snyder. He was sensitive to any slight or insult, real or imagined, and occasionally Richardson even misinterpreted Sid Simpson's best intentions that first season. When Rosario and Yvonne were back visiting El Paso one weekend, Simpson learned Richardson was alone. He invited his coach over for dinner. Simpson's son Mike loved to cook, and Southern cuisine was his specialty.

When he arrived at Simpson's home, Richardson surveyed the spread awaiting him. Fried chicken. Corn bread. Collard greens. Black-eyed peas. Sweet potato pie. Even watermelon. "Ahh hah, I see," Richardson thought. "They're feeding me *soul* food." He sat down cautiously, not sure if he was being insulted or perhaps was the butt of a joke.

Simpson recalls, "Nolan had one eyebrow raised up, checking us out."

Simpson slid into his chair and, without ceremony or comment, tore into the fried chicken. His son grabbed a thigh and attacked it.

"I knew Sid was for real when I saw him eat that night," Richardson says.

———

Richardson learned that coaching in Texas junior colleges could be a rough ride. Once, Western Texas was at Panola Junior College, where Richardson grew more and more incensed with the biased officiating as the first half progressed. After computing the total number of free throws for both teams at halftime, he sent a manager up from the locker room to the scorer's table with an announcement. Western Texas was done. They would not be coming out for the second half, because they were being cheated.

The Panola officials were shocked, then livid; they set up outside the Western Texas locker room to prevent Richardson from exiting to the team bus. Richardson said in no uncertain terms that the referees were prejudiced and wouldn't give a black coach a fair shake. The Panola athletics director tried to calm Richardson down. "We know it's bad out there," he said, only to appease the coach.

"If you know it's bad, why haven't you stopped it?" Richardson said.

"That's just my way," Richardson says now, "to speak out. When I coach, it's me versus everybody. Same with when I played. I kept a chip on my shoulder, and that's something I guess I still carry from Ol' Mama."

Richardson also admits he can be intimidating. "I'm a black man with a big, strong voice. I have a certain physical stature," he says. "There are games within games, psychological games, and that's part of what I'm up to on the sidelines." In characteristic fashion, he adds, "That's something you won't find in coaching books."

Eventually, the Panola boss talked him into bringing his team on for the second half. Although they were behind by twenty points, Western Texas stormed back to win easily. Richardson had proved a point. Or so he thought.

A note was on his door when he got back to school Monday morning: *Please see Dr. Clinton in the president's office, pronto.*

"I heard you had a little trouble in Panola the other night," Dr. Clinton said.

Richardson forced a smile, not sure what to expect. Would he be suspended? Chastised? Fired?

"I'm damn proud of you," Dr. Clinton said. "Don't back down from anybody, Nolan. We don't want you walking on eggshells around here."

It was the first direct vote of confidence Richardson received from his president. "That just made me sure that I could win," he says. "I knew the school was behind me."

It wasn't only the president who was affected by Richardson. "Nolan could have run for mayor of Snyder and won, after his first season," Simpson says.

Later that spring, Richardson began socializing regularly with the employee who told Sid Simpson not to hire the "nigger coach."

One afternoon that first season in Snyder, Richardson called the team into the locker room and singled out a Detroit native, Freddy Davis. Richardson said, "Freddy, that white girl you're dating? You can't be seen in town, at the movies, at a football game. Some boosters have called, and they're going to withdraw their support."

Melvin Patridge recalls, "Nolan put it out to all of us, so we'd know what kind of atmosphere we were in. These are the same boosters that were having us to dinner and smiling in our faces. In El Paso, who you were dating wasn't a big deal. But we saw racism in Snyder, and the look on Nolan's face that day, you could tell it was the hardest thing to tell us."

During Richardson's college days, Don Haskins had called in his friend and teammate, Andy Stoglin. According to Stoglin, Haskins told him to stop holding hands with a white girl around the El Paso campus.

It annoyed both Richardson and Stoglin that Haskins would be involved in this sort of monitoring of their social lives. (Haskins did not recall this incident.) Richardson surprised himself by handling things in Snyder more or less the way Haskins did in El Paso.

Patridge says, "I think that's when the racism thing really raised its head, and he had to adjust. I saw Nolan change there in Snyder, from happy-go-lucky to 'It's me against the world.'"

That pressure carried onto the court. During one game, the Western Texas team was down by eight points at halftime.

"You have to perform," Richardson insisted. "If you don't perform I can't feed my family."

"He had never put it in that context," Patridge says. "That was new."

The family would eat—Western Texas College was winning big, even in Richardson's debut season.

Western Texas qualified for the state playoffs at the conclusion of Richardson's first year. The games were to be in Abilene—the town where Richardson had not been allowed in the hotel with his Bowie baseball team, and Haskins's team had been sent back into the night.

When Simpson gave Richardson his travel itinerary, Richardson had to smile. They had reservations at the same hotel. Every pregame talk takes place in a locker room. This one would take place in front of the hotel. Richardson gathered his diverse squad on the sidewalk and stood on the steps, recounting his shame and anger at twice not being allowed to room in that very hotel. Of course he stressed how he'd hammered two home runs after being insulted the first time.

Then Richardson quoted his ace, Ol' Mama. "There are people who pave roads and others who walk on them," he said. As often would happen over the years, with his us-against-the-world speech, the coach ended with, "Let's go out and beat somebody's ass."

"You feel like you *can* take on the world after Nolan speaks," Dwight Williams says. "First, nobody worked harder than us. We were in incredible condition. Coach talked about pride in our work ethic every day. Second, he instilled confidence in us."

Patridge says Richardson's mindset evolved in Snyder, a town with a practically nonexistent black population. In El Paso, the Hispanic population revered Richardson, considered him one of their own. There was no such comfort zone in Snyder. "When we were at Bowie," says Patridge, "it wasn't ever *us against the world*, but instead it was *us against whomever we played*. Nolan didn't talk about race so much in El Paso."

Western Texas College won the state playoffs, qualifying for the national tournament in 1978. They finished Richardson's first season ranked #13 in the nation.

That summer, Texas Tech assistant coach Rob Evans told Richardson about a high schooler named Paul Pressey. Pressey had quit his Richmond, Virginia, high school mid-career, then returned. As a senior, Pressey was discovered to be too old to compete, and so he slipped under the radar of recruiters.

If Ralph Brewster was Richardson's first great high school player, Pressey was his first college star, first of a long line of versatile wing players who would shine for him. At 6'5", he could dominate inside or out. Pressey later went on to score nearly 8,000 points in his NBA career.

Western Texas would alternate between Glidewell's cat-and-mouse press and Ralph Taskers's full-court frenzy, with Paul Pressey usually on the nose of the press. Richardson's second Western Texas team lost only two games in the regular season. They went back to the national playoffs and made it to the first round of the 1979 Final Four.

Dwight Williams, only 5'9", signed at Texas Tech that spring, leaving behind a more talented team in junior college than he'd join in Lubbock. But Williams, who was friendly with Ralph Brewster from their El Paso days, knew help was on the way. "Paul Pressey, David Brown, Greg Stewart, they were supposed to sign at Tech the next year," Williams says. "That's the primary reason I went there. The plan was those guys were supposed to follow me to Tech."

Lubbock is less than an hour by car from Snyder, and it was impossible for Richardson and Brewster not to keep close watch on each other. Brewster had gotten off to a good start at Texas Tech, but he still wasn't crazy about the town or the basketball arena. "We played at the dingy Lubbock Coliseum," he says. "It was almost like I went back in time being at Texas Tech." Brewster started some games as a freshman, chipping in almost 4 points per game, and 3.1 rebounds. The team was doing reasonably well, too, finishing 19-10.

Brewster often reminded himself of three facts that made Lubbock easier to stomach. First, UTEP continued to struggle through losing seasons, so Brewster could hardly get wistful thinking how much fun he would have had in El Paso—although the Miners certainly would have improved with him patrolling the paint. Second, rumors were swirling about the University of New Mexico program. They were about to go down in flames, destroyed by a transcript-fixing scandal. Finally, Brewster was playing a lot for a freshman. Brewster could just about make peace with himself over his decision.

Brewster's second season in Lubbock was even better. Tech finished 19-11, and just missed the NCAA Tournament. They did earn an NIT bid, but lost to Indiana in the first round. And Brewster was blossoming, scoring 11 points per game to go along with 7.6 rebounds—impressive sophomore stats.

———

Over Christmas of 1979, his third year in Snyder, Richardson returned to El Paso. While attending UTEP's Sun Bowl Tournament, he bumped into the school's director of athletics, Jim Bowden. Bowden was a native of Odessa, not far from Snyder, and knew how difficult the world could be for Richardson in West Texas.

Bowden was out of place as a college administrator. He used the plain language of a ranch hand, and he seemed uninterested in glad-handing El Paso's few rich boosters. He had uncommon common sense, and coaches would seek him out for advice.

When Richardson took a seat, Bowden congratulated him for being undefeated so far that season. "You know," he continued, "the Tulsa job is supposed to open up this year. You should apply."

Richardson told Bowden that he would.

The University of Tulsa's basketball team was in the midst of their fifth losing season in a row. Their coach, Jim King, would resign only eighteen games into the season. His assistant took over, but things didn't get any better. Although no professional teams claimed this medium-size city as home, attendance for the college was less than 3,800 per game. (UTEP, situated in a similar-size city and carrying a losing record that year, averaged more than twice as many fans as Tulsa.)

Tulsa had been sending teams to the court for over seventy years and had garnered exactly one lonely NCAA Tournament bid. They had earned a trip to the NIT on three occasions—in 1953, 1967, and 1969. Tulsa had not won a postseason game in over two decades.

Consecutive bad years can cripple the enthusiasm of boosters, making them desperate to try something new, almost anything to revive hope.

Ed Beshara had hope. Beshara owned a men's clothing store in Tulsa and was closely involved with raising scholarship money for the private university's basketball program. Beshara stubbornly believed the school could compete, although the Missouri Valley Conference was one of the nation's best basketball leagues. A Lebanese-American, Beshara was a relentless worker in his little clothing empire. He was also a stubborn optimist and longed for someone who shared his attitude to lead the Tulsa team.

Ed Beshara's father, Antone Beshara, had emigrated from Lebanon in the early 1900s. Religious persecution of Catholics and the chance for a better life brought "Papa Tony" Beshara and his family to Oklahoma.

But Oklahoma, which became a state in 1907, wasn't always friendly to immigrants or people of color. In Okemah, a lynch mob went after a young black crime suspect in 1911. The mob temporarily settled for the suspect's mother, Laura Nelson, knocking down her cabin door, then accusing her of hiding her son. The image of Laura Nelson, dangling with her son from a steel bridge, was captured on camera, sold as a postcard, and remains one of the few lynchings of a woman on record.

Antone Beshara settled in Haskell County, forty miles from Okemah, where he would raise twelve children. With vigilante justice and white mobs lurking in Oklahoma, Papa Tony Beshara wasn't shocked to find the Ku Klux Klan on his doorstep one evening. The Klan charged him with the crime of running a successful business while not being born in America. But Papa Tony knew how to face down cowards in sheets—he returned to the porch moments later with a loaded shotgun.

The Klan scurried away, lobbing curses and threats over their shoulders. Peering out from behind Tony's leg was his American-born son Ed.

Beshara had a rough time growing up when the family moved to Tulsa. "I would get beat up three times a day on my way to school," he'd say, "and I lived across the street!"

Despite growing to only 5'5", Beshara was a skilled and gutsy football quarterback, who received the equivalent of an athletics scholarship to Washington University of St. Louis. When the Great Depression hit, Beshara's scholarship was rescinded. He was forced to forgo college, moving back to Tulsa to begin working in the clothing business.

In 1950, Ed Beshara Clothing was founded on Harvard Street in Tulsa, where it still stands. Beshara grew to love Tulsa but often struggled with the mentality of the locals and had little patience for racist talk or attitudes.

Blunt and brash, Beshara was well connected around town. He had heard the rumors that Tulsa might consider a black coach, then kept hearing the same refrain from Tulsa business folks—they wanted a white coach. The West Point coach, Mike Krzyzewski, seemed to be the popular choice, and Beshara would have been okay with an immigrant name nobody could spell. But hiring a black coach intrigued him.

"I don't think there's any question that Dad felt sympathetic to a minority coach," his son, Ed Beshara Jr., says.

Beshara, who considered himself a champion of the underdog, got involved.

Richardson's team at Western Texas College rolled on, making it through his third regular season undefeated. Before the junior college tournament even began in the spring of 1980, Nolan Richardson was promised the job at the University of Tulsa—although he had not signed a contract yet.

He went into the playoffs as the most inspired lame-duck coach in history. Western Texas won it all, finishing the year 37-0.

Snyder's fans knew Richardson was Tulsa-bound, but that didn't stop them from having "Nolan Richardson Day" before he left—a mark of both Richardson's charisma and the way he was able to win the town over. But what Richardson recalls most is the drive back to Snyder after winning it all. The team got caught in a blizzard. Fearing for the safety of the kids, Richardson ordered the bus to stop in a remote Kansas town. Doors were knocked on; calls were made. The team was eventually put up in a local church. That's how the championship team celebrated: with hot chocolate, plaid blankets, and cookies in a church basement.

During Ralph Brewster's junior year, as Richardson was winning big in junior college, the Tech team took a step backward. Tech finished 16-13, but Brewster was still a force inside, getting 11 points per game again and pulling in 7.1 rebounds. After three seasons at Tech, Brewster had thrown down 33 dunks, and had big games of 29 points on two occasions. He was also one of the coach's favorites and was often trotted out at Elks Club and Lions Club luncheons as a model Tech basketball player. He was growing into an impressive and self-assured young man.

Brewster was thrilled to learn Nolan Richardson was going to be a major college coach at Tulsa. He was pals with the El Paso players on the Western Texas team, and they kept him informed of their success. Brewster's confusion about choosing Tech—it wasn't exactly remorse—had washed away. His unselfishness and loyalty had paid off for Richardson, and, he now concluded, Tech had, in fact, been the correct choice for him. Brewster even fantasized about Texas Tech meeting Tulsa in the playoffs.

There were problems, though. Brewster heard the first subtle strains of racism. "I'd hear people say to black players, 'You can't major in that,' when someone would express an interest in an academic field." Yet Brewster was reasonably happy. "I wasn't perfect, either," he adds. "I'd oversleep on the road, for example."

Everything pointed to a great final season for Brewster. He was about to have a senior year to remember, but not the one he'd anticipated.

SIX

GOING TO THE TERRITORY

Tulsa has a tangled and tragic history of race relations. Oklahoma earned statehood in 1907, and by 1910, Tulsa numbered ten thousand residents. By 1920, the population had multiplied tenfold. The catalyst for this boom was the discovery of oil nearby, and as the town mushroomed, so did its black population. Many blacks were the descendants of runaway slaves who had fled to Indian Territory. Others came with Native American tribes during the "Trail of Tears." By 1920, more than ten thousand blacks lived in Tulsa. Soon the Ku Klux Klan began to make inroads; a Klan leader from Atlanta attracted a crowd of three thousand as the new decade began.

Most of Tulsa's blacks settled in an area north of Tulsa, which became known as Greenwood. Within the Greenwood district were two newspapers, over a dozen doctors, lawyers, and a thriving black middle class. People referred to the self-sufficient district as "The Negro Wall Street," or, disparagingly, "Little Africa." Tulsa might have been a model for future American cities—although greater

Tulsa was not integrated, both communities thrived independently.

Everything changed on May 30, 1921. Dick Rowland, a black man, was accused of assaulting a white woman in an elevator. Rowland was arrested and held in jail. The next evening the *Tulsa Tribune* ran an editorial with the headline "To Lynch a Negro Tonight."

Sure enough, that evening, a mob of approximately two thousand whites stormed the jail. Fifty black men—many of them World War I veterans—blocked their path. An argument ensued. Shots were fired. The most devastating and deadly race riot in United States history was on.

Given a free hand by Tulsa police and authorities, white mobs terrorized Greenwood, and thirty-five square blocks of buildings were burned to the ground. The *Chicago Defender* reported that a private airplane was used to drop dynamite on Greenwood. Among the destroyed property were six hundred businesses, twenty-one churches, and dozens of restaurants and groceries, as well as a library and a hospital. In all, over a thousand homes were lost, and as many as three thousand blacks, many of them women and children, were killed. The official total of murdered blacks at that time, however, was twenty-six.

No white person was charged with a crime. Neither was Dick Rowland, the accused elevator assailant.

Few towns in America had as horrific an event in their rearview mirror as the Tulsa Race Riots, a black genocide. Many blacks—the ones who survived—left Tulsa. Others lived in tents. Blacks tried to rebuild Greenwood, and it enjoyed a modest resurgence in the late 1920s. Greenwood was partially leveled during the urban renewal of the 1970s.

By then, the Tulsans had made modest progress in improving their ruptured race relations. John Phillips, who later became TU's coach and attended high school in town in the mid-1960s, says, "The races got along pretty well in the sixties and it wasn't really a redneck town by any stretch." The high schools were desegregated by then, and athletics became a place where the races mixed freely. However, there were still powerful elitists resistant to progress.

Tulsa Athletics Director Emery Turner had desperately wanted to hire Lamar University basketball coach and Tulsa native Billy Tubbs to turn the program around. But Tubbs figured Tulsa was doomed to fail and dropped out of the running. Rumors circulated that it was a done deal: Nolan Richardson would be the next coach.

One day in early March of 1980, just before the University of Tulsa offered Richardson a contract, a booster named Evans Dunne appeared in the doorway of Ed Beshara's clothing store. He didn't want a new suit.

"What's on your mind, Evans?" Beshara asked.

What Evans Dunne said became a familiar refrain among Tulsa boosters that spring: "I'll never give another dime to the University of Tulsa if they hire a nigger to coach our boys."

Evans Dunne was one of the University of Tulsa's biggest financial contributors, and he donated huge sums to their struggling sports programs. The Dunnes were considered Tulsa's first family. Evans was the son of an old oil-money family; his wife, Nina Lane Dunne, was the author of *Tulsa's Magic Roots*, a picture book published in 1979 that was on every coffee table in South Tulsa.

Dunne's attitude was indicative of the dilemma in college sports. While students or faculty might have been ready to desegregate, the people pulling the purse strings often were not. Most schools, especially in the South, began adding black players, but not because it was the right thing to do. Rather, they desegregated when they did not want to risk getting beaten on the court or field. It often took a well-established coach, one with a sense of courage and justice, to begin recruiting black players.

An administrator who suggested hiring a black coach would be under enormous pressure. But Richardson's breathtaking junior college teams were averaging over 100 points a game, and that had gotten Tulsa president Paschal Twyman's attention. "Nolan bowled us over with charisma," Twyman told *Sports Illustrated*. "We knew we were breaking some ice here, but we decided to fly with it. We needed to win badly."

Richardson's predecessor, Jim "Country" King, had been a standout player at Tulsa before going on to the NBA. The 6'2" Jim King played plenty for the Los Angeles Lakers, San Francisco Warriors, and finally as a backup on gritty Chicago Bulls teams, their best of the pre–Michael Jordan era.

When Ken Hayes bolted from Tulsa in 1975 for the head-coaching job at New Mexico State, Tulsa asked Jim King, their most visible alum, to take the helm. The school was in a bind, and King—who had no coaching experience—was pulled by loyalty. Only two years into his NBA retirement, and at the age of thirty-five, Jim King agreed to be Tulsa's head coach. After his first season, King was offered an NBA assistant-coaching spot but remained at Tulsa.

King wouldn't enjoy the consistent winning he had helped to generate in the NBA. His best record at Tulsa was in his third season, 1978–79, when he finished 13-14. King even lost eight in a row to its crosstown rival, Oral Roberts University.

By the end of January 1980, Jim King took an early retirement. Bill Franey, his assistant, coached the final nine games of that season. King left Tulsa with a record of 44-82. At the age of forty, his career as a coach was over.

Don Haskins knew a positive piece from popular sportswriter Bill Connors would help smooth the way for Richardson. Connors knew Haskins from his playing days at Oklahoma A&M, took Haskins at his word, and ran a glowing profile of Richardson in the *Tulsa World*.

Richardson continued to make it clear, even to Connors, that he wanted to distance himself from Haskins in terms of coaching philosophy. Richardson never disparaged Haskins personally, but he was quick to criticize the conservative playing style that Henry Iba was credited with popularizing.

Richardson could, however, sometimes be loose with his language. About his El Paso home, he told *Sports Illustrated*, "I'm from a place I never want to go back to." Later, Richardson would clarify this statement. He meant being poor and unknown.

Tulsa's on-court struggles were in stark contrast to the success of its crosstown rival, Oral Roberts University.

ORU was a new school founded by Oral Roberts, the evangelical preacher, educator, businessman, and television personality. The school opened its doors in 1965, and immediately had three winning seasons in a row.

Reverend Roberts was hugely popular in black communities at that time—not only for his willingness to include blacks in his church, but also for his encouragement for blacks to attend his university and play on his basketball team. ORU had three black players on their inaugural team in the fall of 1966.

The state of Oklahoma was relatively progressive in desegregating their college sports teams. Henry Iba desegregated his Oklahoma A&M team in 1957, when he signed Memphis native L. C. Gordon. The other major state school, Oklahoma University, followed suit the next season. Before the 1964–65 season, Tulsa coach Joe Swank signed the school's first black players, a trio of junior college transfers—Sherman Dillard, Julian Hammond, and Herman Callands.

This was a new era, though, and Oral Roberts University fully integrated their team from its inception, putting a premium on black athletes whose style and speed became a hit in Tulsa.

In 1968, a seemingly meaningless home game became one of the most important in ORU history. Middle Tennessee State racehorsed past ORU, putting up 115 points. Reverend Roberts, who was a fixture at ORU games, was smitten with Middle Tennessee's style of play and decided to hire Ken Trickey, their flamboyant coach, the following spring.

Playing in the smaller College Division, Trickey finished 27-4 his first year at ORU. In 1972, his third year, the school entered the University Division and broke out with a 26-2 season and an NIT bid, the school's first postseason playoffs.

But it was more than just the fact that Oral Roberts University was winning. The team was fast-breaking as if the flames of hell were at their heels.

The godfather of Oklahoma basketball was still Henry Iba, whose strict, disciplined style influenced three generations of local coaches. Teams all over the state walked the ball up the court and played a conservative and stifling defense. Nobody, it seemed, wanted to risk irritating *Mister* Iba by playing a fast-paced game. Iba, who retired in 1969, was too diplomatic to speak out about what was happening at the new college in the state, but it must have appalled him.

During Ken Trickey's 26-2 run of 1972, ORU averaged 105 points per game, and even tallied 155 points in a win over Union College.

In 1974, ORU won two games in their debut in the NCAA Tournament. ORU needed to beat Kansas to earn a trip to the Final Four—a remarkable feat, considering it was less than a decade since the college opened its doors. Kansas overcame a 9-point deficit in the game's last few minutes, crushing the hopes of the ORU faithful.

That spring, the Tulsa police busted Ken Trickey for driving while intoxicated. Trickey had already announced his resignation before the arrest, but rumors of a setup spread through Tulsa.

Trickey compiled a record of 118-23 in only five years at Oral Roberts University and was a John the Baptist of the Fast Break—indirectly prophesying the coming of Nolan Richardson to Tulsa less than a decade later.

———

While ORU was welcoming to black players, their administrative approach was typical of the times. Black players were coveted; black leaders were not. Consider that twenty-six players have scored over one thousand points in the school's history. Twenty of them have been black. ORU has had ten head coaches, all of them white.

A few years after Ken Trickey's departure, Oral Roberts himself enticed coach Ken Hayes to leave New Mexico State and return to the city of Tulsa.

Hayes had been successful at New Mexico State, but he decided to return to Tulsa after the reverend made his offer. "You'll be my last coach," Roberts promised. Hayes came back to town just after the NCAA sheriffs penalized ORU with serious sanctions in an effort to get Oral's basketball coach to walk the straight and righteous path.

Hayes kept the pressure on Tulsa University. In his first season, Hayes knocked off his old TU team twice, the eighth win in a row for ORU over Tulsa.

The following spring, Nolan Richardson arrived in town.

Head coaching jobs have always been hard to come by, even for hugely successful junior college coaches. Richardson, who was thirty-eight years old, could not afford to turn his nose up at Tulsa's pauper past.

Tulsa competed in the Missouri Valley Conference, which had been one of the premier basketball leagues in America for years. The MVC at one time featured Cincinnati and Louisville, two teams that had won NCAA titles. Memphis State and Drake had earned berths to the Final Four, while Bradley and Wichita State had illustrious histories.

During the 1960s and 1970s, only one or two nationally televised college basketball games were broadcast a week. The advent of cable television in the late 1980s would slowly strangle the powerful MVC, because none of the schools were in major media centers. They were in Des Moines, Peoria, Canyon. And Tulsa. But before the days of cable TV, the Missouri Valley was a feared conference.

When Richardson arrived, the MVC had just seen Larry Bird at Indiana State lead his team to the NCAA title game. Richardson would face a long list of greats who would later earn jobs in the NBA: Lewis Lloyd, Antoine Carr, Cliff Levingston, Xavier McDaniel, David Thirdkill, Benoit Benjamin, Kevin McKenna, Mitchell Anderson, Hersey Hawkins, and Jim Les.

Nobody believed Richardson could win, especially not win immediately, despite his four fine players from Western Texas College—David Brown and Phil Spradling from El Paso, Greg Stewart, and future NBA star Paul Pressey. They'd be joined by Bob Stevenson, Tulsa's best returning player. Spradling and Stevenson were white.

Richardson still needed a natural point guard, and he settled on Mike Anderson, a relentless scrapper on the Alabama junior college team he'd beaten for the championship. Anderson's team lost any hope of winning when he fouled out. In a classic case of "if you can't beat 'em, join 'em," he signed with Tulsa a few weeks later. Richardson was taken by Anderson's quickness, but it was more than that. Richardson says, "You could tell he was that rare kid, a natural leader and a listener. And tough? He was as tough as could be."

Anderson, who is now the head coach at Missouri, says, "I could see that people just gravitated to Nolan, and he was unique in that way. I was excited about how Nolan played, but my first impression was that Tulsa was the real West, cowboys and Indians."

A decade before Richardson took over at Tulsa, Will Robinson was hired as the first black coach in major college basketball. Illinois

State, also of the Missouri Valley Conference, named Robinson the head coach in 1970, when he was fifty-eight.

Like Richardson, Robinson had begun coaching at the high school level, leading Detroit's Pershing High School to a state title. That team featured Spencer Haywood, who, with Robinson's help, would successfully challenge the NBA's ban on allowing underclassmen into the draft.

Robinson had been a talented high school football quarterback in Ohio and even came in second in the state's golf tournament—although he was not allowed to play on the golf course at the same time the white kids played.

His teams at ISU featured the skinny hotshot Doug Collins, who went on to a long NBA playing and coaching career. Robinson compiled a record of 78-51, and never had a losing season, but got dumped in 1975, his college career over after five quick years. Robinson then hooked on as a scout with the Detroit Pistons of the NBA, but declined an offer to be their head coach in the 1980s. Today, the Pistons locker room is called the "Will Robinson Locker Room of Champions." He died in 2008 at the age of ninety-six.

Neither John McLendon nor Big House Gaines was ever offered a chance to coach at a major white-majority state university. They were seen as Negro coaches at Negro schools and could not liberate themselves from that identity—or, rather, the administrators who hired new coaches at white universities could not free themselves from that prevailing mindset. Ben Jobe has managed to coach at both historically black colleges and majority white universities. Jobe served as the head coach at five historically black schools, the last of which was Southern University. In between those head coaching posts, Jobe was an assistant at two mostly white colleges, as well as the head coach of the University of Denver (then a Division II school).

In 1968, while Jobe was at the historically black South Carolina State University in Spartansburg, campus life was shattered when three young black men were shot in the back by police during a campus bonfire and protest. The incident echoed the killing of students at Kent State University by the Ohio National Guard.

Except that it didn't. Kent State got international media coverage and even inspired a rock 'n' roll anthem. South Carolina State's killings were largely ignored, and this left Jobe mystified and angry. The white media's blindness to State's on-campus slaughter would serve as a twisted metaphor for Jobe's successes. Despite his 524 college wins, he was ignored, too. He was never offered a head Division I job at a white-majority university.

Jobe enjoyed his most publicized success at Southern University, where, in 1993, he defeated an old employer, Georgia Tech, in the first round of the NCAA Tournament. His Southern teams qualified for the NCAA Tournament four times and earned one NIT bid (a rarity for a Southwestern Athletic Conference [SWAC] school).

He won 209 games at Southern, a remarkable total, considering he was forced to play almost ten "guarantee games" a year—games where Southern would travel to play for money, games that would never be "returned" to Baton Rouge, where Jobe's team could enjoy the home-court advantage. Despite this, Jobe never had a losing season at Southern.

An important reason coaches at historically black colleges don't advance to bigger state universities is because their overall won-lost records don't reflect their coaching ability. The Jobes with overall winning seasons are rare. Guarantee games are often necessary for a smaller school's survival. A big state university pays anywhere between $40,000 and $80,000 per game to the smaller historically black college. Never does the big school "return" the game and play on the smaller college's court. (It should be noted that not only the historically black colleges are subject to this prostitution; it might be Sam Houston State or Northeast Louisiana. All these smaller schools very much depend on the guarantee money to keep their programs afloat.)

The big state schools learn that some of the historically black colleges should be avoided. Over the years, teams like Southern and Coppin State have made the big schools regret paying out enormous amounts of money only to get beat on their own court. Because of guarantee games, there will never be a time when, say, two SWAC teams are awarded NCAA bids, since no teams in the league have impressive enough overall records.

Ben Jobe is brilliant, politically conscious, and outspoken. He is also devoid of the verbal clichés required of basketball coaches. He despises the Basketball Hall of Fame, where he ought to be a member—although he claims he'd refuse induction. Jobe lambasts the hall of fame for inducting announcers like Dick Vitale and the inventor of the shot clock. (Jobe: "The man who invented the shot clock should be in the General Electric Hall of Fame, not the Basketball Hall of Fame.") Jobe calls the NCAA a "fascist organization" and blames the NCAA for the destruction of black sports at black colleges.

Like Jobe, Frankie Allen has coached at both historically black colleges and white-majority universities and has some insights in the problems black coaches have advancing. Allen became the first black head coach at a mostly white school in Virginia when he was named coach at Virginia Tech in 1988. He has also been the head coach at Tennessee State, Howard, and is now at Maryland–Eastern Shore.

Allen says that if you want to understand the problems at historically black colleges, follow the money. And not just the guarantee game money. "There is little money coming from the private sector at Tennessee State," he says, "but the white schools enjoy tremendous help from donors." He says that the guarantee games sometimes allow historically black schools to fund the entire athletics department but that the money rarely goes to the basketball programs.

"That all depends on the coach's relationship with his boss," Allen says. "We played at Nebraska and got $75,000, and our AD is going to help us get new lockers."

One of the costs of this bargaining—almost certain losses for guaranteed money—is the sacrificed coaching careers.

The head-coaching jobs in the SWAC or MEAC are mirages at best; graveyards of crushed careers at the worst. Each January, every SWAC and MEAC coach starts his conference season with a losing record after its devastating preseason schedule has been played out. If a coach wins the SWAC, he still might not be above .500 for the season.

Today, a common trend is for big universities to hire a hot coach from a "Cinderella" team that has miraculously made the NCAA Tournament. But no SWAC coach, and just one MEAC coach, has ever gotten that call. One of Nolan Richardson's longtime assistants, Andy Stoglin, got his first head-coaching job at the SWAC's Jackson State University. He made the NCAA Tournament there, but the guarantee games prevented him from having a sparkling record, and he never advanced.

Examining the history of the program at North Carolina A&T affords both a look at the futility of coaching in the MEAC and an insight into how college hoops has evolved ever so slightly.

The MEAC includes schools like South Carolina State, Coppin State, Bethune-Cookman, and the league's traditional power, North Carolina A&T.

Cal Irvin took over at A&T in 1954, and he amassed over three hundred victories at the Greensboro school. He never had a losing season in eighteen years, but never got a chance at the big time either.

During the 1980s, North Carolina A&T was coached by Don Corbett, who led A&T to *seven straight* NCAA bids. His overall record, despite a slew of guarantee games at A&T, was 249-133, including thirty-seven wins in a row at home. Yet no mostly white school in basketball-crazed North Carolina, or anywhere else, would try to lure Don Corbett away—or play on his home court.

Jeff Capel Sr. is the exception that proves the rule. He coached North Carolina A&T for a single season, in 1993–94, and made the NCAA Tournament. He was named the head coach at Old Dominion the next season.

For every modern success story like Richardson's, there are forgotten men, brilliant coaches like Cal Irvin and Don Corbett, whose opportunities were limited by their skin color. Richardson still speaks with respect of his successful-yet-obscure predecessors: Ben Jobe, "Fang" Mitchell at Coppin State, and David Whitney at Alcorn State.

Black coaches, especially assistant coaches, were perceived for years as recruiters who could relate to black players and little more. Recruiting is imperative, but most black coaches consider the label to be belittling at best, as there is a distinct division within the business between recruiters and strategists. The coach who relies on strategy must be smarter, the thinking went, and they were always white.

Reggie Minton remembers those labels well. He was an assistant at the Air Force Academy before becoming the head coach at Dartmouth, then Air Force. Minton attended Wooster College in Ohio, where he began to develop his political consciousness. "In college I had given a speech," he recalls, "and I talked about not only wanting to ride in the front of the bus but wanting to drive and then *own* the bus." It was a speech America's athletics directors and college presidents should have been required to attend.

The Air Force Academy played a PAC-10 school one season when Minton was an assistant. After the game, the coaches went out for beers, but Minton, who doesn't drink, returned to his hotel room. When his boss, Hank Egan, returned, he told Minton what the PAC-10 coach had said.

"Why do you have *that* guy on your staff?" the PAC-10 coach said to Egan, referring to Minton. "Air Force doesn't even have any black guys."

By the early 1980s, Minton was one of the most qualified assistant coaches in the game. That didn't exactly reap huge rewards. He landed the job at Dartmouth for $30,000 a year.

Today, Minton helps direct the National Association of Basketball Coaches (NABC). He thinks today's new generation of African-American coaches simply does not understand their place in history. "They come along and it is all there," Minton says, "and they think of it as a right. In 1980, Nolan Richardson was one of a handful of black coaches outside of the historically black colleges. In 1983, there were eight of us. Eight! It was tight, a brotherhood."

The long-term effects of college basketball's segregated coaching ranks can still be charted. When UCLA icon John Wooden began his long string of championships in the 1960s, not a single black coach was competing for the national title. Today's recently retired coaching legends got their start in a segregated system. Bobby Knight, Don Haskins, Lou Henson, Eddie Sutton, Dean Smith, and Ray Meyer all began their careers well before a black coach could challenge them.

This segregated system has perpetuated itself, distorting the otherwise impressive "trees" of most of these coaches. For example, Bobby Knight had twenty-five assistant coaches who worked under him land head jobs. Only two have been black.

Since no black head coaches worked in powerful places, they were not calling the shots on who might get the *next* promotion, as Eddie Sutton and Lute Olsen did for decades. For a black assistant coach, the wait could be humiliating.

Rob Evans, who helped launch Nolan Richardson's career, worked as an assistant for Lou Henson on highly successful teams at

New Mexico State. Later, after his long tenure as an assistant at Texas Tech, he joined Eddie Sutton at Oklahoma State. All in all, he served as a major college assistant for twenty-four years before he got the call from Mississippi to run their program. Soon after, Evans led Ole Miss to two straight NCAA bids for the first time in school history and was named SEC Coach of the Year.

The system in college ball limited black coaches from even thinking about beginning a career. Imagine a typical black college graduate, who did not come from a middle-class background. Would he sign on as a low-paid assistant coach? Or would he take a job at, say, Marshall High School in Chicago for twice as much money? Since young black coaches did not often have the luxury of calling home for help with the rent, they were simply more likely not to be able to pay their dues. Or, rather, pay any *more* dues.

"Man, they hired that nigger coach."

That became the refrain heard around Tulsa the summer of 1980, and the complaint drove Ed Beshara to distraction. Unbeknown to Richardson, Beshara was able to talk Evans Dunne down, urging him to consider the woeful state of the basketball team, and to not withdraw his support. "Give the guy a chance, let's see how he does," Beshara told anyone who would listen.

Soon after Richardson arrived in Tulsa, Beshara called the basketball office and invited Richardson to stop by for coffee.

Richardson was met at the store with Beshara's standard greeting. "Hoss," said Beshara, "I just want to find out where you stand and who you are." The two men took off for hamburgers.

Richardson and Beshara came back to the store two hours later, laughing like school kids on the playground.

Encouraged by Beshara's upbeat humor, Richardson began looking for fresh ideas to set his Tulsa team apart. He ordered flashy new uniforms, then decorated the dismal locker room. Next, he selected a theme song to be played endlessly: "Ain't No Stoppin' Us." When Richardson learned that some of the few fans would dump their trash in the mouth of the team's bloated mascot, he insisted on a sleeker one.

On Richardson's second trip to Ed Beshara's store, he figured he'd better buy some clothes. He beelined to the sale rack and held a polka-dot shirt to his chest. A row of polka-dot shirts that Beshara could hardly give away lined the wall. Beshara didn't want them ruining the new coach's image. "You don't want that stuff, Nolan," Beshara called, waving him away.

He was too late.

"Check out how these colors look on me!" Richardson said. "How about this? Blue with gold polka dots. Tulsa colors."

"It's totally out of style," Beshara moaned. "We're trying to get rid of those."

But Richardson was grabbing the eye-catching colors by the handful. "I have to entertain, fill the gym with fans," Richardson said, checking for sizes.

"Fill the gym, hoss?" Beshara said. "They only get a few thousand fans a game."

Richardson turned serious. "You better get your tickets now," he said.

"I used the polka dots as an attention-getter, to get myself and my team noticed," Richardson says today. Soon the style—or anti-style—caught on, and a tacky Tulsa tradition was born. The students began wearing them as well, and the fans followed suit. Richardson wore polka dots his entire time with the Hurricane.

"Polka dots became contagious, like a citywide case of the measles," sportswriter Jimmie Tramel said.

Ed Beshara said, "I sold polka-dot shirts like selling ice cream."

In one mid-season contest, Richardson donned a tuxedo, and the team struggled. As he followed his team toward the locker room at halftime, fans implored him to change his outfit. The coach switched to polka dots in the locker room. Tulsa won in overtime. Later, when he again tried to take a detour from the polka-dot path, his daughter, Yvonne, insisted he stick with them.

"That kind of talk—about hiring a nigger coach—wasn't unusual at all back then," Beshara's son says today. "It was my dad who was unusual. He just didn't see color."

Ed Beshara also didn't see basketball. Literally. He rarely went to games at Tulsa, even during Richardson's tenure. "Five games in five years," his son says, quoting one of the few stats he recalls. "Dad wasn't friends with Nolan because he was a coach or famous. If Nolan decided to drive a bus instead of being a coach, they would have still been close."

Tulsa easily won their first two games under Richardson, but on December 4, 1980, Louisville was coming to Tulsa. Louisville was the defending NCAA champion and had four returning starters from the 1980 winners, as well as future NBA star Scooter McCray. It would be Richardson's first big test as a major college coach.

Louisville had swept through the NCAA Tournament field the previous year with a rip-and-run style, beating UCLA for the national title. They were one of the dominant programs in college basketball in the 1980s and an offensive model for what Richardson hoped to assemble: a fast-breaking team that ran its opponents into the ground. Richardson's pep talk to his Tulsa team was simple. The lowly Junior College Champions of Western Texas College were taking on the Division I champions of Louisville. Richardson repeatedly reminded his players of their underdog role, and this was Tulsa's first us-against-the-world challenge.

The fourth-largest crowd in school history went berserk as Tulsa's frantic full-court defense forced Louisville to commit an astonishing thirty-five turnovers. Tulsa won, 68-60.

Two days later, Tulsa beat the University of Oklahoma on its own court.

Tulsa fans were dizzy from excitement. "It was love at first dribble," the *Tulsa World* wrote. Crosstown rival Oral Roberts University was next.

A miracle was unfolding, but not the one Reverend Roberts hoped for. Richardson won at ORU, 72-69.

The ensuing matchup was with the University of Georgia, and future NBA stars Dominique Wilkins and Vern Fleming. Lines formed at the Tulsa ticket office for the first time in decades. But the University of Georgia ended Tulsa's win streak, beating Tulsa by two.

That was okay with the coach—they were going to have to lose sometime. It was not, however, all right with Yvonne Richardson. The eight-year-old did not recall ever seeing her father lose a game. They'd been undefeated the previous year, and rarely lost a home game in Snyder before that. Her father had won forty-two games in a row. When was the last time she saw him lose—when she was five? Six? Richardson couldn't recall either, and Yvonne was disconsolate. She wept for hours.

The Tulsa Hurricane's quick start won over Evans Dunne and his cohorts,

Richardson admits, "It was easy for the fans to say, 'Hey, we've got something here.'" Indeed, Tulsa did have something.

Just before the conference season began, Tulsa beat Purdue, which had been in the Final Four the previous year. The Hurricane cracked the top ten for the first time in their history, and the town was up for grabs. Sportswriter Jimmie Tramel coined the phrase "Rollin' with Nolan," and it stuck.

Polka dots were the most visible change in Tulsa, but something more important was stirring below the surface. Basketball success and improved race relations went together like a screen and roll. In this case, historically white South Tulsa and predominantly black North Tulsa united over Hurricane hoops. For the first time in school history, attendance topped a hundred thousand for the season. Per-game crowds doubled, going from 3,700 a game to 7,300. Tulsa's townies began referring to the Hurricane team as "we."

"A lot of good things happened in Tulsa that had nothing to do with basketball," Richardson says. "Blacks and whites had something to talk about, something good to share."

One fan told Richardson, "I remember going to work and nobody, and I mean black and white, said anything to each other. Now we have a common bond."

"When we beat Louisville," recalls Mike Anderson, "anybody could see that something special was brewing." The Tulsa team and their coach were at the forefront of social change, both on campus and in town. "Nolan used to tell us all the time," Anderson says, "there's just one race. The human race."

In 1982, a Gannett News piece claimed that Tulsa University ". . . may be the number one social phenomenon in college basketball."

Just before Christmas, Richardson would give the fans another gift. Tulsa would complete the in-state sweep by nudging out Oklahoma State.

Nobody seemed to mention the "nigger coach" anymore.

Tulsa finished the 1980–81 season with a record of 11-5 in the Missouri Valley Conference, good enough for a second-place finish. But they lost in the semifinals of the MVC Tournament and got passed over by the NCAA Tournament selection committee, despite their wins over Louisville, Oklahoma, Oklahoma State, Tulane, and Purdue in their nonconference schedule. In fact, Tulsa had finished the regular season at 20-6 against eleven teams that went on to postseason play. It was perhaps the worst snub in NCAA Tournament history.

Only forty-eight teams were invited to the NCAA at that time, and Tulsa was given a bid to the NIT. Because of the sorry state of the Tulsa University facilities, the first few games were to be played on the Oral Roberts campus. Tulsa beat Pan American in their first game to set up a showdown with UTEP and Don Haskins. UTEP was just beginning to recover from three straight losing seasons, the worst of Haskins's career.

The game proved to be an emotionally conflicted one for Richardson, as well as a matchup of contrasting styles. He had, of course, totally abandoned Haskins's philosophy by this time, and it was important for him to have a good showing against his own coach. Richardson's resentment over being smothered on offense by Haskins's system had faded—nearly twenty years had passed, and Richardson was the only former UTEP player who was a major college coach. That made it easier for him to reconcile with Haskins's overbearing control.

With no shot clock at the time, UTEP began the game passing and cutting for a full minute. Tulsa countered by pressing and trapping everywhere, trying to coax UTEP into a faster pace. Tulsa took the lead with two minutes to go. A frantic rally led by an obscure UTEP sub wasn't enough, and Tulsa prevailed.

Tulsa beat South Alabama by one to earn a trip to Madison Square Garden and the semifinals.

New York City was a blur.

Tulsa beat West Virginia by two.

In the NIT championship, Tulsa topped Syracuse in overtime.

It marked the first time in the history of the game that a black coach won the NIT. Tulsa and Nolan Richardson were on the map.

What made the biggest impression on the coach in New York City happened during the cutting-down-the-net ceremony in the midst of the on-court celebration. Somebody grabbed Richardson, embraced him, and planted a kiss on his cheek. Richardson had been getting hugs and handshakes, but no kisses. He turned to see who the hell had gotten his cheek wet.

It was Evans Dunne.

When the team arrived home in Tulsa at 4:30 a.m., two thousand fans were crammed into the airport terminal to welcome them. University president, Paschal Twyman, pronounced Monday an official campus holiday and shut down the college. Governor George Nigh joined ten thousand other fans in downtown Tulsa's Bartlett Square for the victory party.

Richardson refers to that magical year as one of his favorite seasons. "It was maybe the most incredible feeling I've ever had as a basketball coach, seeing how much the city and community appreciated what we had accomplished."

Ralph Brewster, however, was heartbroken in Lubbock, Texas.

He'd grown to tolerate the town, and he very much liked his teammates at Texas Tech. He'd overcome his initial homesickness. Then his patience and dedication had paid off with those two fine seasons in a row, when he averaged double figures as a sophomore and junior. Richardson had steered him to the right place, he believed, because he was a success at Tech.

He'd celebrated privately when Richardson had won the national junior college championship at Western Texas, and he nearly phoned to ask if he could join the guys and transfer to Tulsa. But Brewster knew he'd have some hard explaining to do with his Red Raider teammates. Plus, he'd have to sit out a full year to play just one final season. So he'd stuck around at Tech, anticipating a landmark senior season.

That great season didn't happen. Brewster was shocked to find himself on the bench. Richardson's raucous ride with his crew of El Paso players made him feel worse. Why had Coach Gerald Myers thought the best place for his experienced insider was on the sideline?

Brewster's senior year was a disaster. He was healthy, playing in twenty-seven games that final year, but his playing time was chopped in half, and thus his point totals. He scored only 5.7 points per game. His rebounding also fell off, to 4.1 a game. Brewster was humiliated. He had willingly bought into the Bowie backroom deal, and he'd helped launch Nolan Richardson's career, but he had somehow again gotten caught up in the machinations of college basketball.

With Brewster on the bench, Tech would stumble to its worst record during his four years there, finishing 15-13. "I didn't even understand what had happened," Brewster says, "until years later."

When his college days ended, Brewster played professionally in Mexico, Venezuela, the Philippines, and the minor league CBA. After his professional playing career was through, he became a business-man, traveling all over Texas. Once, he phoned Rob Evans, his old assistant coach, when he had an appointment in Lubbock, and suggested getting together. Evans made a tearful confession to Brewster that night, saying that Myers had grown to despise Nolan Richardson and took it out on Brewster. Brewster still didn't get it—why wouldn't Myers like Richardson?

Gerald Myers believed his recommendation had landed Richardson the job at Western Texas and that there should be another pay-back—signing Brewster out of high school was not enough. "My coaches felt Nolan *owed* Tech," Brewster says. When Myers learned that Richardson was bringing his best players with him to Tulsa—especially Paul Pressey—he took out his frustrations on Brewster. "Whenever he saw me, he saw Nolan Richardson," Brewster says. "Myers suppressed it all, he never said it out loud, but it wasn't the same for me. After that, he was just anti-Ralph."

Brewster remains perplexed by the irony. Tech had essentially *taught* Nolan Richardson to use his best player to advance his career, yet when Richardson took the next step, going to Tulsa, the Tech coach was angry.

Brewster's Tech teammate and El Paso pal, Dwight Williams,

says the contrast in styles between Myers and Richardson was stark, and that made things more difficult for Brewster. "I think Gerald Myers epitomizes college basketball," Williams says. "From the top down, it is a business. But from the bottom up, from the player's point of view, it's a game. Somewhere in the middle you're supposed to meet, but we never got that from Coach Myers." Richardson was different, Williams says. "He will see a man who played at Bowie forty years ago, and know his name."

To this day, Brewster thinks about his decision to attend Tech. "There's a thin line between resentment and wondering *what if*," he says. "Because in truth, the way my career turned out was not to my liking at all. In my adolescent mind, I wondered during that senior season, 'Why did I let Nolan talk me into Tech?'"

Winning the NIT meant the Tulsa program could finally upgrade. Before Richardson arrived, the basketball office didn't employ a full-time secretary; former coach Jim King's wife would volunteer a few days a week. Richardson had only $36,000 to divide among his entire coaching staff his first season. After the big win in New York City, Richardson insisted on raises for his assistants.

The next season, Richardson's team didn't take any chances. They swept through the MVC Tournament by an average margin of 16 points, earning the automatic berth to the NCAA. It was only the second trip to the NCAA in the school's history. Tulsa lost to the University of Houston team, which featured Akeem Olajuwon, 78-74.

Richardson was so confident in his coaching skills that the quick success at Tulsa came as no surprise to him. Besides the breakneck pace his teams played at, there was something else setting Richardson apart. He wanted his players around his home as much as they desired.

This could mean a formal dinner hosting a recruit, a birthday celebration, or simply the guys flopping around his TV room and watching the game of the week, the World Series or the Super Bowl. The total immersion with the players was in complete contrast to most coaches—including Don Haskins—who quickly grew weary of their kids and wanted nothing to do with them once practices were over.

Of course Richardson was winning, and that helped. The open-door policy meant Rose Richardson was always cooking, and young Yvonne was balancing trays of soft drinks. He was cognizant of this void in his earlier years and that plenty of his players came from fractured homes as well. The team quickly learned that Richardson's dissatisfaction or anger on the practice court remained there.

Although Richardson was emotionally closer to his players than the vast majority of coaches, there were occasions where he simply could not solve the riddle presented by some troublesome player.

Such was the case with a chronically overweight Phoenix player named Bruce Vanley. Despite his weight, Vanley was a talented and effective college pivot who once outplayed North Carolina star Sam Perkins when Tulsa tamed the Tar Heels by 10 points. Regardless, Vanley's weight remained a problem. Extra sprints. Jump-rope sessions. Laps. Diet restrictions. Lectures and threats. Nothing helped. It was a mystery to Richardson how an overweight player might remain fat within his frenetic system. Yet Richardson was fond of Vanley, and he made it clear that the pudgy post player, like everyone else, was always welcome at the Richardson home.

One evening, Richardson went to scout a Tulsa high school prospect. By the end of the first quarter, the coach had seen enough. The player wasn't fast enough for Tulsa, and Richardson slipped out a side door and headed home.

When he shook open the back door, Bruce Vanley was sitting at his kitchen table. Below his round face was a pie tin. Half the apple pie was gone. Vanley looked up, his mouth full.

"What the hell is going on here?" Richardson bellowed.

"Hi, coach," Vanley mumbled.

Richardson sprang forward as if to toss the entire table aside. But Rosario appeared at Richardson's hip, and she slid between the coach and the still-chewing Vanley. She pointed her finger at her husband. "This is my kitchen!" she said. "I'm in charge. I do what I want in here."

Vanley shoveled in another bite. Richardson reached for his own plate.

Tulsa would slip a bit during the 1982–83 campaign, finishing 19-12 and earning a return to the NIT. That the players were now disappointed with the NIT bid revealed how far the program had come. Not out to prove themselves as they had been in 1981, Tulsa lost to TCU 64-62 in the first round.

In 1983–84, Tulsa would finish 27-4. Although it was a few years before the three-point line was instituted, Tulsa averaged a blistering 90.8 points per game. The season marked a new high in excitement for Tulsa basketball, and the team's scoring totals were by far the highest in their history.

Tulsa's fans took notice, too. Attendance under Nolan Richardson is still the high mark for the University of Tulsa. Many of the players who competed for Tulsa during those years allude to the era as a time when nothing could go wrong. The team's success seemed preordained in a way, as if they were destined at Richardson's arrival to become one of the most improved teams in the nation.

Only one thing was nagging at Richardson. Yvonne sometimes complained that she didn't feel well. She was fatigued often, and if she had a fever it seemed forever until it came down.

Richardson would finish his time at Tulsa with a home record of 80-6, and Tulsa would win the Missouri Valley Conference in 1984 and 1985. In Richardson's five seasons, he boasted a record of 119-37, a rate of 76 percent.

Just as impressive, and invigorating to the Tulsa faithful, black and white, was the way Richardson disposed of their non-league in-state rivals. Richardson would amass an astonishing record of 17-1 against Oklahoma, Oklahoma State, and Oral Roberts University. He was 10-0 against ORU, a team that had regularly qualified for the NCAA and NIT. That record of 17-1, maybe more than the NIT title and NCAA bids, is what solidified Richardson's hero status in Tulsa.

Still, Richardson's legacy at Tulsa goes far beyond jump-starting a dormant program. While twenty-three coaches preceded Richardson at Tulsa, only one coach made the NCAA Tournament. There have been eight coaches since Nolan Richardson left Tulsa in 1985, and five of those coaches have qualified for the NCAA Tournament, a shocking turnaround even with the expanded field of sixty-five teams today. One other coach, Buzz Peterson, won the NIT in his first and only season before tripling his salary at Tennessee. The Tulsa job is now coveted nationally, and coaches like Tubby Smith and Bill Self, who would also go on to win NCAA titles, have gotten their starts in Tulsa.

Just as important, Richardson paved the way for three African-American coaches: Tubby Smith, Steve Robinson, and Alvin "Pooh" Williamson, who took over briefly in 2005. Incredible progress has been made in Tulsa since the "nigger coach" complaints of 1980.

In March of 1985, the Tulsa team was waiting to hear their matchup in the NCAA Tournament. When Richardson learned Tulsa would be in the same bracket as Don Haskins's UTEP team, his feelings were mixed. Either Richardson or Haskins would be sent home from the NCAA playoffs after a single game.

The next morning, Yvonne Richardson, who had not been feeling well since February, was diagnosed with leukemia. She was thirteen years old.

———

A few weeks later, Arkansas coach Eddie Sutton announced he was leaving to accept the University of Kentucky job. Sutton, like Don Haskins, had played for Henry Iba. In an uncharacteristic display of frustration, Sutton said he would have crawled to Kentucky to be the coach there. Something or someone at the University of Arkansas, evidently, had angered him.

Sutton had taken his 1978 Arkansas squad to the Final Four, the first time a Southwest Conference team earned a Final Four bid with black players.

Arkansas athletics director Frank Broyles phoned to gauge Richardson's interest in Arkansas. Broyles played in Ed Beshara's annual golf tournament, and had heard an earful from Tulsa fans about their black coach.

Yet Richardson originally declined to be interviewed for the Arkansas job, citing his daughter's diagnosis. Yvonne's doctor was there in Tulsa, and that was that. But Yvonne reminded her father of his own complaint, that if he'd just had a better on-campus home court he might win the NCAA championship. She encouraged Richardson to at least listen to Arkansas. He had driven Yvonne to Fayetteville when Tulsa played them in football, and she was astounded by Arkansas's rabid crowd and first-class facilities.

Richardson, as it turned out, was not the top candidate. In a move indicating either the nerve or foolishness of Frank Broyles, the job was first offered to that year's NCAA championship coach, Rollie Massimino of Villanova. When Massimino declined, Bobby Cremins and Gary Williams were approached, but none of the three white coaches had a genuine interest. "They all three used Broyles to get a raise at their own schools," one Arkansas sportswriter says. Richardson was the last one standing, front and center, and Broyles offered him the job.

The coach, though, told Yvonne he had decided he was going to stay at Tulsa.

"No, Papi," she said. "We're going to Arkansas."

Richardson relented and accepted Broyles's offer.

"Two hours later," the same sportswriter says, "Broyles was on a plane that went to Augusta National Golf Club. Augusta is an archaic and blind place," he says, "but that's how Frank was raised and he didn't see anything wrong with it." The home of the Masters Tournament was segregated at that time, and the irony of his Augusta trip after hiring a black coach was obvious to some Arkansas insiders.

Richardson still mulls over his decision today. "Everything was there for Yvonne in Tulsa," Richardson says. "Not just her doctors, but her friends, too."

Years later, Richardson would express remorse to the *Tulsa World*. Despite Yvonne's encouragement, he wondered if the move might not have been the best one for her. "When you think about that, going back over things," Richardson said, "you often ask yourself if you had to do it over again, would you do that? I would have probably not done it. No one was more important than my girl. That was a selfish decision . . . what I really wanted was her."

Haskins couldn't recall much about beating Tulsa in the NCAA Tournament in 1985. He claimed not to have any recollection of setting the NCAA record with fifty-five free throws attempted, although Richardson could not forget that statistic.

But Haskins clearly remembered when Frank Broyles phoned for a recommendation on Nolan Richardson a week later. "I told Nolan that I wouldn't go to Arkansas," Haskins claimed. "I asked Broyles, 'If Nolan gets in trouble, are you going to stand behind him?'"

Broyles's answer, according to Haskins, was, "It's a black man's game."

"That's all he kept saying," Haskins said, "the entire phone conversation, *'It's a black man's game.'* He never did answer my question about standing behind Nolan."

Yet no other large state school in the old Confederacy had ever chosen a black head coach in basketball, and it would be seventeen more years until a black man was picked as a football coach in the south. Regardless of Frank Broyles's assessment of the state of college basketball, his decision to hire Richardson in 1985 was daring.

SEVEN

THE SOULS OF BLACK FOLK

Arkansas joined the Union as a slave state in 1836 and seven years later prohibited the entrance of any new free men of color. In 1853, an editorial ran in the *Arkansas State Gazette and Democrat.* God, the newspaper said, had created Africans to be slaves. Slavery was both divinely sanctioned and legal.

On the eve of the Civil War, 111,000 slaves lived in Arkansas, roughly a quarter of the state's population. But three-quarters of Arkansas slaves lived in the southeast half of the state. That diagonal demarcation is still important today. The Mississippi floodplain to the southeast meant flat lands, big plantations, and slave ownership. The northwest half of Arkansas, with the Ozark and Ouchita Mountains, was less suited to cotton plantations. Northwest Arkansas was both whiter and poorer, with largely yeoman farmers scratching out a living.

Just before the start of the war, the Arkansas legislature voted to expel the remaining free blacks, less than a thousand men. When the fighting began, many slaves fled for the North. A lot of them would return. Between five thousand and fifteen thousand black men from Arkansas fought for the Union before the conclusion of the war.

In 1864, Arkansas's "Organic Law" abolished slavery, repudiated secession, and forbade any law "prohibiting the education of any class." Allowing freed slaves to be educated was a surprising development, but voting was another matter. No provisions were enacted for black male suffrage—not for literate black men, for those who owned property, or even for Union soldiers. And blacks not already living in Arkansas could not take up residence in the state, except in the unlikely case of an exception made by the U.S. government.

Radical Reconstruction had hardly been unveiled before the balance of power shifted back to ex-Confederates. The Ku Klux Klan appeared in Arkansas in 1868, and a wave of lynchings followed, with the precise purpose of influencing elections. The sheriff in Monticello was kidnapped and tied to a black man before both men were shot. Then their corpses were posed, embracing, and left to rot, as a lesson.

When Jim Crow segregation became official in the 1870s, the frequency of lynchings declined, although there would be periodic outbreaks, especially in the southern part of the state. Arkansas became a center of the Back to Africa movement, and Liberia was promoted within the black community as a fine place for freed slaves to live.

Arkansas became a national joke (if you could bring yourself to overlook the lynchings) in 1869, with the opening of a popular theatrical production called *The Arkansas Traveler*. The protagonist was a rustic back-hills character with a muddy Southern accent and laconic wit, initiating the hillbilly stereotype. The production traveled around American stages, a success until it closed in 1899.

The damage to the state's reputation continued in the 1880s, when the widely published newspaper column called—surprise—"The Arkansas Traveler" featured more depictions of hillbillies dispensing wit and wisdom. Soon a magazine with the identical name and goal—making fun of Arkansas—was published and stayed in national circulation for over thirty years.

Arkansans began to adopt attitudes of resentment and paranoia about the East. Of course, Arkansas could be its own worst enemy. The well-known journalist H. L. Mencken, in a lengthy article about the South, made a brief reference to Arkansas, writing that residents were "too stupid to see what was the matter with them." The state's General Assembly leaped into action, passing a resolution that demanded an apology from Mencken.

In the resolution, they misspelled the author's name.

The worst post–Civil War racial episode in the state's history occurred in 1919 in Elaine, Arkansas. Whites feared the organization of a black union there, and when a hundred sharecroppers attended a gathering of the Progressive Farmers and Household Union, violence erupted. Five whites and hundreds of blacks were killed; in fact, the exact number of murdered blacks has never been known.

Probably the most publicized lynching occurred in 1927, when John Carter was accused of assaulting a white woman. He was hung from a telephone pole, set on fire, dragged through the streets, then dumped at the corner of Ninth & Broadway in the heart of Little Rock's black community.

During the Great Depression, two western Arkansas residents created the fictional radio characters that became the *Lum and Abner Show*. NBC bought the program and moved the "rural philosophers" to Chicago, where the show aired for twenty-five years. The Arkansas hayseed backwoods image was now a firmly established nationwide joke.

A few years later, *Reader's Digest* published a note that was supposedly found on a bulletin board at a closed factory up North. The note read: "Pair of shoes for sale; moving back to Arkansas." Despite the lighthearted nature of some of the humor, concern about the state's reputation was of growing importance.

In 1953, Arkansas elected a governor with a progressive background, named Orval Faubus. One of Faubus's best moves was to appoint a Rockefeller to oversee the state's economy. In Winthrop Rockefeller's first year, 1956, over five hundred businesses were convinced that Arkansas would be a great place to relocate.

The University of Arkansas opened its doors in 1871 as the state's land-grant institution. Just a year later, the university's board of trustees announced the school was "open to all without regard to race, sex, or sect."

At least two freed slaves attended UA that year. One, James McGahee, is credited with being the first black student to enroll. (The story of McGahee's enrollment was discovered in 2006 by a graduate student.) The university president taught McGahee himself, so as not to embarrass the teachers.

In 1873, the Arkansas State Legislature authorized a university branch in Pine Bluff to be the school for African-Americans. Then, as the state's politics shifted, the University of Arkansas in Fayetteville began excluding blacks.

That policy of exclusion was unchanged until Silas Hunt applied to the UA law school in 1948. Hunt was an army hero who had fought at the Battle of the Bulge, where he was badly wounded. (Hunt was not, however, awarded the Congressional Medal of Honor. No black soldier would be honored for decades.) Through a coordinated effort with Little Rock activist Wiley Brandt, Hunt was admitted to the UA School of Law in 1948. That same year, Edith Mae Irby became the first black to enroll at the University of Arkansas Medical School in Little Rock.

State laws still prohibited integrated classrooms, so Hunt had to attend segregated classes—meaning that he was the only student in his classroom in the basement. In an odd subterranean show of support, a couple of white students decided to join him. Later, Hunt was allowed upstairs, with a single railing separating the wounded World War II hero from his classmates. He died a little over a year after enrolling, at age twenty-seven, likely from tuberculosis combined with complications of his war wounds.

Although the University of Arkansas was the first major school in the South to enroll a black student, the college continued its policy of rejecting all applications from undergraduate blacks until the *Brown v. Board of Education* ruling by the Supreme Court in 1954. That led to the first black undergrads being admitted at Arkansas in 1955.

Fayetteville High School, as well as the Hoxie District in the northeast corner of the state, immediately began implementing the *Brown* decision in 1954. Seven black students were admitted to Fayetteville High School, making it among the very first towns in the South to successfully desegregate without fanfare or controversy.

There would be plenty of controversy, however, coming up in Little Rock.

The Civil Rights movement targeted Little Rock as a city that could, potentially, quietly withstand the desegregation of its schools. Little Rock was not in the Deep South, the state was largely white, and Governor Orval Faubus was a moderate, so the town appeared to be a good bet. Little Rock had become a focal point in 1942, when Susie Morris, a black teacher at Dunbar High School, filed a lawsuit because she was paid less than white teachers. Morris won the lawsuit but lost her job.

The plan was to integrate Central High School gradually, and only nine students volunteered, due to pressure, rumors, and fear. Yet that made the plan easier to implement. Nearly everyone—newspaper editors, businessmen, school administration—expected an easy and peaceful transition.

During his reelection campaign in 1956, Faubus had hardly referred to race. In Arkansas, the law required the governor to go up for election every two years, and by 1957, Faubus was gunning for a third term. He had a stark choice: empower the tide of integration and lose, or challenge the feds and make himself a symbol of segregation.

In the spring of 1957, Faubus pushed through four segregationist bills. He didn't need a weatherman to know which way the wind was blowing. The segregationist bills passed, 81-1.

With school and desegregation at Central scheduled to begin, Faubus could find no middle ground, the salvation for many a politician. That September he indirectly condoned mob violence by publicly claiming that he, the governor, could not maintain peace. Then Faubus decided to call out the Arkansas National Guard to *prevent* blacks from enrolling at Central High School. The National Guard found itself on the side of the white mobs, and despite specific orders from the district court, kept the nine black kids from entering the school.

What happened in the ensuing weeks is well documented. Eight of the students who arrived were abused and threatened before being turned away by the Arkansas National Guard. The mob had its confidence bolstered, as did the segregationists. President Eisenhower reacted by sending in the 101st Airborne Division to aid the integration process, the first time since Reconstruction that federal troops were sent to the old Confederacy.

Most compelling about the Central High School story was what happened to Elizabeth Eckford that first day. A fifteen-year-old, Eckford had not received the message about the detailed plan for the nine students to travel to Central together. Wearing the new dress she had made herself and bolstered by the morning prayers of her parents, Eckford walked to Central High School alone.

The mob spotted her and mirrored her steps, taunting and spitting on her. Eckford had seen the National Guard ahead and figured she'd be safe. When she got to the guard, though, they blocked her path by raising bayonets to her throat.

With the mob closing in behind with shouts of "Lynch her!" Eckford realized she'd have to reverse directions and walk the gauntlet again. Soon she was surrounded on all sides, with the National Guard behind her. She turned toward a bus stop, and the crowd let her pass, giving her an earful the entire walk. After being encouraged by a *New York Times* education reporter and an elderly white woman, Eckford finally got on a bus and was out of harm's way.

Eckford returned to Central the next day and graduated on time a few years later.

The genocide in Tulsa's Greenwood district in 1921, of course, predated a national television audience. While the story of Central High School appeared in newspapers and magazines, it was the newer medium of the television screen where the meltdown in Arkansas had the most impact.

Central High School was the first showdown between a rabid mob and the force of law to play out on national television. According to David Halberstam's book *The Fifties*, "The images were so forceful that they told their own truths and needed virtually no narration. It was hard for people watching at home not to take sides . . . watching orderly black children behaving with great dignity, trying to obtain nothing more than a decent education, the most elemental of American birthrights, yet being assaulted by a vicious mob of poor whites."

It was hard for people at home not to take sides. While surely not everyone in Arkansas had a television, everyone in Arkansas had to make a decision. Especially its leaders. They had televisions. The white students at Central decided mostly to accommodate the nine black kids, especially as the year progressed.

Black teenagers from Little Rock, without the least bit of power, were acting with tremendous courage. How would the state's leaders, with *all* the power, act?

Frank Broyles arrived as football coach at the University of Arkansas in the late winter of 1958. Fayetteville High School had successfully, if modestly, desegregated, as had the university's law school, medical school, and undergraduate student body. Of course, none of those events were nationally televised.

Broyles, no doubt, took note of the fortunes of Governor Faubus, who during the previous summer had looked unlikely to win a third term. But the Central High School crisis ignited his popularity among the majority, the white voters. A white person of voting age could no longer be for segregation yet against Faubus. In the next election, Faubus beat his two opponents handily—their combined votes didn't amount to half of his total.

It wasn't just Frank Broyles who was watching, of course. Future presidential candidate and segregationist George Wallace also learned from Little Rock, according to Halberstam, ". . . how to manipulate the anger within the South, how to divide the state by class and race, and how to make the enemy seem to be the media." A decade later, George Wallace would win Arkansas in the presidential election as an independent. Wallace won only five states, and Arkansas was the only one not in the Deep South.

Some moderates felt the "lessons of Little Rock" meant that violence would scare away business. That would prove to be true. The negative publicity again set Arkansas back in the nation's eye. Not a single new industrial plant opened in either Little Rock or its surrounding Pulaski County in the year following the crisis. Winthrop Rockefeller, who had championed Arkansas as a great business location, resigned.

But another lesson of Little Rock was that clinging to a racist past at the institutional level could be a popular policy.

Desegregating a high school in the biggest city in the state was one challenge. Getting anyone else to follow suit was quite another. By the autumn of 1963, less than one percent of African-American public school students in Arkansas attended classes with whites. As late as 1967, 83 percent of black students still attended segregated schools.

Any leader interested in keeping the world segregated had to *make the enemy seem to be the media*. But it could be taken in a different direction—befriending and controlling the media could be a smart step, too. Nothing in Arkansas received the same media attention given to the University of Arkansas football team.

In 1963, Governor Faubus announced that he opposed lifting the racial restrictions on athletics at the University of Arkansas. The University of Arkansas Board of Trustees agreed with Faubus, instituting policies that excluded blacks from university sports and dormitories.

"When I heard the board of trustees made that ruling," longtime UA psychology professor Phillip Trapp recalls, "I said the faculty should go on record." They did. The college faculty, as well as the student association, officially endorsed the integration of Razorback athletics.

Trapp was asked to serve on the university's faculty athletics council in 1962. What better place to integrate, he thought, than the place where most of the attention was? "The board of trustees was still solidly against integration," Trapp says. "That's why Frank Broyles was so against it, he'd be going against the board."

Trapp's embracing the ideals of integration didn't sit well with one board of trustees member, Pete Rainey. When Trapp was introduced to him, Rainey turned his back on the professor.

Delbert Schwartz chaired the faculty athletics council for years, and Trapp says that Schwartz wanted to groom him to someday chair the group. Just before a meeting, Trapp cornered Schwartz and told him he was going to make a motion that Arkansas should integrate their athletic teams. "I want it to go into the record," Trapp told him.

"Oh, my God," Schwartz said, "if you do that you'll *never* become my replacement."

"I knew the committee was handpicked by Frank Broyles," Trapp says, "and I didn't have much aspiration that it would pass, but our students had voted that way."

Knowing his proposal was likely doomed, Trapp still made the suggestion that Broyles integrate his team. "I can see this giving us a national title in short order," Trapp said. "We'll be the first major school in the South, and we'll have our pick of black athletes." Black athletes were already dominating on the national stage, and that meant bigger crowds, Trapp reasoned, more money. Many of the top black athletes were from the Old South, but Arkansas was now embracing the principle of segregation at the expense of their basketball team—as well as their balance sheets. Arkansas football was certain to be harmed as well, when the SWC integrated, if they didn't follow the trend of sports being at the forefront of racial progress across the country.

Two board members voted for integration; nine voted against it.

But that was not the most disheartening aspect. "I heard [Broyles] say when I made that proposal that it would be 'over his dead body,'" Trapp recalls. "I think he had a strong race card going. That would be pretty obvious, he came from Georgia, and in fairness, he'd been indoctrinated, but at that time Broyles was very strong against integrating athletics."

A few months later, Trapp would get a final reminder of how popular his ideas on integrating football were. He was removed from the faculty athletics council, with which Broyles worked very closely. "I would guess, and this is a guess," Trapp says, "that Frank Broyles said, 'We don't need that radical on that committee.'"

Trapp was gone from the faculty athletics council by the mid-1960s, but more showdowns were on the horizon, ones that would reveal who held the power at the only major university in the state. Would it be the students and faculty? The board of trustees? Or the football coach?

EIGHT

GOD'S TROMBONES

Rosario Richardson **was** tired of the talk in Fayetteville, and they hadn't even been there a year. Waiting in line at a grocery store, she heard a shopper offering to give away her 1985–86 season tickets. The shopper knew the reason the Arkansas Razorbacks weren't winning. "Because they hired that black coach."

Rose Richardson whipped out her checkbook and tapped the woman on the shoulder.

"I'll buy those tickets," she said.

The lady at the grocery store was not the only disappointed Razorback fan. Former coach Eddie Sutton's crew had won their opening NCAA Tournament game the previous season, and Richardson had two of those starters back. Expectations were enormous—Arkansas was even included in some preseason Top 20 polls. While the team did pretty well in the preseason, once Southwest Conference play began, the Razorbacks stumbled badly.

The team appeared confused under Richardson's system, and they even lost seven games in Fayetteville's Barnhill Arena. Richardson suspended two players for drug use. He realized that he didn't have the talent in place to do much better, and he was already catching heat, particularly from *Democrat-Gazette* writer John Robert Starr. "You have to sweep the house out before you move in," Richardson says. "I didn't do that at Arkansas and it may have been a mistake."

Richardson's time at Arkansas began with a sense of trepidation—he loved Tulsa; Yvonne was sick; then his new team floundered. The traits that made him successful—brazen confidence and his us-against-the-world philosophy—were in stark contrast to Frank Broyles's trademarks. The athletics director was more politic and measured, quick to smile, always positive with his pat answers. Few people were aware then that Eddie Sutton had grown weary of Broyles's strange, overbearing-yet-distant management style.

Richardson found a modest townhouse overlooking a golf course in Fayetteville. The place didn't quite feel like home, partly because the family was returning so often to Tulsa for medical treatment. They kept their house near Seventy-first and Memorial in Tulsa as a base for when Yvonne went in for treatment. Richardson soon came to believe there were not the doctors available in Fayetteville that Broyles had suggested there would be. Little Rock offered better medical care, but Tulsa was an hour closer. The constant return trips to Tulsa reminded Richardson of how content he had been there.

Richardson also came to grips with the notion that leukemia killed the mother he could barely remember, and his nephew Butch was gone just two months after being diagnosed. Richardson badly needed support, but instead felt as though people in Arkansas only cared about whether his basketball team was winning.

Mike Anderson, the point guard on Richardson's first Tulsa teams, joined the staff at Arkansas as a low-level assistant coach. His responsibilities were centered on driving Yvonne back and forth to Tulsa on days when her father could not. Anderson had met Yvonne in 1980, his first year in Tulsa. "She was like my kid sister," he says.

"Yvonne was the inspiration to keep Coach Richardson going," Anderson adds, emphasizing the powerful sway the girl, now in her teens, had over her father.

As her health declined, Yvonne never expressed pity for herself. "She didn't complain," Anderson remembers. "She was optimistic, always thinking God would make a way for her to get well."

Anderson believes Richardson had been so fortunate in his time at Tulsa that the same feeling of optimism initially spilled over into everyone's thinking about Yvonne. "All those championships Nolan had won, all those firsts for a black coach. His life was like a storybook in a way. When Yvonne was diagnosed with leukemia—well, we all just knew she would turn out okay."

As Yvonne deteriorated, she could still find humor in the darkest of times. Occasionally, Anderson would drive Yvonne, along with her mother, to road games on the day the Razorbacks played, so she wouldn't have to be gone as many days as the team. Once, coming back from a loss in Dallas, Anderson found himself in a thick fog. High beams made the fog appear denser. Because he was on a narrow road, Anderson figured pulling over might be even more dangerous. He slowed down then leaned forward over the steering wheel, hoping that might help his vision. Rose, a nervous traveler in good weather, began crying out, "Oh, Lord Jesus!" at every dip and turn.

When the fog lifted, Yvonne began mimicking her mother. Soon, everyone was laughing, even Rose. "Yvonne called me 'Oh Lord Jesus' for weeks afterward," Anderson says.

Yvonne wouldn't let her father—*Papi*, she called him, or *Papito*—pity her, or himself. Instead, she peppered him with inspirational talks or demanded another "interview."

In an attempt to comfort her, Richardson reminded her not to worry, that the Razorbacks would get better and he was doing his best. One day Yvonne told him his best wasn't good enough, a startling thing for a child to tell a father. "You've got to step it up," she said.

When Richardson assured her he would, she let out a sigh.

"I think I can rest now."

Remaining upbeat became nearly impossible for Richardson. The drive to and from Tulsa, which he sometimes did instead of Anderson, gave him plenty of time to second-guess his decision to leave for Arkansas.

On one occasion, Yvonne was retching and vomiting and couldn't stop. Richardson pulled the car over and decided to let her stretch out in the backseat. Tulsa was still over an hour away. Richardson climbed back in and floored the accelerator, figuring if he exceeded the speed limit on a straightaway, perhaps a policeman would pull him over. He could convince the cop to flip on his siren and give them an escort into Tulsa. Instead, he sped into Tulsa unnoticed.

With Yvonne dying, his wife understandably distraught, and feeling pressure from Broyles, the fans, and media, Richardson felt isolated. He was in need of someone who could provide what Ol' Mama did, and he found that guidance and friendship in an old white man named Orville Henry, Arkansas's best-known sportswriter. Henry checked in with Richardson every day during his early tenure in Arkansas.

This is a pattern in Richardson's life, gravitating to older men, who are often white, for advice and friendship. First, Bert Williams, Don Haskins. Then Sid Simpson. Ed Beshara. Orville Henry.

Although Henry was better known as a football writer, he and Richardson became close. Henry was in some ways an Old Southerner but had become more progressive as far as questions about race were concerned. An Orville Henry anecdote: In the late 1960s, Henry and his ten-year-old son Clay went to play golf at the Fairpark Golf Course. On the eighth hole, both Henrys drove their ball from the tee and began walking ahead. Clay saw a black boy about his own age cutting across the fairway.

"Dad," Clay said, "we need to hurry! That boy's going to steal our golf ball."

Orville Henry stopped in his tracks and turned to his son. "You think he's going to steal your ball because he's black, don't you?"

When they got to their golf balls, the black boy, perhaps eight years of age, had passed. They were safe. But Henry called and waved the boy back.

Henry asked the boy if he had ever hit a golf ball. The boy had not.

"Would you like to try?" Henry pulled out his son's five-iron. Then Henry emptied his son's bag of two dozen balls.

"I'm going to give you a lesson," Orville Henry said to the boy—or perhaps both boys. Henry showed the black boy the grip, got him in a stable stance, and showed him the classic shoulder turn, and how to keep his eyes down. Fifteen minutes later, with balls sprayed everywhere, Orville Henry turned to his son.

"Where's your putting ball?" he said. "Let me have it."

Henry presented it to the boy. Then he turned back to his son and said, "Pick up all the balls."

Although Richardson had heard the story on several occasions, he always found it moving. He could have been that black kid cutting across the grass.

One longtime Arkansas sportswriter says that Orville Henry may have been influenced in the same way Evans Dunne was at Tulsa. Although Henry wasn't racist, he says, Henry would have certainly had an older mentality. "At one time, Orville had been asked not to return to Pine Bluff to speak, because of his off-color jokes," this sportswriter says. "Later, Nolan sort of won Orville over. Also, Orville had married a very progressive woman, and that helped."

Richardson's trouble with Frank Broyles began during that first season. Orville Henry was friends with both men, and could sometimes smooth over misunderstandings. More often, though, understanding was beyond Richardson's and Broyles's grasp.

Broyles remembered Eddie Sutton's slower style, and Richardson was radically different. "When Nolan was struggling," one Arkansas sportswriter says, "Broyles was coming down to watch practice, trying to figure out if Nolan could really coach."

Once the disappointing first season concluded, Broyles told Richardson he wanted him to go visit Indiana coach Bob Knight. Broyles felt that Richardson could maybe learn how to teach defense and get his team under control.

Richardson, who was already sensitive about his rabid pressing and *Star Wars*–paced offense being slandered, considered this an insult.

Plenty of coaches still believed Don Haskins to be the best defensive coach in the nation. Knight himself had spent time with Haskins at the 1972 Olympic trials, where Haskins had been an assistant to Henry Iba. "Hell, Knight had all kinds of questions about Mr. Iba's system," Haskins recalled. "Knight could have gone to Nolan to learn my system. Nolan knew it as well as anyone."

Richardson declined to visit Indiana, although he admired Knight.

"Fuck Bobby Knight," Richardson told Broyles. "My daughter is dying and you're bothering me?"

Broyles's pestering Richardson about coaching decisions was not unique to basketball. This was perhaps Broyles's central contradiction— he found great coaches, then could not stop himself from second-guessing them.

One October, football coach Ken Hatfield burst into Richardson's office, fuming, waving a legal pad. "Damn!" Hatfield said. "Broyles is sending me plays to run. First he wants me to fire [assistant coach] Fred Goldsmith, and now he wants me to change my whole attack."

Richardson leaned forward in his chair and smiled at his assistant coaches.

"Let me see those plays," Richardson said. He still loved football and liked to talk the talk with Hatfield. Richardson studied the diagrams for a long minute, flipping back and forth, engrossed in the possibilities. Suddenly he crumpled the pages into a ball and lofted a left-handed shot at the wastebasket. It banked in.

"That's what I do with Broyles's suggestions," Richardson said.

As Yvonne's situation deteriorated, Richardson lost all patience with Broyles. It was one thing to make suggestions about scheduling, the media guide, or uniform styles. But it was quite another to suggest, by offering tactical advice, that Richardson didn't know how to coach.

"I think Frank Broyles had different expectations of black people," Richardson says today. "Look where he came from—the Deep South, Georgia. His ancestors were slave owners, and he had a different view of the duties black people should have."

He finally blasted Broyles over what he believed was his boss's lack of compassion. "You knew I had a sick daughter when you hired me!" he shouted at Broyles his first season. "Don't expect me to ignore her."

Any gesture from Broyles seemed to irritate Richardson. "Broyles did offer Nolan to take a leave of absence with pay," one longtime sportswriter says, "but Nolan misinterpreted that to mean Broyles wanted him gone." Events that would unfold a year later would prove Richardson was right.

Richardson was not the only person who might be baffled by Frank Broyles.

Charles Prigmore was the executive vice chancellor at University of Arkansas Medical Center in Little Rock during the 1970s. Prigmore, a former high school football coach, kept a close eye on Broyles, and sees him as a complex man, a charismatic leader who could border on arrogant and self-serving.

One hot summer day in the early 1970s, Prigmore was in his office at the Medical Center when word began circulating that a Razorback football player, a lineman from South Arkansas, had arrived in an ambulance. He'd fallen out of a pickup truck, and it appeared there might be spinal cord damage. Prigmore hustled down to the neurology floor, where the player had been moved. He was shocked at what he found.

With a whirlwind of commands, the neurology floor came under Frank Broyles's jurisdiction. He lined up the staff as if they were freshmen at fall football tryouts. "Our chief of neurology," Prigmore recalls, "was a quiet and unassuming guy, and he just stepped back when Broyles and his entourage came through. Broyles wasn't trying to medically treat the kid, but he just took over, saying he needed this type of bed and that kind of room, and calling out orders to nurses."

An hour later, without asking anyone for permission, Broyles hosted a press conference in the neurology wing.

The 1986–87 season was a bit better than Richardson's first year, but he was preoccupied with Yvonne. Andy Stoglin would coach the team when Richardson couldn't be in Fayetteville, and the alternating coaches certainly didn't help the Razorbacks. They couldn't get any momentum, although they beat Kansas, Ohio Sate, and Cal, and were 8-4 before the league season. Then Yvonne got worse.

The back-and-forth trips to Tulsa and St. Francis Hospital, where Yvonne had been nearly full-time, were taking their toll on everyone. Transfusions, bone-marrow transplants, chemotherapy, a journey to the Mayo Clinic—nothing improved Yvonne's situation. At one point, fungus appeared on her lung, and that worried the doctors. They had to break her rib to get to the lung.

After the New Year, Yvonne was allowed home from the hospital. She slept between the coach and Rose. But her condition worsened, and she was rushed back to the hospital.

Yvonne Richardson died of leukemia on January 22, 1987. She was fifteen years old.

Richardson's sense of isolation from the state, the town, the university, and the athletics department was overwhelming. He was so distraught that even when well-wishers tried to console him, he could barely bring himself to feel their sympathy.

People close to Richardson believe Yvonne's death altered his level of compassion. Watching his daughter slowly wither away gave him a more empathetic antenna for others in trouble. Ironically, though, after witnessing Yvonne's resilience, Richardson pushed his players even harder. While he understood emotional anguish, seeing a healthy player who wouldn't fight frustrated him.

His empathy for the underdog was natural—who had had to overcome more obstacles? Starting out as the Bowie coach kept him close to his roots, and he identified with the scruffy Segundo Barrio kids as outsiders. The mindset continued as he became one of the few black college coaches in America, first at Snyder and then Tulsa—and finally as the only black coach in the Southwest Conference.

Through Yvonne's illness, Richardson says, Broyles never acknowledged that these were tough times for his family. That hurt Richardson deeply. Then it angered him, especially when he felt as though Broyles was pressuring him to turn his back on his family and focus on the Razorback team.

A longtime employee of the University of Arkansas athletics department confirmed Broyles's attitude, but thinks the bad relationship that had already surfaced had less to do with race than ego over the years.

"Broyles forced out Ken Hatfield as football coach in 1989," the employee says. Hatfield had amassed over a thousand yards in his playing career at Arkansas as a punt returner—his totals led the nation for two seasons—and he was a hero on Broyles's best team, when he coached football for Arkansas, in 1964. Hatfield's coaching record at Arkansas was 55-17, and he was widely regarded as one of the top football coaches in America.

This employee made an appointment to visit Nolan after he lost Yvonne, although he didn't know him well then. "I brought him a plaque that someone had given me," he says. "It wasn't a fancy gift, but it meant a lot to me and I wanted Nolan to have it." The employee waited outside Richardson's office, the gift in his lap, until the coach emerged. The employee presented the bereaved coach with the worn-out plaque and explained why it had given him strength over the years.

Richardson was clearly touched. He wept, and thanked the man.

"Nolan told me he felt like he was all alone, on an island," he continues. "That really surprised me."

Less than a week later, this employee was at lunch with a table full of Arkansas football coaches when Frank Broyles approached and began openly disparaging Richardson's coaching ability. "It just struck me as out of place," the employee says. "I mean, Yvonne had just died, and he was telling us that [assistant coach] Andy Stoglin was a better coach, that Nolan couldn't coach."

Going into their last home game in 1987, less than two months after Yvonne's death, the Razorbacks were 6-7 in SWC play—not exactly where Richardson had envisioned being, after taking the job two seasons earlier. The opponent for the final game in Fayetteville was Baylor, which had beaten Arkansas in Waco. With only three games to go, Richardson badly needed a win, since he'd be going on the road for his final two league games. Baylor wasn't a great team, but their coach was an Iba—Gene Iba, a nephew of Henry Iba—and that ball-control playing style sometimes meant trouble.

Another concern to negotiate was Senior Night. The last home game for any college usually means a chance to honor the players in the final year, both stars and benchwarmers. The Razorbacks' starting lineup that season did not include a single senior. Richardson's predecessor, Eddie Sutton, had traditionally started as many seniors as he could in the last home game.

Richardson did have one senior, a 6'7" Houston kid named Eric Poerschke, a holdover from the Sutton era. Poerschke was simply the wrong player for Richardson's system, a bad fit stylistically, and he found himself on the bench his last season. It wasn't that Poerschke was a bad player. He'd started a handful of games as a sophomore for Sutton. In Richardson's first season, Poerschke led the Razorbacks in field goal percentage, and scored over fifty baskets for the year.

"I realized I wasn't really in his plans my senior year," Poerschke says, "and that wasn't a great thing to go through. But I knew that this was part of life, so I decided to be a good teammate and pull for our other guys."

The Razorbacks had shown plenty of promise before the holidays, but kept stumbling in SWC play. Poerschke says, "Pressure seemed to come when we started losing. But looking back it didn't have much to do with winning and losing at all. It was Yvonne." Now Poerschke can see that the season was incredibly difficult. "I've got three kids now, and you begin to realize—well, Nolan was at practice more than most people would have been. And being the first black coach, there was already overwhelming pressure."

Richardson respected Poerschke, a brilliant student who would graduate with a business degree, although he rarely played him as a senior. "He never complained, never hung his head," Richardson says. "He worked and fought like he was one of our main guys." Yet, because Richardson's first team at Arkansas had sputtered, he was concerned about a late-season collapse again, so the idea of starting a benchwarmer in an important game made him skittish.

Regardless, Poerschke was looking forward to Senior Night. His parents were coming from Houston to see his last game, and it would likely be his last chance to shine before the home fans.

But Baylor controlled the tempo from the outset and wouldn't let the Razorbacks run their fast break. Richardson's assistants suggested giving Poerschke a try, but he didn't seem to hear. Arkansas held on to win by four, but senior Eric Poerschke didn't play a minute.

"I wasn't that upset," Poerschke claims. "We won."

And that, Poerschke thought, was the end of that.

Arkansas finished that 1986–87 season 8-8 in the SWC, and was awarded an NIT bid. Richardson was fiercely proud of his NIT championship team at Tulsa, so it annoyed him terribly when he began hearing Broyles refer to the NIT as "a loser's tournament."

The NIT bid in 1987 offered an unusual matchup for the Razorbacks. They'd face Arkansas State, which they had not played since 1948.

There's a reason the big schools like Arkansas do not schedule the lower-profile in-state schools—a loss would be embarrassing. The afternoon of the game, the president of the university, Ray Thornton, stopped by with Frank Broyles to see their basketball coach. Thornton told Richardson, "Win, lose, or draw tonight, you are going to be our coach." Then Thornton turned to Broyles, and, according to Richardson, said, "You understand that, Coach Broyles?"

That evening the Arkansas State Indians got off to a fast start and built a 21-point lead in Fayetteville. Razorback fans squirmed. Their press wasn't effective, and the game clearly meant more to Arkansas State. After a couple of steals and blocked shots, the momentum shifted, the *Democrat-Gazette* wrote, and the Razorbacks would rally, sneak by, and perhaps save Richardson's job, just two years after he began.

"Nolan has a sixth sense," Mike Anderson says. "He has a feeling about who wants him to succeed and who does not."

Frank Broyles, Richardson believed, did not.

The *Democrat-Gazette* must have had the same sense, writing later, "Arkansas Athletics Director Frank Broyles, spotted before the game, is nowhere to be seen afterward. There are rumors that Broyles was back at his office calling boosters to buy out Richardson. Years later, Broyles denies he was at the game, saying he was out of town."

According to Richardson, this attempted sabotage by Broyles indicated who was in charge in Fayetteville. It wasn't the president, either. "Broyles ran the show," he says. "They couldn't touch him."

Arkansas lost their next NIT game at Nebraska. Richardson returned home believing what the *Democrat-Gazette* obviously believed, that Frank Broyles wanted him gone. The timing of this—with Yvonne recently deceased—was something the coach never got over. And for Richardson, slights or insults are permanent.

"But that works both ways for Nolan," says his longtime friend, El Paso judge Thomas Spieczny. "Any injustice sticks with him, even if it's one that *he* caused accidentally."

Eric Poerschke, who never stripped off his warm-ups on Senior Night, concurs. "The odd thing is, when I see Nolan, he keeps apologizing for not playing me one game in 1987. I've gotten over it, but he can't. It's been twenty years."

NINE

INVISIBLE MAN

Twenty years might seem like a long time to some, but not to Frank Broyles. He served the University of Arkansas as football coach and then as director of athletics for a total of *fifty* years—nineteen seasons as football coach, thirty-five as AD, and four years as both. His football teams in the 1960s, along with the University of Texas, set a standard for excellence in the Southwest Conference. Arkansas was a member of the SWC from 1915 until 1991, and the only team in the league not from Texas.

Broyles was born in 1924 and raised in Decatur, Georgia, just outside of Atlanta. Like Nolan Richardson, he starred in football, basketball, and baseball. Richardson had done that in high school, but Broyles did it in college too. He was named All-SEC a half-dozen times at Georgia Tech, both as a football quarterback and a basketball star. Broyles's Orange Bowl passing record stood for over fifty years. Of course, Broyles never competed against a single black player.

The state of Georgia in that era set clear lines and values. In the 1940s, Georgia invested $142 per year for each white student, as opposed to $35 for each black student. Eugene Talmadge, who was Georgia's governor for much of the 1930s and 1940s, said, "I like the nigger, but I like him in his place, and his place is at the back door with his hat in his hand."

Georgia passed laws to protect segregation before and after the 1954 Supreme Court decision. One candidate for governor in the mid-1950s wanted children to declare under oath whether they preferred an integrated school. If they did, they would be assigned to a mental institution.

Frank Broyles returned to Georgia Tech to join its coaching staff as an assistant from 1951 until 1956. The governor of Georgia by then was Marvin Griffin, who realized the impact Jackie Robinson had a few years earlier and saw athletics as an important place to fight against racial equality.

Broyles was the offensive backfield coach when Georgia Tech was invited to play in the Sugar Bowl on New Year's Day of 1956. Tech would face Pittsburgh, who had a single black player. Tech head coach Bobby Dodd got Governor Griffin's permission to play the barely desegregated game, but a month before the contest, Griffin changed his mind, saying, "There is no more difference in compromising the integrity of race on the playing field than in doing so in the classroom. One break in the dike and the relentless seas will rush in and destroy us." The governor ordered Georgia Tech to stay home.

In a demonstration more indicative of Tech students' love of football than equal opportunity for Negroes, close to two thousand students marched to the capitol building and burned Griffin in effigy. After the Georgia Tech Board of Trustees approved the trip, Governor Griffin backed down. Tech won the game—their fifth bowl game victory in a row—but the leading rusher was Pitt's black star, Bobby Grier.

In 1957, on the heels of Georgia Tech's success, Broyles was named the head football coach at University of Missouri.

Broyles only coached Missouri for one season before accepting the job at Arkansas. Most interesting about his time at Missouri is the fact that on his watch, his football staff signed the first two black players in school history—Norris Stevenson and Mel West. The pair would star on the best teams in University of Missouri history.

Norris Stevenson knew the town of Columbia was segregated before he arrived in 1957. "For one semester I was the only black player," he says, "and in retrospect, the coaches weren't exactly thrilled with the idea."

Stevenson was joined by Mel West the following semester. "This was another time," Stevenson insists. "You'd have to move everybody, physically and emotionally, to understand it. You'd have to recreate the atmosphere, otherwise things we said today would make no sense. We were kids, and half of us didn't know who Martin Luther King was."

When Broyles announced he was leaving for Arkansas after their freshman year, Stevenson and West stuck around to help Missouri to three fine football seasons. The University of Arkansas had never had a black athlete in any sport.

Frank Broyles had a personal connection to the Little Rock Central crisis of 1957. One of the first moves he made at Arkansas was to lure a man named Wilson Matthews away from his job coaching Central High School to become the Razorbacks' assistant coach.

Playing a whites-only schedule, Wilson Matthews led Central High School to ten state championships in his eleven years there. Matthews had an interesting view of what caused the problems at Central. In Terry Frei's book about the showdown between the Texas and Arkansas football teams of 1969, *Horns, Hogs, and Nixon Coming*, Matthews is quoted as saying, ". . . if a bunch of damn soldiers hadn't showed up and got a crowd around, there wouldn't have been any problems." Whether Matthews meant the Arkansas National Guard, who held bayonets on black girls, or the 101st Airborne Division, who opened the school to them, is unclear.

Matthews helped Broyles with the Razorbacks from 1958 to 1968 and was known as the most influential coach on Broyles's staff. A passionate and foul-mouthed motivator, Matthews assumed head coaching duties for the freshman team, the "Shoats," in 1969. Later, he took over the conditioning programs, then moved into athletics administration soon after. He worked as an assistant athletics director until 1992. Because he moved to administration, Matthews never coached a varsity black athlete at the University of Arkansas.

Broyles's debut at Arkansas in 1958 began badly—he lost his first six games in a row. The Razorbacks recovered by winning their last four. They had phenomenal success after that rocky start, especially in the 1960s.

In 1964, Broyles's all-white squad roared through the season undefeated at 11-0. But Arkansas faced only four teams with winning records, so both UPI and AP, the biggest polls, declared Alabama national champs before the bowl games were played, as was their custom at that time.

Alabama devalued that decision by losing to Texas in the Orange Bowl. Then Arkansas beat Nebraska in the Cotton Bowl, 10-7. (Nebraska was the only team Arkansas faced that year that had black players.) Two smaller polls, the Football Writers Association of America and the Helms Foundation, declared the Razorbacks national champions. Today, both Arkansas and Alabama claim the national championship of 1964.

That same year, a black student named Robert Whitfield won a discrimination lawsuit against UA campus housing, and the federal ruling forced the dormitories to be open to all without regard to race. Whitfield and Joanna Edwards became the first two blacks at the University of Arkansas to be admitted to previously segregated dormitories.

Broyles's all-white 1969 team lost a heartbreaker to Texas in the still-segregated contest called "The Game of the Century" by some. The loss likely cost Arkansas a unanimous national title.

Over his career, Broyles's teams won over 70 percent of their games. His Razorbacks appeared in ten bowl games, usually the Cotton Bowl or Sugar Bowl. He would coach only two losing teams in his nineteen years. Broyles's time at Arkansas straddled two eras—the strictly segregated Southwest Conference of the late 1950s and early 1960s, and the quickly integrating teams of the early 1970s.

The black football phenoms of the 1950s and 1960s college scene include an impressive roster of stars who later earned places in the NFL's Hall of Fame: Jim Brown, Gale Sayers, "Deacon" Jones, Willie Davis, Lenny Moore, Roosevelt Brown, Carl Eller, Herb Adderly, Emerson Boozer, Ollie Matson, Dick "Night Train" Lane, and Paul Warfield.

The closest NFL team to Arkansas, the St. Louis Cardinals, featured black Texas native Johnny Roland—who, of course, had to leave Texas to play major college football.

The best black players from Arkansas flaunted their talent before Frank Broyles could even get a foothold in Fayetteville. Bobby Mitchell, Willie Davis, and Elijah Pitts were Arkansas natives who became NFL stars despite being ignored by the state university in the 1950s. Other black players from the state, such as Jim Pace and Sidney Williams, had been all-conference players in the Big Ten.

Any objective observer could figure out that black kids deserved a chance based on ability alone. Few states have as impressive a tradition of black football players, but with mostly segregated high schools and a separate athletics association for the Negro schools, it was rare that whites competed on the same field as black kids in Arkansas.

Only the biggest Negro schools competed in football, because of the equipment needed to field a team. There might be thirty schools competing for the state's Negro championship in any one year, but there were generally eight well-established high school teams. Those teams often had to leave the state to play games. "Separate but equal" was a joke, with the state of Arkansas spending as much as three times more on educating white kids as it did on black kids in some counties. It wasn't until the 1970s that all the black schools were accepted into the Arkansas Activities Association, the governing body of high school sports in the state.

Broyles would have had to go just a few hundred yards to find a great black player to desegregate his team. Fayetteville High School had a star football player named William "Bull" Hayes, who graduated a few months after Broyles arrived in 1958. Bull Hayes was the first black athlete in the state of Arkansas to play against white competition in high school.

Hayes had to deal with more than the usual high school hassles. When the Fayetteville team bused into Harrison for a game, an effigy of a black man was hanging from a tree in the town square. According to the *Democrat-Gazette*, Harrison star Don Branison said his team was told to stop Bull Hayes no matter what it took. "We tried to kill him. . . . We tried to hurt him real bad," Branison said.

Fayetteville beat Harrison anyway. Branison was awarded a scholarship to the University of Arkansas the following year.

Bull Hayes had offers from Oklahoma State and Tulsa, where Arkansas played regularly. To avoid the embarrassment of a local black player making them look bad, the Arkansas staff arranged a full ride to University of Nebraska for Bull Hayes.

TEN

THE EDGE OF CAMPUS

Richardson's task as the first black coach in the old Confederacy was not fully appreciated, and most newsmen didn't see the significance. "They didn't understand that this was another world," TV journalist Steve Narisi says, "this was the Southwest Conference." The fact that Richardson didn't have the instant success he did in Tulsa compounded the trouble.

Yvonne's decline, of all things, caused Richardson problems with the fans and Broyles. "He'd miss games with Yvonne sick," Narisi says, "and people would get down on him for that. From the very early days Richardson was on the wrong side of some of the fans. I don't think Nolan ever got over that. If he was a white coach under those circumstances, the fans and media would have been far more patient."

Another source of trouble was the speed at which Richardson was pushing his team to play. Wally Hall, whose *Democrat-Gazette* columns irritated Richardson for years, says, "I will be the first to admit that I didn't embrace Nolan's style. He was a pioneer, and it took me two years to appreciate that." Hall says both the media and the fans had grown accustomed to the Iba-influenced style with which Eddie Sutton succeeded.

With two major newspapers in Little Rock, numerous television stations, and his first teams spinning their wheels, Richardson was confronted with a different media presence than that in Tulsa. Richardson's relationship with Arkansas journalists was complicated. During his first few years in Arkansas, there were two statewide papers, the *Democrat* as well as the *Gazette*. An aggressive battle for readership meant inflammatory articles were sometimes the norm. John Robert Starr was especially critical of Richardson, and when the Razorbacks made dramatic improvements over the years, Starr took credit for that in print, claiming his mean-spirited attacks made Richardson a better coach. In the late 1980s, the papers merged, but Starr continued his critiques.

The games at Arkansas brought a surprising yet familiar face on a regular basis—Tulsa clothier Ed Beshara, who had rarely attended games at TU.

Richardson had talked Beshara into a road trip to attend a Tulsa game at West Texas State in the early 1980s and invited him to sit on the bench. With the score tied, and just seconds remaining, Richardson took a time-out. As he started to set the play, he became aware of a commotion in his own huddle. It was Ed Beshara, jumping around, red-faced, yelling, "Get the ball to Ricky Ross!"

Ross hit the winning shot moments later. After that, though, Richardson figured Beshara was too excitable.

Nevertheless, Richardson was comforted to see Beshara appear at every home game in his early days at Arkansas. With Yvonne dying and the team struggling, Beshara was more than a fan. Richardson loved and trusted him.

"Suddenly you're a real supporter," Richardson joked. "Why didn't you come to the games at Tulsa when it was ten minutes away?"

Beshara answered straight away. "You didn't need me at Tulsa. You need me here at Arkansas, hoss."

"Everyone deals with death in different ways," Mike Anderson says. "Rose's job, like a lot of mothers' jobs, was to raise her child. Then Yvonne wasn't there. Basketball was going on, and that was Coach Richardson's focus because the players were family, too."

"I don't think I've ever met anyone who gave so much of herself as Rose," says Madalyn Richardson about her stepmom, "especially after Yvonne passed."

Several people close to the couple suggest that Rose in particular is still, twenty years later, struggling with the loss of Yvonne.

When Richardson was gone recruiting or at a speaking engagement, Rose would often remain in her bathrobe all day, living in a corner of their bedroom. She would switch on the television, letting the noise distract her. Sometimes she would go days without even venturing outside the townhouse, let alone into Fayetteville.

Some say, however, that Richardson himself carried the grief around even longer.

"After the loss of Yvonne," one player says, "Coach could always go to basketball, and when you're playing or coaching there's that feeling nothing else is going on. His team could substitute for the family."

After reading about Yvonne's death, Temple University coach John Chaney phoned Richardson. Chaney is in some ways Richardson's northern alter ego. His résumé is another testament to how difficult advancement was for black coaches of that era.

Chaney played ten seasons in the Eastern Basketball League, the only minor league below the NBA, and was named that league's MVP in 1959 and 1960. The MVP awards never led to an NBA career; most teams still had quotas limiting the number of black players.

Temple University hired Chaney in 1982. It was seen as a risky move—he was fifty years old, and despite his incredible success as a Division II coach, he had not a single minute of experience at the Division I level as a player or even assistant coach. The gamble paid off, as his Temple teams were usually nationally ranked.

Chaney has had some controversial moments. During a rough-and-tumble game against Saint Joseph's in 2005, he sent substitute Nehemiah Ingram into the game and ordered him to foul intentionally. Chaney, whose team recorded more fouls that night than field goals, would regret the move. Ingram badly injured a Saint Joseph's player. Chaney suspended himself for the remainder of the season.

Chaney refuses to sidestep these incidents. In the Temple media guide the following season—obviously controlled and written by Temple with his guidance—one of the topics in the "Chat with Coach Chaney" section is "On last year's incident with Saint Joseph."

Chaney can be blunt, charming, and funny. He's part philosopher, part social critic. When questioned about his career accomplishments, he declines to mention the five-hundred-something games he won at Temple. Rather it's "To cause the NCAA to sit down and listen to us about the needs and changes that should be made for many of our young athletes who are predominantly black. That is the fight that I have not stopped fighting."

Chaney and Richardson would cement their friendship in Virginia in the late 1980s, where a new organization called the Black Coaches Association was holding one of their first meetings.

Talks with Chaney helped Richardson regain his focus. By the autumn of 1987, the beginning of his third season, Richardson felt a sense of urgency to get Arkansas back to the NCAA Tournament. His Razorbacks responded, going 21-9, including 11-5 in the SWC. They were rewarded with their first NCAA Tournament appearance since Eddie Sutton left Arkansas.

The Razorbacks drew Villanova in the first round and lost 82-74. Richardson was now 0-4 as a coach in NCAA Tournament games, including his time at Tulsa.

Broyles, still not convinced Richardson could coach, suggested after that season that Richardson hire Bob Weltlich as an assistant coach. Richardson knew the reason. Weltlich, who had stumbled as head coach of University of Texas and was fired, got his start as an assistant to Bob Knight. It exasperated Richardson that Broyles wanted him to hire a coach whom he had little trouble beating.

Instead of a staff change, Richardson gathered his assistants a week after the Villanova loss to talk about intensifying their recruiting. Richardson was blessed with a terrific staff—several of his assistant coaches would one day be head coaches. Andy Stoglin, Scott Edgar, Mike Anderson, and his son, Nolan "Notes" Richardson III, all coached Division I teams after leaving Arkansas.

Richardson had his own style of dealing with prospects. Whether it was at a high school gym or campus visit, Richardson would have an assistant coach gather the recruit or his family and bring them to him. Former Tulsa coach John Phillips says, "Nolan would never get up and go to the player. He was establishing early on that if you want to play for him, it was going to be on his terms."

In the spring of 1988, Richardson and his staff signed one of the best recruiting classes in school history. The group included Todd Day, Lee Mayberry, and Oliver Miller, a trio who would win three consecutive SWC regular-season and tournament titles.

The following year, the Razorbacks finished the 1988–89 season at 25-7, including 13-3 in the SWC. Richardson won his first NCAA Tournament in 1989 over Loyola-Marymount.

Richardson created a new award at the conclusion of the 1989 season, for the Razorback with the best attitude and grades. He called it the Poerschke Award. Eric Poerschke, who was glued to the bench on Senior Night in 1987, was now forever a part of Razorback lore. Richardson recognized himself in the underdog, even if the guy was a well-to-do white benchwarmer with straight A grades.

Richardson's sense of justice was becoming tied to memory—by reminding everyone of past injustices, even his own, he could make things better.

Despite the Razorbacks' gradual improvement, Richardson could still find himself frustrated by the Arkansas mentality. It had been difficult to change old habits, and not only with his players. The university and townspeople sometimes left him flummoxed.

The northwest corner of the state, where Fayetteville is located, still had a far greater percentage of whites than the rest of Arkansas. Many towns in the northwest had unofficial laws forbidding blacks from living in them at all.

The town of Alix had a sign at its city limits that read NIGGER, DON'T LET THE SUN GO DOWN ON YOU IN ALIX until 1970. Nearly one hundred "sundown towns" existed in Arkansas through the 1960s. Towns like Paragould and Springdale—practically a twin city of Fayetteville—were also sundown towns. A Springdale steak house called Heinie's had paper placemats that read, THIS IS AN ALL-WHITE CHRISTIAN COMMUNITY. Harrison, a Klan stronghold, was a sundown town until 2002.

All of these towns are a short drive from the University of Arkansas.

One morning, during Richardson's early years at Arkansas, his secretary, Terri Mercer, announced that he had some visitors: representatives from a black fraternity and sorority. The young lady was crying. "They ruined our social on Saturday," he heard her say to Mercer.

Richardson invited them in. The police had arrived at the party, she sobbed, and brought things to a halt. That wasn't unusual on any big college campus. Richardson handed her a Kleenex and checked his watch. It was a Monday morning, and he had plenty to do.

"Dogs!" she said, finally getting her composure. "They raided the house with dogs!" Police, responding to a call, had cleared out the social event with a K-9 unit, the snarling German shepherds scattering the black college students.

Richardson felt his face get hot. He called his secretary back in and instructed her to find Lonnie Williams, a black administrator on campus.

"It was just a fight after the dance, some pushing and shoving that escalated," Williams recalls. "Since black students had been involved, Nolan felt like we had to go down there and do something."

"I couldn't believe it," Richardson says today. "I'd seen Bull Connor in Alabama on television, breaking up marchers with dogs and hoses. But this was the 1980s."

Williams arrived at Richardson's office minutes later, and they hurried over to the campus police station. Richardson had golfed with police chief Larry Slamons before and got along fine with him, but the coach was seething as he entered the station.

"What is the policy on using dogs to raid a home?" Richardson demanded.

The chief was perplexed. What dogs?

"Do you use dogs to raid white fraternity parties?" Richardson asked.

"Of course not," said Slamons.

"Then you shouldn't be doing that shit with the black fraternity either," Richardson said.

Slamons excused himself, made some calls, and learned that dogs were indeed used to raid the black fraternity. A young campus cop called for backup, and the Fayetteville *city* police brought the dogs.

"Chief Slamons was truly sorry," Williams says, "and just as much in the dark as we were." Instead of the campus police intervening, the Fayetteville police arrived. "They used incredibly bad judgment," Williams continues. "Just the sight of the dogs created bad feelings, and dogs were never needed to disperse that type of a crowd."

Lonnie Williams was inspired, however, by Richardson's response. "Nolan was very animated and authoritative and simply would not budge until we got some answers," he says. "How many coaches do you know would have personally gotten involved, or not stopped at the phone call?"

There was no player accused. No victory hung in the balance. No referee's judgment could be questioned. It was an important moment in his time at Arkansas, an awakening of sorts that had nothing to do with basketball.

Richardson's direct style in confronting injustice in the 1980s contrasts greatly with that of Hall of Fame coach—er, contributor— John McLendon.

When McLendon attended the University of Kansas in the 1930s, the campus was segregated. Degree requirements in McLendon's major included proficiency in swimming and lifesaving. The school had an unusual policy, though. Black kids were given an automatic "A," to keep them from polluting the whites-only pool.

McLendon decided not to accept the free grade and went to the pool anyway to fulfill his requirements. Friends of McLendon collected over a thousand signatures on a petition that said they did not mind swimming with Negroes.

But the word was out, and the attendant had already drained the pool before McLendon arrived. When signs started appearing on campus, reading DO NOT SWIM WITH THE NIGGER, McLendon collected the signs and gave them to his advisor, and basketball's inventor, Dr. James Naismith. Naismith, in turn, took the signs to the university president and said if another sign appeared he would find work at another college.

McLendon then went to the head of the physical education department, who happened to be Phog Allen, the basketball coach. Allen claimed that the pool rules were simply for McLendon's safety. McLendon cut a deal on the spot with the KU basketball coach. Keep the pool open—for everybody—for two weeks. If violence or any ugly incident between races occurred, McLendon would retract his request.

McLendon had a plan. Rather than meet the Neanderthal segregationists head-on, he gathered KU's four dozen black students and instructed them *not* to go near the pool for two weeks.

At the conclusion of the allotted two weeks, McLendon returned to Phog Allen. Since no racial incidents had occurred, McLendon—with the help of Dr. Naismith—held Phog Allen to his word.

McLendon's gentle touch slowly helped make room for more aggressive changes decades later. In 1987, the Black Coaches Association elected a popular assistant coach from Iowa, Rudy Washington, as their leader. One BCA goal was to increase the number of head coaching jobs being offered to African-Americans, especially assistant coaches. The BCA enjoyed enormous growth in the next seven years and wielded surprising power.

The group quickly established ties to Nolan Richardson, John Chaney, John Thompson at Georgetown, and George Raveling at USC—the most visible of the nation's black head coaches. Raveling would later retire to work in the gym-shoe industry, leaving the outspoken trio of Richardson, Thompson, and Chaney.

Another issue was Proposition 48, which called for rising requirements of SAT and ACT standards. Chaney—and many experts—insisted the tests were culturally biased against minority students. The issue of reducing the number of men's basketball scholarships from fifteen was also a concern. Any reduction in scholarships in basketball would have profound effects on African-American high schoolers, who made up nearly two-thirds of the talent in major college basketball. With over three hundred member schools, the NCAA cutting a single scholarship from each team could affect as many as two hundred potential black students across the country.

On January 14, 1989, John Thompson walked off the court at the beginning of a game, protesting the exclusion of black kids from the game due to Proposition 48. Thompson's exit was broadcast nationally. John Thompson was, at that time, the country's most visible and successful black coach in any sport.

Richardson had an epiphany watching the replays of Thompson's exit. "I felt so bad," he says. "I didn't know what to do. I might not have been a college player or coach if I'd have had to pass the SAT back then."

Thompson's dramatic move—along with the police dogs incident—reinvigorated Richardson. By all measuring sticks, he had "made it," but he was beginning to sense that success threatened to distance him from his own past. Thompson's protest somehow made him aware of what his choices might be.

Richardson grew more reflective about his own history. Decades removed, he didn't feel so very far from the Segundo Barrio, despite all his success. Clinging to the fence in the heat at a segregated swimming pool. Watching his Bowie teammates file into a no-Negroes hotel. Listening alone to the radio static of the all-white tournament in Shreveport. These events still felt very current to Richardson.

ELEVEN

TELL ME HOW LONG
THE TRAIN'S BEEN GONE

Frank Broyles's willful blindness in the 1960s became the stuff of legend in Arkansas black communities. The list of qualified black players who prepped in Arkansas *while* Broyles was coach—and refusing to desegregate—is damning. Dozens went on to star at other colleges.

Arkansas natives Willie Frazier, Eugene Howard, John Little, and Clarence Washington all had productive NFL careers. Still, the University of Arkansas clung to its backward policies. None of these talented players were allowed to play at the only major school in their state.

It wasn't just Broyles who was ignoring Arkansas black talent. The basketball coaches at the university were blinded, too. Eddie Miles was good enough to play ten NBA seasons but was ignored by Arkansas. Frank Burgess was not recruited by the Razorbacks but led the entire nation in scoring in 1960 when he racked up over 30 points per game at Gonzaga.

The University of Arkansas did not recruit Oliver Jones of Rowher. He went to Albany State instead, where he grabbed over a thousand rebounds, an incredible total, in the early 1960s. The repercussions of ignoring Oliver Jones were enormous, and expose recruiting cycles—or ruts—and the difficulties in overcoming them.

Albany State named Oliver Jones as head coach a few years after he graduated. He'd win nearly four hundred games at Albany State. And for *eighteen seasons* in a row, one of his younger brothers started at center for Albany State: Melvin Jones, Wilbert Jones, Caldwell Jones, Major Jones, and Charles Jones. The Jones brothers weren't just good college players. They would combine for over twenty thousand career points in the NBA or ABA.

Caldwell Jones, who desperately wanted to attend the University of Arkansas, played seventeen years in the ABA and NBA. When Arkansas went cold on him, it sealed things for the next Jones boys in line. Charles Jones won two NBA championships in his fifteen years in the league.

There's no telling how good Arkansas could have been had they hauled in the best black players—especially the six Jones brothers, who surely would have started a basketball dynasty in Fayetteville.

Yet basketball was far ahead of Frank Broyles when it came to pursuing black players.

In Broyles's autobiography, which was published in 1979, he dances around the issue of integration like Gene Kelly in a cloudburst.

"We did not recruit black athletes until the late 1960s," he wrote. "When I came to Arkansas, there were no black players in the Southwest Conference . . . Nothing written in a Board policy stated that we were to avoid recruiting blacks, but it was very clearly (though informally) conveyed to me that we would not.

"It was a matter out of my hands and I didn't think about it a great deal.

"I assume there was a feeling on the part of some of our board members that if we unilaterally integrated our athletics program, SEC schools would use it against us and open recruiting strongholds in certain areas of Arkansas."

It was the SEC's fault, as well as the enigmatic Board, whom Broyles, sadly, had no influence over. While future NFL players were denied a chance to play at the state's only major university, Broyles used the excuse of protecting his white recruits from those vicious vultures to the southeast.

"We fell behind," Broyles wrote. "All of a sudden it became an issue and people wanted to know why we weren't recruiting black athletes. Our conference had an image to overcome."

All of a sudden it became an issue.

Blacks within the state either resented the University of Arkansas or became apathetic. Broyles's deafness to the Civil Rights movement would come back to haunt him in recruiting.

Lyell Thompson was a professor of agriculture at the University of Arkansas for years. Thompson, who is white, found himself on campus at the same time the new football coach arrived. An army veteran, he tried to spark a desegregation movement as early as 1958.

Working to end segregation at the University of Arkansas would prove to be a discouraging battle. Thompson was surprised to discover one summer that he would not be getting the raise everyone else in his position was entitled to. "I went four years without a raise, and I was told by the dean, and then the vice-president, that I should go north, where people looked on blacks in the same way."

In fact, says Thompson, the president and board of trustees were all strongly against desegregation. So was the football coach. "Frank

Broyles was a Southerner, and he didn't want to integrate at all," Thompson says.

It was his church affiliation, of all things, that got Thompson into hot water. "I had grown up a Methodist, but I had lost my orthodoxy. My Unitarian church group met in the university building on campus. I realize now that we shouldn't have met on campus." Technically, the meeting was against school policy.

What kind of radical plots were these Unitarian zealots up to? "We came out with statements about desegregation," Thompson says, and word soon spread around campus. "Frank Broyles brought up the fact that a religious organization was meeting on the university campus."

The feared Unitarians were exiled and forced to meet elsewhere.

After Texas Western and their all-black starters won the NCAA basketball title in 1966, even the Texas universities began recruiting black athletes. So did the mostly white colleges in the state of Arkansas.

Were they following the leadership in Fayetteville?

Not a chance. Not only would Frank Broyles be slower to desegregate than anyone in the Southwest Conference, the famous coach at the big university was slower than virtually all of the other colleges in Arkansas. Ten white-majority colleges within the state of Arkansas desegregated their sports teams before the University of Arkansas:

1. The College of the Ozarks, which dropped football in the years before they integrated, had a black basketball player in 1963.
2. Ouachita Baptist had a black basketball player in 1965, and had a black football player two years later.
3. Harding College had eight black basketball and football players in 1966.

4. Henderson State added two black basketballers in 1966, two footballers in 1967. (Henderson's Bill Lefear played four seasons in the NFL.)

5. Arkansas Tech had a black football player in 1966; in 1968 they added a black basketballer.

6. Arkansas-Monticello played a black basketballer in 1967; football in 1968.

7. Central Arkansas played a black basketball player in 1967; football in 1968.

8. Hendrix College (with no football after 1960) had a black basketball player in 1968.

9. Arkansas–Little Rock (who had no football team in the 1960s) featured a black basketball player in 1968.

10. Southern Arkansas desegregated basketball in 1967, football in 1969.

Only nearby John Brown University was slower than the University of Arkansas. They added a black basketball player in 1973. John Brown the abolitionist is not, obviously, the school's namesake.

On top of that, Arkansas AN&M in Pine Bluff was sending players like L. C. Greenwood to the NFL. (At the time, three historically black colleges were in the state: Philander Smith College, Arkansas Baptist, and Arkansas AN&M, which today is UA–Pine Bluff.)

The Razorback basketball team finally would sign their first black player, T. J. Johnson, in 1967. When would Frank Broyles and Arkansas football follow the lead of virtually every team in the Southwest Conference and every other college in the state?

The plights of the first African-American athletes in the 1960s Southwest Conference foreshadow the experience Nolan Richardson would have as the first person of his race in a leadership role. While the pressure on Richardson would not be nearly as dramatic, a quick study of the SWC's most important recruit of the 1960s sheds light on the mindset of the league and Frank Broyles.

TCU played the SWC's first black basketball player, James Cash, during the 1966–67 season. Cash led TCU to the SWC title when he was a junior; he would later become a professor at the Harvard Business School.

It was an undersized speedster, however, who changed the face of the Southwest Conference. In 1962, Southern Methodist University hired an assistant named Hayden Fry to be the new football coach. Fry, the least experienced coach in the league, began working to sign an African-American player who perhaps could lift SMU football out of the cellar.

Fry found that player in Jerry LeVias of Beaumont, Texas. While he was not the first black football player to take the field, LeVias was the first superstar in the SWC.

A mere 5'9" and 170 pounds, LeVias was an electrifying halfback and receiver. Like every black kid in Texas at that time, he'd played in the Prairie View Interscholastic League, the Negro poor sister to Texas's all-white University Interscholastic League. Although highly recruited nationally, LeVias chose SMU, which was 1-9 in 1964. He signed with SMU in 1965, but since freshmen were not eligible to compete, LeVias would play for the first time in September of 1966.

Fry knew exactly what kind of impact LeVias would have and appeared to be challenging his SWC rivals. In SMU's press release announcing that LeVias had signed, Fry said, "I hope this signing will open the door for future Negro student-athletes in the Southwest Conference." SMU claimed a total of five black undergraduates on their campus LeVias's first year. He was one of two African-Americans playing varsity football in the SWC in 1966.

LeVias became perhaps the greatest player in the league history up to that time, and without question the most influential. He caught 155 passes and scored 25 touchdowns in his career. On three occasions he was named All-SWC and would go on to play six years in the

NFL despite his small frame. LeVias was also named to the dean's list at SMU.

LeVias was the subject of abuse from students, and that included his teammates in his early days. He overcame myriad obstacles—hate mail, his teammates yelling "get that nigger" at a Purdue running back, and harassing phone calls.

Death threats were common. One game, LeVias was instructed by Fry to stand in the center of the SMU huddle the entire contest so a threatened assassination would be more difficult. The abuse took a huge toll on him. At a symposium in 2002, when asked if he would choose to do things the same way—sign at SMU, become the first African-American player in the league—LeVias said he would not.

SMU put together two 8-3 seasons with LeVias. They tied for the SWC conference title in his first season, and he led the league in points scored.

Jerry LeVias was a consensus All-American after his final season.

Yet Arkansas football still had not put an African-American player on the field.

And SMU's coach, Hayden Fry, had not come from some liberal Yankee school with progressive tendencies. Fry had been Frank Broyles's assistant at Arkansas.

The final two SWC schools to desegregate their football teams were the most powerful programs—the University of Texas and their coach Darrell Royal, and the University of Arkansas.

Former Arkansas appellate judge and UA graduate Wendell Griffen likes to quote Dr. Martin Luther King when the subject of segregation in Arkansas sports comes up: "Cowardice is a submissive surrender to circumstance."

"Had it not been for Jerry LeVias," Griffen adds, "running rings around Royal and Broyles, heaven only knows when black athletes would have been allowed to play at those institutions."

Fate intervened to permit Arkansas to continue their disgraceful segregationist policies. In 1963, the University of Arkansas Board of Trustees came out with a statement of policy. They were shrewd enough not to say "No blacks allowed." Instead they instituted a gentler "Keep things as they are" policy. This was the biggest civil rights story in Arkansas since the Little Rock crisis, and it was announced on November 21.

On November 22, John F. Kennedy was killed, and the Arkansas story disappeared.

TWELVE

THE FIRE NEXT TIME

Nolan Richardson brought a feeling of urgency to the 1989–90 regular season. Arkansas entered the NCAA Tournament as a No. 4 seed in the Midwest Regional. Wins over Princeton, Dayton, North Carolina, and Texas landed Richardson in his first of three Final Fours. The Razorbacks dropped the semifinal game to Duke 97-83, finishing the year 30-5, including 14-2 in the SWC.

The Final Four appearance gave Richardson a new measure of respect, both nationally and within the state.

Arkansas's last season in the old Southwest Conference was 1990–91, and they finished it by winning the regular season at 15-1, then taking the SWC Tournament championship. They scored over one hundred points in an astounding eighteen games. The Razorbacks went into the NCAA Tournament as a No. 1 seed, but Kansas ruined their hopes of a Final Four repeat, beating the Razorbacks 93-81. Arkansas finished 34-4.

Also in 1991, assistant coach Mike Anderson and his wife welcomed the birth of a daughter. They named her Yvonne.

In 1991–92, Arkansas finished its first season in the SEC at 13-3, winning the conference. That first year included a 103-88 rout of Kentucky at Rupp Arena. The final game for the trio of Day, Mayberry, and Miller took place when Memphis upset Arkansas in the second round of the NCAA Tournament. The Razorbacks finished 26-8. Day, Mayberry, and Miller, whose combined four-year record in Fayetteville was 115-24, became first-round NBA draft picks.

Richardson has always had a disdain for what he calls "book coaches," a reverse snobbery. When Larry Gipson was a new assistant at Tulsa, he delivered detailed scouting reports about upcoming opponents in Richardson's office. Gipson was no fool. He'd coach his own national championship junior college team in the 1980s, and years later he'd win the Division II national championship at Northeastern State of Oklahoma.

Gipson recalls, "Nolan would look through the report for a while and snort. Then he'd toss it back at me. 'Book coaches,' he'd say."

Richardson acknowledges that there's plenty to learn from a book about basketball. "But it's getting it from a book to the players' heads," he says. "That's the key. That's coaching."

He pioneered a run-and-trap system, but he may have trapped himself into a stereotype. "For years, the theory has been that if you play fast, you aren't really coaching," he says. "But my experience is that it takes more discipline for kids to play fast. For example, as good as Ralph Tasker's teams were in Hobbs, in some ways his press was predictable. I wanted my players to think on their own, not be robots. It takes *more* discipline, and smarter players, to play with that kind of freedom."

One of the primary paradoxes of Nolan Richardson is that he

disdains an academic approach, yet wants to be respected by "book coaches."

He was irritated by the status bestowed upon Rick Pitino. While Richardson was winning with a *Star Wars* pace before Pitino was ever a head coach, Pitino has put out several videotapes and DVDs about coaching. He's even written self-help books for coaches. Richardson has shown less interest in marketing his playing style or coaching philosophy, but he's never turned down an offer to make an instructional video or book. He simply has never been approached.

Wally Hall of the *Democrat-Gazette* says, "Nolan *was* an X and O coach, but he put it in during practice and had everyone programmed. Then he pushed the button in the game. But you had to go to practice to see the strategy."

Todd Day, who became the school's all-time leading scorer, says, "Nolan was the king of up-tempo, pressure basketball. We hardly practiced offense. It was defense, defense, defense." Day claims that practice was much different than game day. "Nolan was a great motivator on game day," he says, "but the strategy was implemented in practice."

In this respect, Richardson mirrors Don Haskins, whose game-time philosophy was to avoid complicating things—victories were won during practice, Haskins believed. Haskins disdained the concept of "game coaches."

Richardson heard the way successful black coaches were described by the media, and it stung. Black coaches had the talent, the horses. They were great recruiters and could relate to the players. Rarely was a black coach acknowledged as a strategic genius.

"I've studied the so-called X and O guys, and people are now emulating what Coach Richardson did since junior college," says Mike Anderson, listing the prominent programs that are clear descendants of "Forty Minutes of Hell." Richardson rarely gets credit for the changes that he helped bring about. "I know that sometimes hurts him," Anderson says.

This situation—whites getting credit, blacks getting ignored—is not unique to coaching. Pete Maravich adopted a flashy, black playground style—something that Earl Monroe and Nate "Tiny" Archibald from the same era could do—and brought it to a mostly white conference and audience. Maravich became the subject of books, films, and instructional videos. While Monroe and Archibald won NBA championships, Maravich got more notoriety and bigger paychecks.

Richardson responds to this kind of snub by attacking the club that won't grant him full membership. "I remember Jud Heathcote from Michigan State raving to me about his match-up zone defense," he says, "and he was getting all kinds of attention. But I played nearly exactly the same zone."

This is a Richardson trademark. Attacking the attacker, or disdaining the disdainer. In an interview with the *Sporting News*, the writer Bob Hille wrote, ". . . [Richardson] always seems to be saying he doesn't give a damn about what you think of him, yet always finds time to defend himself against criticism or perceived slights."

Richardson could be hypersensitive if the slight came from a rival or antagonist. Frank Broyles sent an interoffice memo to Richardson that, according to Richardson, said, "I envision you being athletics director here someday."

Richardson remains angry about the memo. "He signed his name *Frank*. He didn't even have the decency to write his last name."

Richardson rarely drank and never frequented bars in Fayetteville. Instead, the coach and his wife immersed themselves in laid-back lunches and weekend barbecues during the Day, Miller, and Mayberry years. The team could generally be found hanging out on the couches in their coach's condominium, especially after Yvonne died.

Around that time, Richardson bought a ranch outside of Fayetteville from former Olympic track star Mike Conley. The ranch, with its horses and sprawling hills, also became, for the Richardsons and the players, a place to escape.

"I think Rose wanted some of the team around as much as possible," Todd Day says, "and that was because Yvonne was gone. Rose had less to fall back on, and she was such a long way from El Paso."

Richardson's hands-on approach with his players sometimes had hilarious results. During road trips, bed checks and curfews were routine. One night before an important game, Richardson decided to make the rounds himself. He checked on Oliver Miller's room last.

Miller was not a typical Richardson-style player. Nearly 6'10", Miller tipped the scales at close to three hundred pounds. The Fort Worth native was also unusual in that his parents were moderately well-off compared to most of the team. Miller's weight was as baffling as Bruce Vanley's had been at Tulsa. But Richardson admired Miller, who relished, and often won, his battles with LSU's Shaquille O'Neal.

During that evening's bed check, while Richardson was saying good-night to a couple of freshmen at one end of the hotel hallway, a Domino's Pizza man hurried by.

The deliveryman tapped on Oliver Miller's door. Richardson saw money change hands, as well as four large pizzas.

The coach took a deep breath, walked down to Miller's room, and knocked.

Nothing. Richardson knocked again, louder. "It's your coach. Open the door."

"Just a minute," Miller cried.

Richardson paced the hallway. When the door popped open, Miller scurried back inside and sat down.

"Lights out in ten minutes," Richardson said. "And turn down that TV."

"Sure, coach," Miller said, muting the sound. "I'm almost ready for bed."

Behind Miller was a pile of sweat suits and practice gear. "What's under those warm-ups?" Richardson said, moving around Miller.

"Nothing, coach." Miller stood and shifted, as though setting a screen.

Richardson reached below Miller's feet and uncovered the cardboard boxes.

"Oh!" said Miller. "Right. I ordered those for the rest of the team. They're not even for me."

"Great," Richardson said, sliding the pizzas past Miller. He whipped out his rooming list. "I'll take them down to the guys and you can get some sleep."

"Wait!" Miller cried as the coach closed the door behind him.

Any observer of a Nolan Richardson practice could sit in the back row and be shaken by his booming voice, a tool he would wield like a hammer. He'd demand respect from the strongest kids, instill fear in the weaker ones.

Respect was more important than affection, despite the open-door policy at the Richardson ranch. "I never worried if the players liked me," Richardson says. A major component to his big recruiting pitch was what he'd tell their mothers: "If you send me a boy, I'll send you back a man."

That respect—or fear—doesn't die easily. Todd Day returned to Fayetteville with his agent one year, and as he walked into the arena, Day appeared to be frantically scratching his ears. The agent asked him what the trouble was. "I'm trying to get these earrings out before coach sees them," Day said.

Don Haskins said, "I think there was an element of fear because Nolan got his guys to play so hard."

After Haskins retired, he was invited to come watch the Razorbacks practice. Because of his own grind-it-out style, his typical practice agenda was primarily based on stopping the opponent's fast break. He'd stress both the clogging half-court defense and his annoyingly patient offense. A Richardson practice—the laboratory for "Forty Minutes of Hell"—was as foreign to Haskins as a three-piece suit.

"Everything was done full-court," Haskins said. "Shooting drills, man-to-man offense, hell, you name it. They started on one end, and they raced like hell to the other. There wasn't a single thing that didn't involve the length of the court."

Haskins prided himself on knowing exactly what his players should be doing at all times. "Nolan was different," he said. "He wanted them to rely on their own instincts. That would make them very difficult to scout, because nobody could tell when they were going to trap." The pace of practice, according to Haskins, was exhausting. "I've never seen so many guys running so hard for so long. And they didn't dare complain."

As the Razorbacks began to scrimmage, something happened that initially had Haskins perplexed. One of the Razorback guards caught the ball behind the three-point line. Richardson yelled, "Layup!"

"What in the hell is Nolan yelling *layup* for?" Haskins wondered. "That wasn't a goddamn layup. That was a twenty-footer." Each time the player received the ball behind the arc, Richardson hollered the same thing: "Layup!"

Haskins was aware he had cut Richardson's scoring average in half in the early 1960s—Richardson could now finally joke about that remarkable statistic. But Haskins was unaware that even Richardson's free-throw percentage, something unrelated to style of play, dropped. Before Haskins's arrival, Richardson was shooting a respectable 64.5 percent from the free throw line. Under Haskins that first year, he dipped to 56 percent. His senior year, his shooting confidence further shaken, he finished at an abysmal 54 percent.

Sitting in the second row of the Arkansas arena, Haskins had an epiphany. "Nolan was making that guard think it was an easy shot," he said. "He meant the three-pointer for that kid was as easy as a layup! That stuck with me, the way Nolan can instill confidence."

Richardson's deliberate injection of confidence in his best shooters was a direct reaction to his own career, the way Haskins had clamped down on him.

Richardson would tell the Razorbacks, "I'm an old-school guy. I'm not a damn psychologist."

"But in reality," says Pat Bradley, Arkansas leader in career three-pointers, "Nolan could have had a PhD in psychology."

Richardson wanted his shooters to be brazenly confident. Yet the Haskins-like intimidation remained an important factor. "The team loved him," says a man who was close to the Razorback program for years. "But there was also fear. You can't discount that. Nolan was very, very tough and sometimes mean." Many of Richardson's former players use the word "fear" as often as "love" when describing him.

Pat Bradley says there was another peculiar Richardson trait in practice—his kindness to freshmen. This was also the only time Don Haskins showed any generosity on the court. "He'd encourage the freshmen all season," Bradley says. "Once they were sophomores, though, look out."

Still, at the heart of Richardson's motivation during practice was the constant us-against-the-world speech. How would that sit with someone like Pat Bradley, a white kid from Massachusetts? "I think nearly everyone has inside them," Bradley says, "a feeling for the underdog. I know for me, I was constantly trying to prove I belonged in the SEC, and Nolan never stopped appealing to that. I believed in *him*, because he believed in *me* in a way that nobody else did."

Clint McDaniel, who would star for Richardson's best teams, says the coach's charismatic power pushed the players beyond their limits in practice. "Have you ever seen somebody sprain both ankles at the same time?" McDaniel asks. One substitute, Reggie Merritt, did just that, coming down hard on someone else's high-tops. Merritt, however, refused to be carried off the court by the trainer. "Merritt kept trying to play. He was so pumped up he refused to stop," McDaniel says, "but when he tried to walk, he just kept falling over. That's the kind of motivator Nolan was."

Dave England, the basketball trainer, says, "It's hard for people to understand. The players loved Nolan. *Loved* him."

THIRTEEN

BLUES FOR MISTER CHARLIE

Haskins's hollering and Ol' Mama's wisdom echoed constantly in Richardson's head—his speech, playing style, and career reflected his own history. While he'd play a lot faster than Haskins, and he'd host his players as though they were sons, the aggressive anger his teams played with seemed to be a modern descendant of both Haskins and Ol' Mama. Richardson's past clung to him like a hyped-up defender with plenty of fouls to give.

The same could be said for Frank Broyles, an icon of the Old South, but his past was very different from Richardson's.

Although Jackie Robinson joined the Brooklyn Dodgers in 1947, the South—the white South—was not impressed. Professional sports teams had little or no influence there, even into the 1950s. Atlanta had no professional teams. St. Louis was the closest franchise to many Southern schools.

However, the Civil Rights movement was slowly creeping up on schools like the University of Arkansas and coaches like Frank

Broyles. At times, Broyles must have felt that modern America was encroaching on his tradition of all-white teams, but he clung to his system and his enormous success of the 1960s. As college sports integrated, Broyles became an outsider by the end of that decade. Pressure would even come from the mediocre basketball program on his own campus. In 1966, basketball coach Glen Rose announced to the media that he would be willing to recruit a black player. Broyles refused to endorse those sentiments.

Basketball was more difficult to desegregate simply because of the nature of the game. Football players are covered with helmets and padding, while basketball players have much more skin exposed. The proximity of the fans leaves no doubt as to a basketball player's race, and blacks were also easier to reach with racial taunts or hurled objects. Also, the number of football players—as many as one hundred on a team—should have made football's integration more viable.

Otto "Bud" Zinke was a University of Arkansas physics professor for three decades. He arrived on the UA campus in 1959, a year after Frank Broyles. Although he was a diligent antiwar activist in the Vietnam War era, he does not consider himself to be a radical, especially along racial lines. "I came back from World War II, and it wasn't so much that I was involved with blacks," he recalls, "I simply didn't want to live in a country that had second-class citizens."

He's no dreamer. "I don't get into fights unless I think I can win them," he says. He worked to quietly integrate the Fayetteville swimming pool, as well as the Ozark Theater.

He was a young member of the senate council, the ruling body elected by the faculty senate. Nearly everyone on the faculty was in favor of integration, according to Zinke, or at least the more modest concept of desegregation. Zinke says he will never forget a senate council meeting in the late 1960s.

The university had slowly begun making steps to change the face of the campus, but Zinke and his colleagues knew that football and Frank Broyles were the symbolic center of the university. The senate council decided to confront Broyles.

"If Frank Broyles had said we were going to integrate, nobody would have challenged him," Zinke says. "So we called Broyles in, and asked him to integrate his team."

The room got quiet as Broyles stood. "The faculty was challenging his eminence," Zinke says.

According to Zinke, Broyles said, "I'll go home to Georgia before I have any niggers on *my* team."

A stunned silence followed. "I'll never forget the day," Zinke says. "He just stood there very brazenly, and said that with his slow Southern drawl."

Thomas "T. J." Johnson of all-black Menifee High School signed with the Arkansas basketball team in the spring of 1966, becoming the first black athlete to do so. Freshmen were not eligible to play, but when his sophomore year began in 1967, the coaches decided to "red-shirt" Johnson, holding him out of games while he continued to practice. When an older player on the varsity got hurt, Johnson figured the coaches would change his status. They did not, and Johnson, frustrated, transferred to Central Arkansas, where he led the team in scoring his final two seasons.

His time at UA was mostly without incident, although he told the *Democrat-Gazette* that he hated when the fans in Fayetteville waved Confederate flags. "That always took the wind out of my sails," he said.

Another black player, Vernon Murphy, joined UA during the same semester, but was declared academically ineligible.

After T. J. Johnson and Vernon Murphy did not work out as planned, struggling new basketball coach Duddy Waller set his sights on Fort Smith native Almer Lee to buoy the program. Almer Lee became the first black athlete to earn a varsity letter in any sport at Arkansas. The unassuming Lee had spent a year at Phillips Community College, then transferred to Fayetteville in 1969.

Lee's high school had already integrated, and Duddy Waller believed that would make his transition easier. So would the fact that Lee's high school coach was the highly regarded Gayle Kaundart. Lee had other important pluses. He was a flashy ball-handler, a great scorer, and fun to watch. Lee quickly became a star, pouring in 19.2 ppg in 1969–70. Unfortunately, the Razorbacks weren't very good, finishing 5-19 overall in Coach Waller's final season.

Lee rejects the idea that his first coach in Fayetteville was fired for integrating the team. "Duddy Waller didn't have a very good record," Lee says.

The next year, Lee again paced the Razorbacks in scoring under a new coach, Lanny Van Eman. The team was not very good that year, either, finishing 5-21. As a senior, Lee blew out a knee and never really recovered. A tryout with the Chicago Bulls didn't last long. Lee had a superb, if brief, playing career in Holland.

Lee insists his time at Arkansas was fairly ordinary. No threats. No fights. No name-calling. His teammates liked him, and nearly every Southwest Conference team had a black basketball player by then.

"If there were racial slurs," Lee says, "I didn't hear them. I was treated just like the white players. Of course there was some prejudice in Fayetteville," he says, "but the team stuck together." Instead, Lee took abuse for something he hadn't anticipated.

"The fans called me a hot dog," he says. "They were shocked to see the things I could do with the ball. There was very little behind-the-back or between-the-legs dribble then. They would say 'he's a Harlem Globetrotter!'"

"Almer's style was very suited to the present day," Van Eman says. "He could really handle the ball and shoot, and was like Pete Maravich in some ways."

Van Eman had five black players when his tenure ended in 1974. But it wasn't the challenges of integrating, or the remote location of the university, that presented the biggest struggle. "It was a laborious battle because football was so popular," Van Eman says.

Frank Broyles and Arkansas finally offered a scholarship to an African-American football player named Jon Richardson (no relation to Nolan), a speedster who played from 1970 to 1972. Broyles told the *Democrat-Gazette*, "We wanted to make sure the time was right."

Jon Richardson was an instant sensation. In his debut, a nationally televised game against Stanford, Richardson grabbed a 37-yard touchdown pass for his first of eleven scores that season. But a broken leg in 1971 slowed him, and he became primarily a kick returner the rest of his career—a dangerous and nerve-wracking position.

Jon Richardson got heat from whites and blacks; whites who feared a wave of athletes of color, and blacks who called him an Uncle Tom.

Steve Narisi, an Arkansas native who was later named sports director for Channel 29 in Fort Smith, remembers attending radio-listening parties as a boy whenever the Razorbacks would play. No regional television existed then, and football tickets were gone years in advance. Jon Richardson's debut season still stands out to Narisi. "When Jon Richardson was first there, you'd hear the 'N word' everywhere. He hurt his wrist and he was having trouble, so he fumbled a few times. You'd really hear it then."

FOURTEEN

SOLEDAD BROTHER

J on Richardson was the first black football player to *play* for the Razorbacks. The desegregating of Arkansas football is complicated by the incredible story of Darrell Brown.

Darrell Brown attended a tiny "training" school—a code word for Negro school with poor resources—in Lockesburg, Arkansas. Brown was the star of the track team, a sport that had little in the way of equipment. He practiced the shot put using a heavy stone; he hurdled over carpenter's wooden horses.

In 1965, his school consolidated with the local white school, and team sports like football were available to the Lockesburg kids for the first time. He wanted the chance to fully experience high school athletics, so he asked his schoolteacher father if he could delay his graduation for a year. But it was too late for Darrell Brown, already in his senior year. His father told him he had to go on to college. Brown was in the wrong place at the wrong time. It would happen again.

Brown knew he had outstanding speed and quickness from his

success in track and field. But he longed to play organized football and got the peculiar idea that he could be the first black football player at the University of Arkansas.

When he arrived on campus, he went straight to the football coaches' offices and asked to try out as a "walk-on," a non-scholarship player.

"I'm Darrell Brown," he announced, "and I want to play football."

No black kid had ever been that bold before. Brown informed the coaches that he was a running back. "After a long pause," Brown recalls, "they finally brought me a uniform and some pants. 'This is great!' I thought. I'm going to walk on."

Darrell Brown was not aware of the 1964 Student Association endorsement of integrating the athletic teams in Fayetteville. He knew nothing about the college faculty or their senate council, which had also voted in favor of integration, or that the governor, the board of trustees, and the football coach resisted.

Darrell Brown just wanted to play football for Arkansas.

Being a college walk-on in a major sport is a difficult road. Earning a scholarship—room, board, tuition, and books—is often the ultimate goal, but few reach that payoff. During the 1960s, some major college football coaches had the budget to award scholarships to as many players as they saw fit. Anyone whom the coaches truly wanted was usually awarded a full ride before even enrolling. Walk-ons who impressed the coaches might earn a full ride the next year.

Walk-ons are at the mercy of the coach's discretion and sense of fairness.

A coach can directly discourage or encourage walk-ons. In basketball, just sitting a player on the bench during scrimmages sends a message. Benching a player during, say, shooting drills can be even worse. There are plenty of perks that can be used to reward—or withheld to punish—walk-ons. Free shoes, sweat suits, or travel gear go to the most appreciated walk-ons. There are other carrots, as well. Team meals, team pictures, a photo in the media guide, a seat on the airplane to road games, complimentary tickets, off-season weightlifting. Playing time in varsity games, or a full-ride scholarship, means a walk-on has arrived.

It doesn't take a walk-on in any sport very long to get the message "I'm wanted." Or, "I'm not wanted."

"Let me just sum up my history with Arkansas football," Darrell Brown says. "As a running back, I was simply a tackling dummy."

There's nothing more dangerous in football than receiving a kickoff or punt, and Brown was often assigned that role in practice. The assignment was radically different from normal, though.

Brown became the target of a bizarre meanness, something as grotesque and obscene as the "Battle Royal" scene in the novel *Invisible Man*, where twelve black boys were blindfolded and pushed into a boxing ring. "There were times," Brown says, "I'd be placed on the field to run the ball on a kickoff or punt without *any* offensive players in front of me to meet eleven defenders." One player, with the ball, trying to get through an entire team sprinting directly at him.

Brown absorbed both the abuse and the obvious message from the coach. "I was a country bumpkin," he says. "I just wanted to be at the University of Arkansas and break that color barrier, get what I missed out on in high school."

Frank Broyles, of course, oversaw every practice. "He *wanted* them to do what they did," Brown says. "It all came down from the power that Broyles possessed. I remember him being up in the stands when I was running back kicks against eleven of them, and he'd shout out, 'Why is it that you can't catch that nigger?'"

Brown persevered through that hellish autumn despite feeling as though a bull's-eye was pinned on his jersey.

Sometimes he would have ten other players on his side during practice, but that wasn't a big help. "On the practice field and in the few [freshmen] games in which he played," Richard Pennington wrote in his book about the desegregation of SWC football, *Breaking the Ice*, "his offensive teammates sometimes refused to block for him and even engaged in racist group chants."

Brown never advanced beyond his role as the human punching bag, and never made the varsity. "But he might have if Frank Broyles had made it clear to everyone that Brown was to be treated fairly," Pennington insists. Instead, Broyles's silence condoned the cruelty.

Brown says, "I never had a playbook, was never taught a play. I was placed on the field without knowing any part of the system." That didn't stop Brown from working his way to the front of the line. "The coaches might say, 'I need a defensive back!' and I'd just raise up my hand."

No personal interaction took place between Brown and Broyles. "What I heard from Broyles came to me indirectly," Darrell Brown says, "when he talked about me."

Brown became a member of the Shoats, the UA version of the freshmen team, which featured walk-ons, transfers, and players waiting to earn eligibility or varsity action. "I'd get in and say, 'Where am I supposed to run?' I wouldn't ask about hitting the one-hole, or the two-hole. They'd never taught me that. I was just asking if I was to run right or left."

In *Horns, Hogs, and Nixon Coming*, Brown credits Wilson Matthews as being the running-back coach who encouraged him. Today, he's fuzzy on it, and not sure exactly who that coach was. Matthews was never the running backs' coach; he was usually in charge of linebackers. Matthews is quoted in Frei's book as saying that he has no recollection of any Darrell Brown. The Arkansas football media guide names Bill Pace as the running backs' coach that year. "Only one coach was encouraging to me," Brown says today. "That particular one had responsibility over the running backs."

In fact, Matthews would find himself in the Arkansas administration before Frank Broyles finally desegregated his team.

Lanny Van Eman was named Arkansas basketball coach in 1970 and watched as Broyles began signing black football players. Despite Van Eman's endorsement of Broyles ("a great athletics director"), he believes there was a specific reason Wilson Matthews wasn't on the field when integration took place.

"[Wilson Matthews] used the word 'nigger' in his day-to-day conversation," Van Eman says. "It made me totally uncomfortable." Van Eman suspects the reason Broyles promoted Matthews, making him an assistant athletics director, was simple. "To get him away from the players," Van Eman says, when Broyles was forced to desegregate.

As the vice chancellor at the University Medical Center, Charles Prigmore was often around the football team. Prigmore confirms the fact that Matthews used that kind of language. "Wilson Matthews was a crude guy," Prigmore says. "He was on the staff when we played Georgia in the Sugar Bowl, and I was a part of the official travel party. He didn't have the polish that Frank Broyles had. Matthews would always be spouting off."

One former Arkansas basketball coach before the Richardson era says, "Matthews talked like that, but his heart was better than Broyles's." (Matthews died in 2002 at the age of eighty. Today the Arkansas football stadium has a 3,800-square-foot Wilson Matthews "A" Club room for the big-money boosters.)

Darrell Brown resided in Humphrey Hall, one of the first integrated dorms, and he ate at Brough's Commons. The dining hall there closed at six p.m., which was when football practice usually ended. The scholarship players were half a block from their cafeteria, but Brown would have to run uphill for a half mile, then often find his cafeteria closed. He slept without eating the first few weeks. Later, he realized he needed to get to know the ladies in the lunchroom, and he began doing what blacks in the South had known to do for years. "I'd knock on the kitchen door," he says, "and ask if there was anything left to eat." The cafeterias at that time were totally staffed by black help, and they were sympathetic to Brown's plight.

Being the first black football player took a terrible toll, yet in Brown's understated manner, he says, "I had reservations about continuing on the field. It wound up being a positive experience because it opened my eyes. There was a big shield of resistance to having a black player at Arkansas. Their [the players] words were, I heard some of them say, 'Why do we need a black, we just won a national championship?'"

Any fairness on the football field stood out to Brown. "David Hargis was one of the few players who never called me 'nigger,' and he would stand up for me. I considered him to genuinely believe in the right thing. He'd say, 'Give Brown a chance.'"

Hargis came from southern Arkansas and later was accepted to the UA law school, where he was named editor of the *Law Review*. Today Hargis is a successful trial lawyer in Little Rock. He declines to say "nigger," even when quoting someone, always using the phrase "N word" instead.

Hargis recalls Brown's ordeal vividly. "Darrell Brown displayed a whole lot of courage in doing what he did," he says. "The fact that he didn't have a scholarship, that made it even more daring on his part. They were sending a brutal message to Darrell. When the ball was snapped, it was like he was the only player left on his side. He'd come back in the locker room and he'd have been beaten up every day."

Although it appeared a systematic ostracizing of Brown was in place, Hargis believes it was not orchestrated. "Darrell was never exactly singled out and mistreated in an organized manner," he says.

It was often spontaneous, with the players chanting "Get the nigger." "I heard it back then," Hargis confirms. "It'd be when they were trying to tackle Darrell, and sometimes his teammates wouldn't block for him."

Hargis insists on pointing out cultural and historical differences and the danger of judging the past with today's more progressive mindset. He is also sensitive about Arkansas's portrayal in print. "I'd hate to contribute to Arkansas being viewed as backward," he says. "I don't want to condemn anyone. This was a different era. I'm not blaming or faulting anyone, retrospectively. There were people who had not been confronted with these issues, who hadn't thought about these things. If confronted today, I think they'd regret what they had done."

That may be true. Yet it's important to understand that this was the kingdom that Frank Broyles ruled, the athletics program where Nolan Richardson would arrive two decades after Darrell Brown.

It's also true that Elizabeth Eckford and her spit-drenched homemade dress represented enormous courage, regardless of any sociological analysis or historical context. She returned to Central High School the next day, and the next few years. Darrell Brown was the Elizabeth Eckford of college football.

Football, though, is only part of American society, Hargis notes. "Lots of blacks were exposed to far worse away from sports. They were brutalized," he says. "There's a big difference between being called a name on the field and having a Coke bottle smashed against your head in the street. It's difficult to judge Frank Broyles or Adolph Rupp by today's standards. Our own fathers and grandfathers, some of them, without ill will, entertained racism."

The old Razorback football coach has changed some over the years, Hargis says. "Broyles displayed a lot of racism, but he's softened, and he's done some things that are pretty commendable, especially with Alzheimer's research funding." (Hargis also admired Wilson Matthews and defends him, too. "You could count on what Matthews said," Hargis says, and he never heard Matthews use what he calls the "N word." "Why would he? There weren't any black players around to speak of.")

Hargis is quick to apply modern standards to Darrell Brown's situation in one regard, though: "Darrell had superb athletic ability, based on his speed and quickness," he says. "He wasn't big, but he was very strong for his size. In today's world, Darrell Brown would have played for the Arkansas Razorbacks."

"I made it through the year in 1965," Brown says, "then went out again the next fall."

It is nearly beyond belief that Brown would return to the Razorbacks, but in some ways he was luckier the second year. "I got hurt in practice," he says. That gave him time to reflect on the futility of his quest and make a decision. "I turned away, because of my dream being shattered," he says. Brown's hope of being the first black scholarship player, or the first black to take the field in a Razorback uniform, was over.

Brown concentrated on academics. "I remained frustrated," he says, "because I felt I was just as good and fast as anyone who was playing."

Two years later, Martin Luther King and Bobby Kennedy were gunned down, politicizing Darrell Brown. He was accepted into the University of Arkansas law school. After a long career as a Little Rock attorney (he took President Bill Clinton's deposition at one time), he retired to a farm in Horatio, Arkansas, near his childhood home.

Brown's daughter is employed today with University of Arkansas's athletics department. "She played basketball and ran track," Brown says, "and I all but told her and my son *not* to go to Arkansas. But I think they wanted to prove something, prove that they could make it."

The bond that Brown and Hargis forged kept them in touch for years. In the late 1980s, Brown teamed up with Hargis, but not on the football field. This time it was to play a little golf.

At that time, country clubs in Little Rock remained segregated. Hargis invited Brown and two other prominent black lawyers, Les Hollingsworth and Richard Mays, to play at the Pleasant Valley Country Club. Hargis says the three played without incident and, soon after, Richard Mays applied for membership at Pleasant Valley, bidding to become their only black member.

The Pleasant Valley doctor who conducted the application interview asked Mays why he wanted to join the club.

"I like to play golf," Mays answered.

"But who would you play *with*?" the doctor asked.

Darrell Brown can still get emotional when talking about his time as a football walk-on for Arkansas. He says he's had so few personal interactions with Broyles that he remembers them all clearly. "I saw Frank Broyles one time at a function, and I said to him, 'You don't remember me, do you?'" Then Brown explained that he had been practice fodder, a human tackling dummy as a walk-on in 1965 and again briefly in 1966.

"That's right," Broyles told Brown, "you were the first one!"

In *Horns, Hogs, and Nixon Coming*, Frei writes, "Broyles long has said the state board informally made it clear to him when he arrived at Arkansas that he could not recruit black athletes, but he felt integration was inevitable and right." This claim ignores a number of issues, such as the way Darrell Brown was treated. Also, the fact that the basketball coach at Arkansas beat Broyles by three years in desegregating his team. And virtually every college in the state and SWC desegregated before Broyles.

Yet, according to Frei, "Broyles said he didn't ask the university or athletics administration for permission to begin recruiting blacks."

Thus, in manipulating even the modern media, Broyles made himself simultaneously the victim and the hero of Arkansas's belated desegregation. The board wouldn't let Broyles *and* he ignored the board. Frei even states in the opening of one chapter that Broyles's having a single walk-on in 1969—who never played a minute or even suited up for the games—meant that the Arkansas team was "integrated." Frei makes the same ludicrous assertion about Darrell Brown's time in 1965, saying that Brown had ". . . briefly integrated the program."

"Don't confuse integration with desegregation," Judge Wendell Griffen cautions. "They're not the same thing."

"If you played football, you remember those awful days of sweaty football practice," says Richard Pennington, whose *Breaking the Ice* remains the only book on the integration of the Southwest Conference. The coaches start drill, maybe a one-on-one or two-on-one drill. Every player is standing there, watching. The coach asks for a volunteer to go first. "Well, that volunteer is the guy you want on your team," Pennington says. "He has guts and courage. You know who the wimps are? The cowards? They're at the back, hiding from the drill. That's what Frank Broyles and Darrell Royal were both doing in the 1960s, hiding in the back of the line!"

Pennington was never able to get access to Frank Broyles. The Arkansas coach was the only one who stonewalled him. "Royal and Frank Broyles—and, for that matter, 'Bear' Bryant at Alabama and others—were cowards," Pennington says. "They were simply afraid to lead and do what needed to be done, no matter how difficult, and preferred to let people like Hayden Fry take the heat." Broyles finished 1-9 in his last ten games against Texas, which makes it harder to believe that he would not recruit blacks sooner for practical, if not ethical, reasons.

An unknown walk-on who never scored a touchdown or played a single minute of varsity football at Arkansas is in elite company. Jackie Robinson. Jerry LeVias. Darrell Brown. "What these men did was so very important not just for black people but for whites, too," Pennington says. "What all this shows is how incredibly narrow-minded and parochial white people were back then. If those in power let these black guys compete fairly, they were going to rise to the top. Hell yes, they were afraid."

FIFTEEN

GO UP FOR GLORY

The 1992–93 Razorback basketball team went into the season with low expectations—after all, three of the best players in school history now were being fitted for NBA uniforms. However, a surprising group of newcomers, led by freshmen Corliss Williamson and Scotty Thurman, as well as junior college transfers Corey Beck and Dwight Stewart, made it to the NCAA Tournament's Sweet 16 before losing to eventual national champion North Carolina. Arkansas finished 22-9, including 10-6 in the SEC, and celebrated its last win in Barnhill Arena.

Richardson and Bud Walton, one of the founders of Wal-Mart, became better friends around this time, although they had met soon after Richardson arrived in Arkansas. Wal-Mart is based only a twenty-minute drive from the university, and Bud Walton, who loved the Razorbacks fast-break style, often made the drive to Fayetteville for lunch with the coach.

One October, Richardson had an idea for their annual exhibition game. He usually divided the players into a red and a white team and let his assistants coach. Richardson would watch from the stands to evaluate. Since the university was continuously courting donors, Richardson suggested to Frank Broyles that Bud Walton be asked to coach one of the teams.

Broyles told Richardson he'd already invited Bud Walton, and that Bud declined. "But I didn't believe it," Richardson says, "because coaching half the team, even in an intra-squad game, was an honor."

Richardson ignored Broyles and asked Bud Walton himself. Walton accepted and coached that year against one of the Tyson Foods bosses. This invitation to coach brought Bud Walton and Richardson even closer, but pushed Richardson and Broyles farther apart. This incident was one of several occasions where Broyles's pride trumped his wisdom—anything that would have kept Bud Walton pleased with the university would have been worthwhile.

When the University of Arkansas decided it was time to build a new basketball arena, the Waltons were a natural choice to help. Bud Walton reportedly gave $15 million for the construction of the arena, which was ready for the 1993–94 season. When it came time to make decisions about the design of the arena, Bud Walton went directly to Richardson for input. What color tile for the locker room? What kind of seats for the biggest donors?

In building Bud Walton Arena, the university was rolling the dice, hoping Richardson's Razorbacks would double the size of their crowds. One important stipulation from Bud Walton was issued when the arena was built—only Razorback men's and women's basketball could use the facility. No concerts. No pro wrestling. No volleyball. No circus. The one exception could be the annual convention for Wal-Mart.

Bud Walton Arena, with a capacity of 19,200, opened in 1993. The Razorbacks led the nation in attendance in its inaugural season. The arena remains one of the ten biggest for college hoops in the country. Richardson's squad would be ranked in the top ten in attendance eight of the nine years he competed there.

The team's success and its bond with one of the richest men in America may not have helped Richardson, ultimately. "Bud Walton loved Nolan," says Sid Simpson, "but Broyles was afraid of that, resented it."

Bud Walton Arena also became home to Razorback supporter Fred Vorsanger.

Vorsanger had served as vice president of finance and administration, a role that meant all of athletics was under him, including then-football coach Frank Broyles.

In 1989, Vorsanger became mayor of Fayetteville. After his term as mayor was complete, he felt that he still had the energy for another job. But in Fayetteville, Arkansas, few jobs were more prestigious than mayor. In 1992, Broyles offered him the job of managing the new basketball facility. It seemed like a step up.

Vorsanger liked Richardson immediately. When the coach heard how Vorsanger was the son of German immigrants in Chicago, bullied as a boy for his accent, the two got to be friends. They joked and teased each other constantly. Once Richardson was walking outside Walton Arena with a visiting golf pro when he spotted Vorsanger coming out of his office. Richardson whispered to the golf pro, then waved to Vorsanger.

"Fred, I want you to show this golf pro your swing," Richardson said.

The golf pro had his clubs with him and handed Vorsanger a driver. Vorsanger loosened up his shoulders, took his stance, reached back, and swung.

Richardson turned to the golf pro. "What do you think? Does he have any hope?"

"No," said the pro. "There's no hope for this guy."

Richardson grabbed the club and they walked away. Richardson and the golf pro stifled their laughter until they got outside.

Sometimes Richardson would joke with Vorsanger about his coaching situation. After hearing that an NBA coach was being paid lots of money not to coach his team any longer, Richardson said to him, "That's what we need, Federico. A long-term contract, then we screw up and they have to pay us anyway."

"He was joking when he said it," Vorsanger says. "He'd laugh and say, 'I wish they'd just pay me my money and I could go away, Federico.' I never took him seriously."

Richardson prepared the Razorbacks for the 1993–94 season with his usual brutal regimen that forced the players to grow up or go home.

One player, Alex Dillard, nearly joined the Marines out of high school—few options were available for a 5'5" kid in the world of sports. Instead, Dillard took some time off, then enrolled at a local junior college, where he sprouted up to 5'9" and emerged as a hot-shooting guard. He signed with Arkansas and arrived in the fall of 1993, but wasn't fond of the coach at first.

"We're going to be the best-conditioned team in NCAA," Richardson told the team, and Dillard wasn't emotionally prepared for what that entailed. By October of 1993, he was no longer planning on being a Razorback. Dillard instructed his father to call a list of coaches who had been recruiting him before he signed with Arkansas. He was planning on transferring at Christmas. Arkansas was like boot camp, Dillard says. "We ran and ran. The first month we had to be in the locker room at five fifteen in the morning." That was difficult enough, Dillard says, but they had to return in the afternoon for more.

Strangely, Dillard continued to grow that fall, sprouting two more inches in a single semester. That coincided with his evolving attitude.

Dillard decided not to quit. "You had to be tough," Dillard says. "He made Bobby Knight seem like a saint, he was so hard on us."

Instilling confidence and fear simultaneously is a Richardson paradox, and Alex Dillard acclimated, then erupted into the most productive scorer-per-minute in school history. Dillard would later score 19 points in seventeen minutes in a single NCAA Tournament game.

The fear-confidence combo sparked a new nickname for the coach, something the team called Richardson behind his back, and an echo from his past. Dillard says, "For four hours a day, he was the meanest motherfucker—excuse my language—that ever walked. Then afterward he'd open his home to us. We called him 'The Bear.'"

The Razorbacks were unaware that "The Bear" was Don Haskins's nickname.

Richardson had a fine team in place going into the 1993–94 season, but he was focused on more than his full-court pressure. He spent an increasing amount of time advising the Black Coaches Association.

The NCAA had decided to phase in something they called Proposition 16, a stiffening of the standards set by Proposition 48. Under the proposed new rules, a freshman would need a 2.5 grade point average in thirteen core classes. The NCAA was also proposing a "sliding scale" for the college board exams, the SAT or ACT. For example, if a student scored as high as 900, he could be permitted to play with a high school GPA of 2.0. The standards were more challenging, but the NCAA felt that, over time, high school students would meet the raised bar.

The Black Coaches Association rejected the new proposals. The BCA released a statement claiming that the NCAA had ". . . turned its back on socially and economically disadvantaged people . . ." When the proposal was passed, many athletic teams would have higher entrance requirements than the rest of their respective universities.

A challenge was issued back in 1989, when John Thompson walked off the court at an opening tipoff. The NCAA backed down then, and the ruling was rewritten. This time, Richardson and Chaney vowed to appeal to civil rights organizations like the NAACP.

Would higher admissions standards improve the graduation rates of athletes, especially black basketball players? Almost certainly. Fewer top athletes were being declared ineligible over the years, and it appeared that kids were adapting slowly to the new higher standards.

However, the most experienced black coaches relied on their historical perspective. To Richardson, any rule change that would exclude black kids was a disturbing move backward.

The BCA began calling for a boycott of the NCAA Tournament that spring. The target date for the discussed boycott was initially set for January 15, the birthday of Martin Luther King Jr. Members of the Congressional Black Caucus met with the BCA in Washington, DC, and they were able to convince the coaches to delay a protest—the Black Caucus thought it was too strong a move. When the boycott didn't materialize, Richardson was quoted nationally as saying, "I've always been a pioneer myself, and growing up like I did, I learned a lot about surviving. There will be a boycott." The NCAA Tournament was six weeks away.

The Black Caucus agreed to begin dialogue with the NCAA that would address the BCA's concerns. The reduction of total basketball scholarships from fifteen to thirteen over a decade was still a sore spot.

By the end of March, the threat of a BCA-sponsored boycott was a very real possibility—a boycott planned for the midst of the NCAA Tournament. Rudy Washington, the BCA's executive director, told the *Sporting News*, "We have the ability to stop work now . . . the NCAA kept saying, 'Yes, we'll put a committee together. We'll study it. We'll do this, yes, yes.' And then we say, 'We're not going to play basketball anymore.' . . . Call it a crisis, a dramatic gesture, if you will . . . We were forced to do this. This isn't something we wanted to do."

Washington was also critical of how long it took for African-American athletes and coaches to wake up. "Unfortunately, most of our people, meaning African-Americans, will die like they lived their lives: asleep. They never know what's going on around them. I just feel a real need to take a step and make some things work for us."

Reactions to the boycott by some black coaches were not so supportive. Ben Jobe, then coaching at Southern University, was frustrated that some of the most visible African-American men in America found time to battle for basketball scholarships. Jobe rejected the notion of a boycott to the *Sporting News*. "This is not the Civil Rights movement," he said. "This is not the war on poverty. This is not ethnic cleansing. This is not pro-life or abortion. This is not crime. This is not the killing of black youngsters by black youngsters. I'm not going to be wasting my energy . . . on fighting for a fourteenth scholarship for a kid who probably doesn't want to be going to school in the first place. If you have an important issue, call me. If not, don't bother me."

The Black Coaches Association, along with the NABC, began to hammer away at the NCAA in 1994 about four major concerns.

The first concern was the reduction in basketball scholarships. Second was the shocking absence of African-Americans in the NCAA's own headquarters. Third, there were few African-Americans serving in upper-management positions at colleges. Fourth, the BCA noted that more white males were coaching women's basketball than African-American females.

The Arkansas media jumped into the fray, and, as was often

the case, they irritated Richardson. John Robert Starr wrote in the *Democrat-Gazette*, "If the [Arkansas] players play, their chances of winning the tournament are considerably enhanced if Richardson, one of the poorest bench coaches in the land, is back in Fayetteville, sulking in his tent."

The Razorbacks quickly established themselves as a great team during the 1993–94 season. They lost only twice in the SEC season, by a total of three points. They were ranked #1 nationally for much of the year. The state-of-the-art Bud Walton Arena even attracted President Bill Clinton, an Arkansas native and former law school professor, who attended four regular season games that year.

Arkansas lost to Kentucky in the SEC Tournament and went into the NCAA playoffs ranked #2 in the nation. They beat historically black North Carolina A&T, then Georgetown, Tulsa, and Michigan to get to the Final Four.

When senior sub Roger Crawford got hurt, Richardson decided to honor Crawford by having #31 sewn onto the shoulder of every Razorback jersey—a sort of "No Hawg Left Behind" policy.

Three thousand Arkansas fans made the trip to Charlotte for the Final Four, where the Razorbacks would meet Arizona.

Richardson, an outsider all of his childhood and professional life, seemed unable to accept the accolades. Despite the national ranking and the notoriety the team had earned, the coach hammered the us-against-the-world story into their heads over and over. The team came to believe that they were not, in fact, getting the respect they deserved—despite being ranked #1 most of the season.

In the semifinals, Arkansas guards Clint McDaniel and Corey Beck harassed Arizona's backcourt, regarded as the best offensive duo in America, into making just two of twenty-two attempts from behind the three-point arc. Arkansas beat Arizona, 91-82.

Richardson held court after the Arizona game, lecturing the

media. In the *Sporting News*, he was quoted as saying ". . . if I would win games and some of the other black coaches would win, we would never win because of our brains and our techniques and our teachings. . . . it was always because 'Well, they've got the best athletes' and 'Man, look at those athletes that guy's got out there.' Wait a minute, I said, look at my team and look at Krzyzewski's team and put us on paper and just ask how many they want of their All-Americans as opposed to us—they don't know us, they don't know anything about us—and see whose team they're going to pick, whose players they're going to pick. That was the thing that used to bother me more than anything." The Duke coach, Richardson believed, had his pick of the nation's top high school players, while Richardson relied on under-recruited sleepers.

What raised even more eyebrows was what Richardson said on national television to color analyst Billy Packer immediately after the Arizona game. Packer had irritated Richardson plenty in the past; not directly, but through what Richardson felt were his veiled comments about black coaches and athletes—the very same things he would be lecturing the media about a few minutes later.

Minutes after the game ended, Packer lobbed a softball question to Richardson. "Gee, Billy," Richardson said, "a blind man could see that."

Don Haskins believed Packer had an East Coast bias. "If you weren't from the ACC [Atlantic Coast Conference], Billy Packer thought you didn't know anything," he said, but Haskins would never challenge Packer, or anyone else, on live television. Haskins thought Richardson's comments, both with Packer and to the media, were a distraction. "I don't think he needed to do that," Haskins was quoted as saying. "He kicked Arizona's ass, and he should've left it at that." With the NCAA championship still to be played, Haskins in his day would have been anything but political. Richardson had emerged as even more politically conscious and outspoken with the national title at stake.

———

The Razorbacks would play Duke, the NCAA champs in 1991 and 1992. Duke had a host of great players, but their star was Grant Hill, a consensus pick for national Player of the Year honors.

The day before the championship, Richardson grew pensive. He was reasonably proud of his accomplishments, but something was nagging him. Richardson had been the underdog so long that despite his team's yearlong national ranking, he still felt dispossessed. He found himself pondering one of Arkansas's little-used substitutes, a senior named Ken Biley.

Biley was an undersized post player who was raised in Pine Bluff. Neither of his parents had the opportunity to go to college, but every one of his fifteen siblings did, and nearly all graduated. "I had already learned that everybody has to play his role," Biley says of his upbringing.

As a freshman and sophomore, Biley saw some court time and even started a couple of games, but his playing time later evaporated and he lost faith. "Everyone wants to play, and when you don't you get discouraged," he says.

On two occasions, he sat down with his coach and asked what he could do to earn a more important role. "I never demanded anything," Biley says, "and he told me exactly what I needed to do, but we had so many good players ahead of me. Corliss Williamson, for one."

Nearly every coach, under the pressure of a championship showdown, reverts to the basic strategies that got the team into the finals. But Richardson couldn't stop thinking about Biley, and what a selfless worker he had been for four years. The day before the championship game against Duke, at the conclusion of practice, Richardson pulled Biley aside. Biley had hardly played in the first five playoff games leading up to the NCAA title match—a total of four minutes.

"I've watched how your career has progressed, and how you've handled not getting to play," Richardson began. "I appreciate the leadership you've been showing and I want to reward you, as a senior."

"Thanks coach," Biley said. He was unprepared for what came next.

"You're starting tomorrow against Duke," Richardson said. "And you're guarding Grant Hill."

Biley was speechless. Then overcome with emotion.

"I was shocked, freaked out!" Biley says. "I hadn't played much for two years. I just could not believe it."

Biley had plenty of time to think about Grant Hill. "I was a nervous wreck, like you'd expect," he says. He had a restless night—he stared at the ceiling, sat on the edge of his bed, then flopped around trying to sleep.

Richardson had disdained book coaches for years. Now he was throwing the book in the trash by starting a benchwarmer in the NCAA championship game.

On the day of the game, *New York Times* columnist William Rhoden wrote a column titled "A Coach and a Player Climb a Mountaintop." The article profiled Nolan Richardson and Duke star Grant Hill. It was April 4, the anniversary of the assassination of Martin Luther King Jr., and the coincidence was not lost on Rhoden.

Rhoden wrote of the volatile political and social climate that meant college sports were being more closely examined than ever. This was a "basketball season that became a civil rights movement, and a tournament that, largely because of Richardson, has forced the news media to at least hear, if not address, festering sociocultural issues striking at the foundation of college sports." Who would play, coach, write about, and profit from college basketball? These issues were now at the forefront.

Rather than win gracefully, Richardson had used the NCAA

triumphs to ". . . drive home the BCA's message of giving African-Americans the same off-the-court opportunities that they command on the court." Rhoden also called out the media on what he called a "manufactured morality play," something that had bothered Richardson for so long—the perception journalists had helped foster, that Arkansas had "talent" while Duke had "intelligence."

Rhoden marveled at Richardson's influence. "Richardson has talked so often and so loudly," Rhoden wrote, "that athletes are beginning to hear what he's saying." Of course, nobody heard more about it than the Razorbacks.

Near the end of Rhoden's piece, he asked a question that would prove prophetic: "Why do black coaches who get fired have such a difficult time resurfacing, if they resurface at all?"

Ken Biley had admired Grant Hill's skills countless times when Duke played on television. He made a conscious decision—he wouldn't back off Hill or give him too much respect. He'd deny Hill the ball whenever he could, crowd him, and try to overwhelm Hill with aggressiveness. Fatigue wasn't going to be a factor, since he figured he'd get limited minutes. "I didn't want to save anything. I always tried to contribute with defense and rebounding, anyway."

Biley was quite aware that this was not the ideal time for a coach to pay tribute to substitutes with good attitudes. "It was risky," he says. "What might it do for our chemistry and our tone for the game?"

Minutes before the game, Arkansas radio spotter Bob Carver watched to see what the reaction might be with the media as one of Richardson's assistants penciled in Ken Biley as a starter at the scorer's table. "Press row lit up!" Carver says. "You could see them thinking, 'Has Richardson lost his mind?'"

As expected, Ken Biley would play less than four minutes and did not score a basket. But he harassed Grant Hill, using his long arms and great lateral movement to hassle the All-American. Hill played point guard at the start, and was off his game. He would throw the ball away nine times that night.

Arkansas guards Clint McDaniel and Corey Beck set the tone with their furious defensive pressure. Corliss Williamson grabbed seven offensive rebounds and put in ten field goals. Scotty Thurman—from Ruston, Louisiana, where Ol' Mama was born—drilled a three-pointer with under a minute to go. That shot sealed the Arkansas victory. Arkansas beat Duke, 76-72. Nolan Richardson had won the national title.

The following week, Curry Kirkpatrick wrote about Richardson's NCAA title run for *Newsweek* and reflected on what he called the coach's manipulation of the media, whom ". . . Richardson plucked like a Stradivarius in motivating his team to overcome what the coach—though seemingly nobody else—perceived as slights based on racism."

Kirkpatrick felt the national polls were enough respect. Richardson insisted the polls were not—it wasn't respect for his team he was looking for. Richardson never suggested it was all a ploy to motivate his team—he remained the defiant outsider, reminding the respected writer of the ugly history in the rearview mirror.

"I know who I am," Richardson railed. "We [black coaches] can recruit, motivate, teach . . . but are we good coaches? I never hear that."

Later, John Thompson told the *Sporting News*, "The game is defined differently for a black coach. Truthfully, it's hard to explain that to a white person. . . . There's no such thing as the game for the sake of the game. It's not a luxury but a necessity; it's a means to an end, it's a means to an end for a lot of people. Nolan understands that."

Thompson was later quoted nationally as saying, "Nolan can never compete as 100 percent coach. He has other responsibilities as a black man. I hear people say they're in it for the love of the game. He can't go in feeling that way; no black man can."

Frank Broyles didn't make the trip to the Final Four in Charlotte because he was hospitalized briefly. He recovered enough to address the crowd at Bud Walton Arena the next week. The two men would embrace in front of the hysterical Razorback fans.

Scotty Thurman says Richardson never discussed his relationship with Broyles, but that the tension was obvious, even after the championship. "You could tell they didn't like one another," Thurman says.

Todd Day, by this time an established NBA star, says, "Frank Broyles had run Arkansas for forty years, and here comes this outspoken black man disagreeing with him. Nolan would stand up for what he thought and challenge Broyles."

There was one powerful person from Arkansas, however, for whom Richardson had no animosity. On June 15, 1994, the Arkansas basketball team was honored in the Rose Garden by President Bill Clinton.

Clinton had made a brief speech in the locker room after the Duke game, and had even posed on the cover of *Sports Illustrated* sporting a sweat suit Richardson had given him. "Nolan Richardson has done a lot of remarkable things in his life," Clinton said to the team, "often against all odds. . . . And so I say to him and all the players, you did your state proud. You made the president happy. But more important, you showed America the best of what college athletics should be. And we are all very proud of you."

Despite the praise from the president of the United States, Richardson had a difficult time enjoying himself. "You create a monster," Richardson told the *Sporting News* after the season. "I know that I've created a monster."

SIXTEEN

IF BLESSING COMES

Nolan Richardson was the first black man in power to openly challenge Frank Broyles, but the ground had been shifting under Broyles's feet since the mid-1960s.

The University of Arkansas campus was not exactly a bastion of radicalism then, but attitudes began changing. The student body and faculty confronted Broyles, and by 1969 he'd been forced to finally offer a scholarship to Jon Richardson. A modest antiwar movement had even emerged on campus, led in part by Professor "Bud" Zinke. In 1969, Gordon D. Morgan and Margaret Clark became the first black faculty members.

The school yearbook reflected the shift on campus. One photograph of Broyles in a late 1960s yearbook had the caption "The best football coach in America. Just ask him." Another photo featured a new group on campus, Black Americans for Democracy (BAD), whose objective was to raise the number of blacks enrolled at

Arkansas. Another full page was devoted to marijuana growing and smoking among white students.

Whether it was because of Arkansas's reputation as a stronghold of segregation or a lack of recruiting effort, Arkansas football just couldn't seem to attract the best black players. After 1967, Broyles would not coach another first-round NFL draft choice.

Broyles claimed to have been handcuffed by the board of trustees, and also to have ignored them on the subject of desegregation. Did he have the power to simply desegregate when he wanted? Or did the board of trustees insist that Broyles be last among colleges in Arkansas and teams in the Southwest Conference?

By 1961, Broyles had won three straight Southwest Conference titles. He was thirty-seven years old and one of the hottest names in all of football. Broyles won at least part of a national championship in 1964 and was named the national Coach of the Year. He was acknowledged by both supporters and detractors as perhaps the most powerful person in the state of Arkansas. The university, dorms, and basketball teams were already desegregating by the time Broyles made a move.

In other words, Broyles likely could have desegregated whenever he wanted to, and definitely after being named national Coach of the Year.

Certainly Broyles lived in a different place than, say, Don Haskins in El Paso, where half the city was Hispanic. Yet Arkansas has never been considered the Deep South. What if Broyles had the courage needed simply to announce he was going to break the color barrier first in the SWC, or look for a job elsewhere?

Fort Smith native Joe Neal, a passionate antiwar activist, rattled the establishment in the late 1960s by leading demonstrations outside UA football games. "The peace movement and the Civil Rights movement were interwoven," Neal says today. "One day we were out trying to stop the war, the next we wanted the campus newspaper to cover black issues."

Neal understood the emotional heart of the university was Frank Broyles's football team, and his blocking of desegregation needed to be challenged. At home football games, Neal and his crew stood in an area outside Razorback Stadium with signs reading WE WANT RAZOR-BLACKS.

"We set up where people were walking into the stadium," Neal recalls, "so they'd have to see us. We operated on the assumption that if Broyles wanted blacks on the team, he could have had them. Broyles was an extreme exemplar of the establishment and Arkansas was way behind the country. But in retrospect, they were trying to always raise money in parts of the state that wouldn't have wanted black football players."

The "Razorblacks" demonstrations were one of a quick succession of events that rattled the slowly awakening campus. Next came the occupation of Hill Hall, which housed the school of journalism and campus newspaper. Black and white students were angry that the school's weekly, the *Traveler*, would not print a letter rebutting an earlier one criticizing Dr. Martin Luther King Jr. Hill Hall later burned, but nobody was ever charged with arson. School president David Mullins's office was occupied by thirty black students who were frustrated with Arkansas's lack of progress.

Not everyone within those progressive movements was in agreement. "There was tension between well-meaning white liberals and others who were closer to the street," says Neal. "There were a lot of people around campus on both sides who felt threatened by black activists."

One of those black activists was former football walk-on Darrell Brown. Brown and a group of other black students bonded together in an attempt to get the school's band to stop playing the Confederate anthem "Dixie" every time Arkansas scored a touchdown or took the field. The song had irritated the first black basketball player on scholarship, T. J. Johnson, and that revulsion was typical of black students. In 1969, black students threatened to storm the field during the nationally televised showdown with Texas if the band didn't stop playing "Dixie."

On the weekend following the Arkansas v. Texas game, Darrell Brown was on the front page of the *Traveler*, along with the Razorback football team. Neither Brown nor the football team had good news to report.

Arkansas had lost to Texas in the white-guy version of the self-proclaimed "Game of the Century."

Darrell Brown had been shot, hit in the leg by an unknown sniper near campus after a meeting about the "Dixie" issue. The president of the university hadn't bothered to check on the wounded student, despite a personal plea from Gordon Morgan, UA's first black professor.

President Nixon was in attendance, as was George H. W. Bush and Bill Clinton. The shooting of a black student was the last kind of publicity the state or university needed. As it turned out, the administration didn't need to worry about Arkansas's image. Darrell Brown's shooting was not mentioned on television. The Razorblack protest didn't make it on national TV. Neither did "Bud" Zinke's antiwar crew.

The band director, acting independently, had decided to quit playing "Dixie" altogether, so black students did not storm the football field. Soon after, the student senate voted to recommend the song be dropped from the band's repertoire.

Brown's law school dean offered a public reward leading to the arrest and conviction of the person responsible for the shooting, but nobody was ever charged with the crime.

———

Arkansas avoided national exposure when Darrell Brown was hit by sniper fire, and they'd work hard to avoid embarrassment in the future. "I can't say that Frank Broyles was prejudiced," Arkansas's former basketball coach Lanny Van Eman stresses. "But there was one incident where a *Sports Illustrated* writer I knew came down for a spring football game, in 1970 or 1971." Broyles called Van Eman to his office and said, "A friend of yours is coming to town."

Broyles was concerned about the way Arkansas—the state, university, and football team—would be portrayed. *Sports Illustrated* had done a blistering series called "The Black Athlete" a few years earlier, and nobody was safe from criticism.

"Broyles was really scared," Van Eman continues. "He said, 'This is a *Northern* guy.'"

Arkansas was likely to be a top-ranked team in the coming season, so, naturally, ticket sales for the spring game were brisk. Van Eman attended with the *Sports Illustrated* writer, happy to be outside on this sunny spring day. But Van Eman was perplexed when he noticed a small tent set up next to the field.

With no threat of rain, the tent near the sideline seemed strange. Why? Maybe a player had an embarrassing location for a nagging injury—perhaps a pulled groin that would need constant treatment.

"At that time," Van Eman says, "there were just three blacks on the football team. Two were on scholarship and the other was a walk-on. Every so often the walk-on would run into the tent. I just couldn't figure out why."

Then it became apparent. The black walk-on would dash into the tent wearing #23. When he came out, he was wearing #41. Next time it might be #35.

The deceptive costume changes were intended, of course, to make the *Sports Illustrated* writer believe that Arkansas had plenty of black players.

The book *Untold Stories: Black Sports Heroes Before Integration* profiles many of the black athletes in Arkansas whose careers were ruined by the segregated system. Darren Ivy edited the collection, which includes many of his own articles, originally written for the *Democrat-Gazette*, researched and written when he was only twenty-four years old. The book was published by the *Democrat-Gazette*, and at first glance seems like a remarkable historical document. Then a pattern emerges—the players were never asked how they felt about being ignored by the University of Arkansas, or what impact segregation had made on their lives.

In fact, in the entire book of nearly a hundred chapters, there is just one single mention of, or quote from, Frank Broyles. His unwillingness to speak about the racist system he empowered, and the inability of the local press to ask him difficult questions, is astounding.

Ironically, the book tries to use Broyles's name to sell copies.

"Now, in this era of equal access," the book's back cover says, "it's difficult for some to remember that at one time there were two worlds of sport, delineated by pigment." Difficult for some, alright.

Just below that is the only Frank Broyles quote, a rather strange one. "It was like a blur," Broyles's quote reads. "It just happened, and you can't remember when it wasn't."

When Darren Ivy was given the assignment to both write and collect the articles by the *Democrat-Gazette*, he had to find his own way. Ivy was just out of school and not even an Arkansas native. Few records and no film could be found about the black sports heroes, and many of the best players only seemed to exist as legends. So Ivy, who worked at the paper from 2000 until 2004, got busy, relying on word of mouth. Outdoor dirt courts, patchwork uniforms, cracked backboards—one story led to another and soon enough, the *Democrat-Gazette* had a series. Ivy interviewed Broyles and used the quote—"It just happened and you can't remember when it wasn't"—in an early piece.

Later, when Ivy asked about Fayetteville star "Bull" Hayes, the black player who was steered away to Nebraska, the conversation with

Broyles came to an abrupt end. "He started getting all defensive and upset," Ivy says. "He got pissed off and he hung up on me."

That article changed everything for Ivy. "After we wrote the story on Bull Hayes, that was one of the most controversial. The series stopped at that one. It made me realize we're living in Arkansas, where racial issues are still pretty prevalent."

The black players during the era of segregation in Arkansas had been stifled. Years later their voices and stories were, in effect, still censored, because the difficult questions were not being asked. Anyone asking uncomfortable questions about that time was being stifled too.

There was a cost to this segregated system of keeping these young men on the outside. Not the touchdown totals or cutting down the nets at the Final Four, but a very real human impact. At least one story was begging to be told, one that connected Frank Broyles and Don Haskins.

Among the first pieces in *Untold Stories* is a profile of Bobby Walters, a running back who scored a mind-boggling ninety-six touchdowns in his high school career. Near the end of the article, it mentions that Walters was the guy who had coached Tim Hardaway in Chicago. A few years later, of course, Hardaway went to El Paso to play for Don Haskins.

Few people knew what kind of football hero Bob Walters had been in high school, because he kept it to himself. Instead, in his adult life, Walters was known as the Carver coach, then as Tim Hardaway's coach.

Walters scored thirty-two touchdowns as a senior, which should have been counted as the state record. Since McCrae High School of Prescott did not have films, or even detailed statistics, they had a difficult time getting colleges to believe Walters's amazing touchdown total. Bob Walters's brother Shelton believes the stats might even be too conservative. "I have to take that as official, since there were no records or films," Shelton says, "but if Bob scored *fewer* than four in any game it would be considered unusual."

The University of Arkansas, where Frank Broyles had just completed his second season, expressed no interest—despite the fact Walters was also ranked #3 in his class academically. Broyles would have never had a chance to see Bull Hayes play; Hayes's season at Fayetteville High School was finished by the time Broyles moved to town, so that would have been a handy excuse. Bob Walters may have been the first great black player in Arkansas whom Frank Broyles ignored.

Northwestern University of the Big Ten took notice, though. Their star, Irv Cross, was a cousin of Walters's coach.

Each school year in Prescott featured their annual talent show and awards ceremony. The spring of 1959, Walters's senior year, would not be any different. There would be all kinds of acts, but the topic on everyone's mind was where Walters would go to play football. When McCrae football coach Joseph Hale tapped the microphone in preparation of an announcement, people got quiet.

"Everyone should know," Coach Hale announced, "that Bob Walters left today on his official visit to Northwestern University." The gymnasium, filled to capacity, roared its approval. "Bob Walters will be the first Negro player from the South to go to Northwestern, and he's going to have the opportunity to play on television." Again, the crowd went berserk.

Distance was not going to deter Walters from taking a shot at the big time. His father, Johnnie Walters, was likely the only black car salesman in the state of Arkansas, and he always had access to a dependable car. "They didn't let him wear a shirt and tie," Shelton says, "but he was allowed to sell cars, mostly to blacks, and that was a big deal."

So was the opportunity to play sports in the Big Ten.

That August, Bob Walters made the journey to Northwestern for preseason football. While he was immediately homesick for Arkansas and overwhelmed by the new surroundings, Walters was happy to be out of Dixie.

But something happened after the first week of practice at Northwestern. One of the coaches told Walters, "I expect you to keep your nose clean and not date the white girls."

Walters was not so much interested in white girls. He was, however, interested in escaping the mentality of the South. The orders from an assistant coach dredged up years of being treated differently because of his skin color. Now Walters realized that the North could be nearly as oppressive. He got discouraged and quietly left campus at the end of the week; a homesick small-town kid, Walters's promising football career was suddenly a wreck.

Walters had few options. Without film or statistics, hundreds of miles from home, he was in a bind. A former Northwestern assistant who'd become the coach at Augustana College asked Walters to go to the small school in western Illinois. Walters went.

Augustana was just as frustrating. "There was absolutely nothing for him to do at Augustana but play football," says Shelton Walters. "Bob had no life at all."

Regardless, Walters played, and his family would pile into a couple of cars and make the journey to see the games. The trips reminded the family of home in a way. The police in Rock Island would follow their car, both going into the city, then again on their way out of town. Shelton says, "Part of it was harassment and part was to send a message. It was to keep you in your place."

Walters quit Augustana after playing just one year.

A depressed dropout from a small college, Walters was running out of options. He bounced around in Chicago in the early 1960s, working odd jobs and attending two junior colleges. In late August one summer, he went back to Augustana for less than a week, but then enrolled at tiny North Central College in Naperville, near Chicago.

Walters was an instant sensation at North Central, and his family again began loading up the family car. But a pattern was emerging, even in Illinois. "Naperville was a small town then, not a suburb," Shelton Walters says. "The police would be waiting at the edge of town, and they would follow us into the city, into the stadium, made sure we left out of town. The police were always in our rearview mirror."

Even at North Central, Bob Walters may have been headed toward a professional career. His coach there had played in the NFL and had the connections to get Walters, by far the best player on his team, a serious tryout. But during the fourth game of his senior year, Walters tore up his knee.

"Bob's talent would have gotten him in professional football," his brother Shelton claims, barring that injury, "if the NFL would have been fair and objective."

With football in his past, Walters began a career teaching and coaching basketball at Carver High School. He rarely mentioned his stellar prep career in Prescott, and being snubbed by the University of Arkansas was nearly forgotten. But Walters would one day get a chance to thumb his nose at Razorback football.

Bob Walters's nephew Danny was only five when he moved from Arkansas to Chicago. The boy was already interested in sports, and over the years he learned bits and pieces about his uncle Bob's high school exploits from family members remaining in Prescott. Meaning, from everyone except his uncle. "Bob never talked about himself," Danny says.

When his parents divorced, Danny moved in with Bob Walters and his wife for a couple of weeks. That experiment went well, so throughout high school Danny would stay with Bob Walters's family on the weekends. During those times Bob would clear the kitchen table, take the phone off the hook, yank the television plug out of the wall, and go over schoolwork with Danny. Danny might try to change the focus to sports, but Bob rarely fell for it—unless it had to do with attitude. Bob's influence and control over Danny mushroomed.

During the Chicago summers, all the Walterses would return to Prescott. Now that he was becoming more interested in focusing on football, the stories Danny would hear about his uncle began to resonate. They always ended with the same refrain—"There's never been anyone as good as Bob Walters."

On these pilgrimages to Arkansas, Danny also became intrigued with the state's big university. Razorback shirts, posters, and fans were more prevalent in Prescott since the team began adding black players in the early 1970s.

In the summer of 1976, before anyone was aware of his own status or potential, Danny wrote a letter. He wanted to express his interest in attending his dream school on a football scholarship. The letter was to Frank Broyles.

Likely, Broyles received hundreds of letters a year asking for a chance to play for the Razorbacks. But Broyles retired from coaching and never wrote back to Danny Walters.

By Danny's junior year in Chicago, he emerged as the star of Julian High School's powerhouse 1977 football team. An explosive hitter with great quickness, Danny was ranked highly by every national recruiting service and was one of Chicago's top prospects.

One day, a letter from Arkansas showed up at Julian High School. Then several more. Lou Holtz, whom Broyles picked as his replacement football coach, sent an assistant named Bob Cope to recruit Danny that year. Cope wasn't the only recruiter to show up. Famed Ohio State coach Woody Hayes came. So did coaches from football factories like Michigan, USC, and Oklahoma. Naturally, Danny began seeking Bob Walters's advice about what school he should sign with.

Bob Walters finally had his chance, twenty years later, to get even with the University of Arkansas.

As the frequency of the phone calls increased, and the pressure was building, Bob Walters came to a realization. He wanted his nephew Danny to play football at Arkansas, despite the way the university ignored his unofficial record-setting career in 1959.

He never suggested stonewalling Arkansas, according to Danny Walters. "Bob wasn't that kind of person," he says. "He wasn't reared that way."

"Bob *encouraged* Danny to go to Arkansas," his brother Shelton says, "because it was something that he could not do himself. Bob felt a sense of accomplishment that someone from his bloodline would play for the Razorbacks, especially after he was not allowed that opportunity."

So Danny Walters did what Bob Walters could never even consider—he signed with the Razorbacks.

Twenty years after his family had driven to North Central College games, Bob Walters found himself on the reverse journey, driving back to Arkansas to follow Danny's Razorback career up close. Legions of the Walters family came up regularly from southwest Arkansas as well.

While Danny was off to a fast start as a cornerback for the Razorbacks in 1980, Bob Walters got bad news. He was diagnosed with cancer and subsequently had most of his colon removed. He continued coaching at Carver the next few years. His enthusiasm for his team got a big boost in 1981, when he first witnessed hotshot freshman Tim Hardaway dribbling the basketball between his legs as though it were on a string.

With the cancer gnawing at him, Walters still occasionally felt strong enough for the six-hundred-mile trip to Fayetteville. The Razorbacks earned three bowl game bids with Danny at defensive back. Danny would later be named to the University of Arkansas All-Decade team for the 1980s, then played five years with the NFL's San Diego Chargers—where, coincidentally, Nolan Richardson had tried out in the 1960s.

When Bob Walters came to Fayetteville, he never referred to his past, and instead was caught up in the excitement of Danny starring for the Razorbacks. "Nobody would have ever known about Bob's high school heroics," Shelton says. "Even Danny hardly knew the exact details."

While Walters remembered how the segregated system had forced him to go north, he didn't dwell on it. "I don't think Bob lost one minute of sleep over Frank Broyles," Shelton says. "Bob never expected to be recruited by Arkansas. That was part of playing in the South." While Danny was one of the team's best players, Bob Walters never met Frank Broyles.

As the cancer got worse, Walters could manage fewer trips to Razorback Stadium. He'd sleep in his car while his wife drove, gathering his strength for the Saturday showdowns. Then the unofficial leader in career high school touchdowns for the state of Arkansas would put on his red sweatshirt and cheer anonymously for his nephew and the University of Arkansas.

By the time Frank Broyles finally decided to desegregate, it was too late for the good of his team. Broyles had blown his recruiting advantage of being the only major school in the state. Terry Nelson, Cleo Miller, Ike Harris, Roscoe Word, and Ike Thomas were all black Arkansans who starred at other colleges before earning spots on NFL teams.

Yet retired professor Phillip Trapp credits Broyles with rapidly adjusting in the early 1970s. "He changed his tune and quickly began to integrate athletics," Trapp says. "I think Broyles dragged his feet, but realized that integrating was the only way he could continue to have a winning team."

And Trapp is correct about Broyles at least trying to adjust.

By 1974, two years before he quit coaching football, his Arkansas team had *twenty-eight* black players on the squad, a huge jump from the lonely Jon Richardson days of 1970. This represented 23 percent of Broyles's team, second highest in the Southwest Conference and a remarkable improvement.

Bud Zinke is long retired from his physics professorship. Today, the reluctant radical is moderately happy about the progress his university made after the senate council meeting when Broyles shocked the faculty with his "I'll go back to Georgia" declaration. "The university integrated pretty gracefully after that," Zinke says. "At that time, the football team was first and everything else was second. But Arkansas has done really well—football is not as popular as it used to be."

Zinke scoffs at any notion that Broyles championed integration at Arkansas, though. "It's really funny. After he realized that he was going to have a second-rate team, he got with it pretty smartly, but that isn't the way he started out."

Broyles was never close to being as successful once he integrated. He won six SWC titles during the Jim Crow era of Arkansas football but could manage only one SWC championship in the integrated 1970s. Regardless of integration issues, by 1976 it was clear that Broyles had become a victim of his own success in the segregated 1960s. In his final five seasons, the Razorbacks were 32-21 with three ties. He lost the last four games of his career.

Broyles still had an incredible run before that to be proud of. His teams appeared in ten bowl games, and his overall record, including his brief time as Missouri coach, was 149-62, with six ties. Within a decade of his retirement he was inducted into College Football Hall of Fame.

The willingness Frank Broyles displayed in changing his team from a publicly racist program to a pretty well-integrated one reveals what some feel is the true nature of the Arkansas icon: everything is business to Broyles. Despite his public statements at faculty senate council meetings, other behind-the-scenes moves, and the brutal humiliation of Darrell Brown, many people think Frank Broyles was mostly concerned about money. Big money boosters didn't want black athletes? Broyles would comply. The rest of the Southwest Conference was passing Arkansas, and it was hurting attendance? Broyles would recruit black athletes.

In any case, Broyles resigned from football in 1976 to concentrate solely on administrative duties. He would reinvent his career by becoming perhaps the most successful and powerful athletics director in college sports.

SEVENTEEN

ONLY TWICE I'VE WISHED FOR HEAVEN

Despite the glow of the 1994 NCAA basketball championship, another misunderstanding between Broyles and Richardson was festering. This one would irritate both men for years. In 1995, Broyles amended Richardson's job title to head basketball coach *and* assistant athletics director. Richardson was thrilled. At first.

Broyles was now in his seventies, and the question of who his successor would be was often a topic of conversation in Arkansas. Broyles told Fred Vorsanger: "If Nolan ever applies for another job, either as a coach or administrator, it will help him."

Richardson asked Broyles what his new duties would entail. Broyles admitted that there wouldn't actually be any extra responsibility. That fall, although Arkansas had a dozen assistant athletics directors and as many meetings, Richardson was never invited. Broyles told him it was a token position. Richardson says, "That was the word he used. 'Token.'"

Vorsanger says, "Broyles thought he was helping Nolan."

Richardson simply did not believe it. "I didn't need a résumé for other jobs," Richardson says. "I wanted to stay at Arkansas."

"This place is not very good at communicating," Vorsanger adds.

On the eve of the next season, with a terrific team in place, Richardson went on the offensive. "When I was playing running bas-ketball, they called it niggerball," he told Alexander Wolff of *Sports Illustrated*. "When Rick [Pitino] did it, it was called up-tempo. If I lose, I can't coach. If I win, it's because my athletes are better."

"He seems to make a system of anger," Wolff wrote. "Players with something to prove identify with his sense of aggrievement and thrive."

Scotty Thurman agreed. "Coach talked about how nobody respected us. He was adamant about that."

Often, before playing a nationally ranked team, Richardson would work his way through the locker room, asking the players one by one if the university they were facing had actively recruited them. Since there were dozens of highly rated programs, the odds were always against it, but Richardson would still rub their collective noses in it—"Did Duke recruit *you*?"—reminding them that they were under-appreciated.

Thurman says, "He used our past and under-recruitment in high school, then brainwashed people to get them to do what they needed to do."

In February of 1995, while Richardson was revamping his Razorbacks for another NCAA title run, the BCA got some unusual help from a college president.

The BCA's executive director, Rudy Washington, hinted publicly that the threat level was elevated now. It wouldn't be the coaches who acted as if the boycott planned in 1994 were still to occur. This time it would be the students. More than one hundred students marched onto the basketball court at halftime of a Rutgers game and refused to budge. The game was canceled.

Much of the furor was caused by a statement made by then-Rutgers-president Martin Lawrence, who was quoted in the *New York Times* as saying, "Do we set standards in the future so we don't admit anybody? Or do we deal with a disadvantaged population that doesn't have the genetic, hereditary background to have a higher average?" Naturally, the unfortunate folks with poor "genetic, hereditary backgrounds" were likely 6'9" and could dunk a basketball with either hand. Lawrence later backpedaled on his remarks, saying that he did not believe racial heredity could forecast academic success.

John Thompson was not buying the retraction. "This was a deep statement," he told the *New York Times*, "interjected in conversation that was intended to be handled subtly or privately."

The BCA finally got their wish, yet there was no next step. The coaches were so involved with their own teams as the NCAA Tournament approached that they couldn't muster a unified response. Writer William Rhoden saw it as a wasted chance. ". . . [T]his time the BCA missed an opportunity to ignite a movement it actually predicted. . . . The BCA has run out of threats and, in the case of Rutgers, come up short on providing direction as well," Rhoden wrote. "There was a movement in Piscataway, ready to be ignited. The BCA wasn't prepared to strike the match."

In early spring of 1995, feeling the pressure of expectations for another NCAA title, an obviously frustrated Richardson called Razorback fans "turds and assholes." The *Democrat-Gazette* printed the quote verbatim. Richardson quickly apologized, saying a very small percentage of supporters had upset him. His earlier comments about creating a monster were coming true—the fans, media, and especially the coach, all expected another NCAA title. Nobody from the university administration questioned or counseled him about the "turds and assholes" quote.

In a *Sporting News* interview in 1995 with Bob Hille, Richardson softened his tone. "There are some good, beautiful, wonderful people in Arkansas," he said. "There's a few who are always going to stick—" At this point, Richardson checked himself, concluding, "They don't want me to be successful, so they'll do anything they can or say some things that are going to affect that."

The 1994–95 Arkansas team was the favorite to win a second national title, with nearly everyone back from the 1994 title team, including the usual starters. Arkansas lost in overtime to Kentucky for the SEC Tournament championship, but that didn't hurt their tournament seeding. Then, in the NCAA playoffs, the Razorbacks struggled before beating Texas Southern, Syracuse, Memphis, and Virginia by a total of 15 points to get to the Final Four. Two of those wins were in overtime.

Just as the NCAA playoffs commenced, the United States Basketball Writers Association gave Richardson the award for Most Courageous Coach. The justification for winning the award was as much for the coach's emotional recovery after Yvonne's death as for his pioneering career. Receiving the award, however, left him raw, retrospective, and saddened. He may have been psychologically unprepared for the Final Four.

The Razorbacks beat North Carolina in the national semifinals, but they were denied a second consecutive NCAA title, losing to UCLA 89-78.

Corliss Williamson and Scotty Thurman decided to declare for the NBA draft after the season. Both were juniors, eligibility-wise. This proved to be the right move for Williamson, but Thurman went undrafted and never played a minute in the NBA. In 2007, ESPN rated Thurman as one of the "Top ten players who should have stayed in school" of all time.

The 1995–96 Razorbacks went into the season with a recruiting class that was ranked first in the nation, but the group featured mostly junior college players who would have a rough transition. In January of that season, leading scorer Jesse Pate and leading rebounder Sunday Adebayo were declared ineligible by the school because of allegations their junior college grades were improperly certified. This controversy set off an eighteen-month NCAA investigation. Despite these troubles, the Razorbacks made the NCAA Tournament, barely, as a #12 seed. They defied the odds by making the Sweet 16 after wins over Penn State and Marquette.

"There were questions by the University of Missouri, which had tried to recruit Adebayo and Pate, about their transcripts," one Arkansas insider says. "Arkansas reviewed it all, but by January they still couldn't figure out the transcripts. So it was Arkansas who made them ineligible, and it was Frank Broyles's decision, not the NCAA's. Nolan felt that Broyles had fucked him."

What happened next further angered Richardson.

"When this conflict over Pate and Adebayo became an NCAA investigation," the insider continues, "the NCAA came back and said that those kids, Pate and Adebayo, *should* have been eligible."

The Razorbacks suffered when Jesse Pate went on to the minor league CBA. Richardson believed that the school's compliance staff within the Arkansas athletics department fought for his program, but that Frank Broyles did not.

Arkansas self-imposed some penalties, most of which were mild. But one of the sanctions—no junior college players allowed for two seasons—infuriated Richardson yet again.

The story got stranger when Sunday Adebayo transferred to Memphis during the transcript trouble. While at Memphis, he led them to victory over his old school. Then he petitioned the NCAA to reconsider his grades and won the appeal. Adebayo then transferred back to Fayetteville, where he powered Arkansas to a win over, ironically, Memphis.

The following season, 1996–97, featured a stripped-down Arkansas team without junior college recruits. It also marked the first time in ten seasons that Arkansas did not earn a bid to the NCAA Tournament; instead, they settled for the NIT. They bumped off Northern Arizona, Pittsburgh, and UNLV before losing in the semifinals at Madison Square Garden. Arkansas finished the year 18-14, and 8-8 in the SEC.

In 1997, the University of Arkansas introduced Dr. John White as its new chancellor. Each of the branches within the Arkansas system—Fayetteville, Pine Bluff, Little Rock, and Monticello—has its own chancellor, but the premier job within that system is in Fayetteville. John White was excited about coming back to his alma mater after his combined twenty-two years as a Georgia Tech faculty member and dean of engineering. Nobody speculated that it might have helped White's application that Frank Broyles was a Georgia Tech graduate.

John White was a natural fit; he was bright, congenial, and had strong ties within the academic and business communities. White males, however, have traditionally dominated engineering, and his hiring raised concerns within Arkansas African-American community as to how sensitive White would be to racial issues.

White, an introspective and thoughtful academic, recognized that and understood the problems with race relations were entrenched at the university. Fortunately, White had an interesting background in seeking diversity. He'd attended the National Science Foundation convention in 1988 and looked at the national data in regard to women and minorities in his field. He returned to Georgia Tech with a fresh view. "I got very concerned," he says. "You could count on one hand the number of graduating engineers each spring who were black or female."

While in Atlanta, White had been working on something called "The Committee of 100," which was attempting to double the amount of women and minority faculty. Atlanta mayor Andrew Young and White became close and would work together to recruit top black doctoral students.

The results raised eyebrows within the field of engineering, particularly at MIT, which was losing its own graduates to Georgia Tech's graduate school. White was framing it as a choice for prospective black students between Boston and Atlanta. "We were simply using Atlanta to its fullest potential," he says.

Fayetteville, where the African-American population was under 4 percent, was a world away from Atlanta. At his first major press conference, a journalist asked Chancellor White what he would miss most about Georgia Tech.

White knew Arkansas had an African-American population of only 16 percent. "It's more about Atlanta," White responded, "and what I miss is the diversity. This place is too white for me."

The response was palpable. "You could have heard a pin drop in that room, and everybody got big eyes," he recalls. But White had done his research. Like a crafty coach, he had statistics to back up his claim. "There's only one black employee on this floor," he said, "there's none on the second floor, there's one on the first floor. We're going to have to do things to improve diversity."

Frank Broyles would not have been thinking about "diversity" when he offered the job to Nolan Richardson in 1985. Yet Broyles's hiring of Richardson was dramatic, unprecedented, and historically significant.

No other majority white university in the old Confederacy had ever hired a black head coach in any major sport—basketball or football. It took tremendous nerve to be the first, and Broyles certainly had that. He had consolidated power over the years, and although his later teams' records damaged some of his mystique, by the early 1980s Broyles controlled the purse strings.

Neither would Broyles have hired Richardson because he thought it was time for a black man to finally have an opportunity, or have selected Richardson as a way to redeem himself for throwing wrenches into the wheels of integration throughout the 1960s. Black players had been dominating basketball for years, and Broyles must have figured a black coach would give Arkansas a recruiting edge. Does that make Broyles simply a smart, albeit cynical, businessman?

Sid Simpson, Richardson's old boss who has resided in Arkansas for years, makes his feelings on Broyles plain. "Broyles is a racist," Simpson says. "I know from talking to Broyles that the *only* reason he hired Nolan is because he was black."

Over Christmas in 1964, Broyles earned the honor of coaching in the North v. South all-star football holiday classic. It was his first time ever coaching a black player in a game. During the game, the South was trapped on the one-yard line, and Broyles called for a simple off-tackle dive on second down, trying to inch his way up field.

But the black running back—the future NFL star Gale Sayers—busted loose for a ninety-nine-yard touchdown. Sayers would later score twenty-two touchdowns in his rookie season with the Chicago Bears, including six touchdowns in a single game.

According to Nolan Richardson, Broyles concluded the Gale Sayers story by adding, "I said, damn, I've got to have me some of those."

When Southern Cal pounded still-all-white Alabama in football in 1970, USC's black star Sam "Bam" Cunningham ran wild, scoring three touchdowns. After the game, one of the Alabama coaches reportedly said that Sam Cunningham had done more for integration in two hours than Martin Luther King Jr. had done in twenty years—a statement suggesting the basis for integration in sports was often not idealistic but exploitative.

Getting "some of those" might have been exactly what Broyles was up to when he hired Nolan Richardson. The hottest coach in the nation at that time was John Thompson, who had won the NCAA title in 1984, becoming the first black coach to do so. In 1985, Villanova squeaked by Georgetown. With Villanova's coach Rollie Massimino no longer interested, Broyles began looking for another candidate. Thompson wouldn't leave Georgetown, but Broyles decided to nab the next-hottest African-American coach.

Regardless of Broyles's motivation, his knack for hiring great coaches is nothing less than incredible, and in hiring football assistants, Broyles stands alone. His former assistant coaches have gone on to win five national championships, over forty conference titles and have combined for over two thousand victories in college. He has had forty assistants go on to be head coaches in college or the NFL.

The Rotary Club of Little Rock sponsors the only national award for assistant football coaches, the Broyles Award. The trophy depicts the coach kneeling in front of his former assistant, Wilson Matthews.

The Broyles Award reflects the lack of racial progress in college football. The selection committee members who choose the award winner are nine white men, including Broyles. No black man has ever been on the committee.

The award began in 1996. It took four years before a black man was even one of the five assistant coaches nominated. There has never been a time when more than one black man was a nominee. Sixty-seven assistants have been nominated overall. Six were black. That comes out to 8 percent, while 33 percent of assistant coaches today are black. Only once in the twelve-year history of the award has the winner been a black man. Randy Shannon of Miami won in 2001.

At the time of this writing, Randy Shannon is the only black head football coach at a top sixty-four BCS university. Like the award's namesake in the 1960s, the Broyles Award Committee can't seem to locate qualified black men.

The most obvious sign of Frank Broyles's impact on the Arkansas campus today is its incredible athletics facilities. Razorback Stadium is a breathtaking tribute to the power and place of sports at the University of Arkansas.

Next to Razorback Stadium sits the old Barnhill Arena, basketball's old home. Past that is Bud Walton Arena, the state-of-the-art basketball facility. Then the Smith Golf Center. Next is Walker Pavilion, an indoor football practice field. There is McDonnell Field for the track team, and also the Tyson Track Center for indoor races. Baum Stadium looks like a Major League baseball park.

Don't worry, many on campus assure. Athletics isn't taking a nickel away from academics, and it's not like the money would have been donated for education. "All of the facility improvements have been financed through private donations without a dollar of tax revenues," an Arkansas media guide says. In the past thirty years, with Broyles as boss, the athletics program has spent nearly $250,000,000 on building or improving athletics facilities. Athletics has an annual budget around $40,000,000.

Over the years, Broyles has ingratiated himself to the biggest money people. He is a member of Augusta National in Georgia, one of America's most affluent and exclusive golf clubs. Membership to Augusta, which is on the site of an old plantation, is by invitation only; there is no application process. Only about three hundred people are members at any one time. Augusta admitted its first black member in 1990, nearly seventy years after it opened, and no woman has ever been a member.

Yet money talks at Arkansas and in the world of college sports. After decades of covering college sports in the area, the *Tulsa World*'s longtime sportswriter Bill Connors named Frank Broyles "Best Athletics Director" in his farewell column of 1995.

EIGHTEEN

SHADOW AND ACT

In 1999, the University of Arkansas Press published *Bitters in the Honey*, a book about the Little Rock crisis of 1957 and the civil rights views of Arkansans. Beth Roy, the author, concluded, "One finding of my study in Little Rock is that white racist attitudes continue unabated, their forms and codes changed since the fifties, but not their intensity."

Chancellor John White had plenty of work to do. "Fayetteville was stunning to me," he says. "I started calling out the cheerleading squad and the pep band. There wasn't a single black student involved! I just kept hammering at it."

White set out on what he saw as part of his mission, scoring some major victories in the hiring of African-Americans. The vice chancellor of student affairs. The dean of the library. The dean of the law school. All were African-American. Nevertheless, White knew his best recruiter and spokesman could be his boisterous basketball coach—not just for athletics, but as a representative for the entire school. "One reason I felt so good about Nolan was having him here, and working with him to get across the message of how great an institution it was for everyone; it really didn't matter about your skin color."

The Razorbacks jumped out to an 8-0 start in the 1997–98 season. Their 11-5 record in the SEC scored them a return trip to the NCAA Tournament, where they topped Nebraska before losing to Utah. Arkansas finished the year 24-9. It was a satisfying year, although Richardson's team got beat by his old friend Rob Evans, who had taken over as the first black head coach at the University of Mississippi.

Richardson was already a hero in his native El Paso. Before the next season, El Paso made it official when Nolan Richardson Middle School opened in northeast El Paso.

Some of the glow of the national championship was beginning to wear off in Arkansas, though. The 1998–99 Razorbacks went 23-11 and landed another NCAA Tournament appearance. Arkansas beat Siena in the first round but lost to Iowa. Richardson was now four years past his glorious Final Four runs.

The frustrations of high expectations sometimes became apparent in Richardson's day-to-day dealings. That May, on an airplane flight, Richardson vented to football coach Houston Nutt, calling Frank Broyles both untrustworthy and a "white-haired devil."

In 1999, Head Coach and Assistant Athletics Director Nolan Richardson received a letter citing statistics from the National Association of Basketball Coaches president Jim Haney.

Haney, who is white, was disturbed. "African-American employees are the academic advisors, equipment managers, facility managers, strength coaches, and compliance coordinators," he wrote. "The athletics administration at the core management positions, administrative jobs that have the most influence on the success of the athletics department, are for white men and women only!"

According to Haney's study, African-Americans filled only 6.5 percent of "core management jobs" in Division I schools. (Division II and III were even worse.) Part of Haney's concern was that African-American basketball players, who then made up over 60 percent of the participants, would conclude that their chances for important jobs after their playing days were nearly nonexistent.

At the time of the study, 30 percent of basketball coaches—assistant and head—were African-American. But did core management opportunities actually exist for them? Or was there a ceiling? Haney asked, "Can we name African-American basketball coaches who have had the opportunity to move into athletics administration in the last five years? I cannot."

The only issue the BCA felt had been fairly addressed by the NCAA was that they had successfully sought out African-Americans for management jobs at their own headquarters. Little or nothing had been done at the university level.

Writing in his *Courtside* column for the NABC's newspaper, Haney was astounded. "Rightfully, you may ask where is the outrage? Where are the powerful voices within the NCAA structure that champion legislative changes on this matter? Where are those who would call the NCAA institutions into account for the abysmal hiring of African-Americans and people of color to core management positions?"

Richardson read Jim Haney's column and accompanying statistics, then brooded. With Christmas of 1999 only five days away, he composed a letter to Frank Broyles. In part, Richardson wrote:

> *During our meeting, you commented that you viewed*
> *my appointment as Assistant Athletics Director as a "token"*
> *appointment. The more I think about this, the more it frustrates*
> *and disappoints me. I viewed my appointment back in 1995 as a*

*significant advancement in my career. I looked forward to learning
more about the inner workings of the entire athletics department
at the University of Arkansas. As you may recall, I previously
served as Athletics Director at Western Texas Junior College,
and as Assistant Athletics Director at Tulsa. I particularly looked
forward to offering you my services and skills in negotiations, and
my knowledge of endorsements to assist the department when you
were dealing with shoe and apparel contracts. This of course did
not come to pass, and I now understand why.*

Richardson wanted a clarification of his assigned role—or, rather,
he wanted an authentic role, and not a token appointment. He was
now considering whether or not to resign from this appointment,
given its lack of substance. His letter continued:

*Like you, I love the University of Arkansas and want to help
the school in many ways, but not as a token.*
*I have never looked upon any position I have had in my life
in a token way. I have worked my entire career to prove that I
deserve every opportunity that I have been given. I would never
accept a position just for the sake of appearances.*

Three days later, Broyles faxed a letter back to his basketball
coach. "I have received your letter and I understand your feelings,"
he wrote. "I will respond to you after the holidays."

Another burr in Richardson's boots was that Broyles undercut
the shoe deal Richardson had with Converse, working out an agreement with Reebok to outfit all of the university's athletic teams. Shoe
companies buying up entire athletics departments is common today,
but at that time it was a new development. Richardson felt he had
earned his shoe money; the lesser sports, which would benefit so

greatly, had not. Later, the university would buy out Richardson's Converse deal, which helped monetarily, but the coach could not help but feel sabotaged by Broyles again.

On January 15, 2000, still waiting on a response to his letter from Broyles, Richardson went public about his "token" status as an assistant athletics director. He simply did not want to be used as a statistic if there were no extra duties—or pay. Richardson's complaints were reported only in local newspapers.

Then, on January 17, 2000, Richardson again brought up his situation in the *Morning News* newspaper. When the journalist pointed out that other assistant ADs, the white ones, had been in similar circumstances, Richardson remained unconvinced. "Those guys can go ahead and stay that way because they've got guys their color doing things for them," he said. "What about me? Who sits in that hallway up there to represent us? I don't. Do I help make decisions? No, sir. I've never been asked a question, I've never been in a meeting. So why use me as an assistant AD for affirmative action? I'm not an Uncle Tom."

On January 25, 2000—now the wait for Broyles's written response was gnawing at him—Richardson wrote a second letter. The subject this time was the disparity in pay between basketball and football assistant coaches. Richardson had raised the issue in a 1997 letter, and Broyles had justified the pay differences then by citing experience. Broyles couldn't use that excuse this time. The pay differential had become even greater when Houston Nutt became football coach in 1998. Richardson's top assistant, Mike Anderson, had more experience than any of the football assistants, and had been coaching in Fayetteville for well over a decade.

Richardson copied the letter to both Chancellor John White and University of Arkansas system president Alan Sugg.

———

Richardson could not have picked a less opportune time to challenge the Arkansas power structure. His 1999–2000 team struggled all year. They finished the regular SEC season at 7-9, Richardson's worst mark since joining the more competitive league.

On February 17, 2000, Broyles addressed Richardson's second letter, admitting to the obvious. Pay disparities existed between Arkansas's assistant football and basketball coaches. Since experience could not logically be cited, Broyles attempted to justify the difference by saying it was "required by the marketplace"—an odd logic indeed from the man who controlled the money within the entire multimillion-dollar business that was Arkansas athletics. There was yet to be a written response to Richardson's pre-Christmas letter.

Broyles also forwarded copies of his own letter to John White and Alan Sugg. But he included a cover letter to them, saying that matters of this nature should be resolved between Richardson and himself. Broyles said that by sending White and Sugg a copy of his letter, Richardson had followed "inappropriate protocol." Richardson was not sent a copy of Broyles's cover letter to his superiors.

That same day, Richardson got into a heated discussion with Wally Hall, the sports editor of the *Democrat-Gazette*. Hall and Richardson often reverted to the usual complaints about each other: Hall wasn't fair; Richardson was too sensitive. Near the end of the argument, Richardson claims he called Hall a "redneck." That is not how it was reported in the next day's news. Hall wrote that Richardson had called the Razorback *fans* "redneck SOBs."

The following day, former football star and board of trustees fixture Jim Lindsey claimed he got a call from an irate fan demanding Richardson be fired for the statement. Lindsey, who was close with Broyles, phoned his former coach to express those concerns. The fan was never identified, but suddenly the feelings of the fans—which had mattered little in the firing of successful UA football coaches over the years—became paramount. Broyles never asked Richardson about

Wally Hall's column, or if the quotes were taken out of context.

The annual banquet for senior football players was that very evening. Broyles approached a table of media representatives—all white, of course—to grumble about Richardson's comments. Just a few days earlier, Broyles had complained to the chancellor and system president about Richardson voicing grievances through inappropriate channels. Now Broyles was about to do the unthinkable.

Broyles asked one of the writers at the table to publish an article that equated Richardson's use of the word "redneck" with a white person using the word "nigger."

The media table was dumbfounded, both at Broyles's public use of the word "nigger" and at his bizarre request. One writer later said that Broyles was animated and raised his voice. Black football players were seated at the next table, and the writer reached for Broyles's arm, asking him to lower his voice. Later that night, Broyles cornered the writer again, saying that the article needed to be written.

Redneck = nigger.

Of course, he emphasized, the comparison should leave out the name "Frank Broyles."

The writer later confided to Richardson that Broyles had tried to push him into doing that article. Richardson asked the writer to record his recollection on tape, and the writer agreed.

What would remain a source of debate in Arkansas was not that Broyles publicly used the word "nigger," and wanted major Arkansas media sources to write about niggers and rednecks. Rather, the question centered on whether Broyles *himself* compared the two terms or if Broyles was *reporting* on the feelings of mysterious "fans."

Paul Eells, the sports anchor for KATV and host of Richardson's weekly television show, later said he was shocked by Broyles's prodding of the journalists and believed the comments to be Broyles's own sentiments. Other media representatives understood the comments to mean Broyles was quoting someone else.

"Frank thought he was made of Teflon," one of Arkansas's longtime sportswriters says. Indeed, Broyles was. Not a single media member wrote about Broyles's bizarre request or criticized him in print.

On February 28, 2000, Broyles wrote back to Richardson again, this time to answer Richardson's letter from over two months earlier. Several factors, Broyles wrote, contributed to this delayed response. ". . . [T]he holidays, the football postseason activity, blocked arteries . . . football stadium debates." Broyles also wrote about ". . . the unexpected nature of your letter, both in timing and content."

Broyles pointed out that Eddie Sutton and successful track coach John McDonnell held the role of assistant athletics director while they were coaching. "In each instance," he wrote, "the title was assigned as a symbolic gesture of respect for contributions to our athletics programs. . . . This title designation . . . has never been and is not currently intended to change any job duties. Given these circumstances, please let me know your decision regarding the title."

In regard to NABC boss Jim Haney's claims, Broyles said that ". . . each and every point is well taken and should be an area of concern."

Broyles could not resist a final parting shot. "One of the virtues of Chancellor White's emphasis on increased graduation rates is the increased availability of qualified former athletes who have attained their degrees."

Was Broyles taking a swipe at Richardson for the graduation rate among black players? Probably. In two years, Richardson's players' graduation rate during his championship years would become a national story. But for Broyles, the solution was simple and easy. If Richardson would simply *graduate* more players, then Broyles would *hire* them as associate athletics directors.

———

Tensions between Broyles and Richardson had reached the boiling point. With the Razorbacks playing their worst ball in a decade in February of 2000, Broyles felt that he had the upper hand. He could have removed Richardson before the SEC Tournament but likely figured the coach would fall on his face—and prove to everyone in Arkansas that he had lost his touch. Just like in 1987, Broyles began quiet preparations to dump the coach, although this time Richardson was acutely aware going into the SEC Tournament that Broyles wanted him gone.

The Razorbacks played Georgia first, but even if they won, they'd have to get by three teams, including powerhouse Kentucky. Despite winning an NCAA title and three Final Four births to his credit, Richardson had never won the SEC Tournament title.

Arkansas rolled over Georgia, then the nationally ranked Kentucky and LSU. In the SEC finals they beat Auburn, and the Razorbacks were the 2000 SEC Tournament champions. The state was awash again in praise for Richardson. Sophomore guard Brandon Dean was voted the tournament MVP, and the team was back in the NCAAs. Despite losing to University of Miami in the first round the following week, Richardson's renewed popularity kept Broyles from firing him.

Broyles likely learned a lesson. With Richardson on the sideline, even a weak Razorback team could not be counted out of the SEC Tournament. He wouldn't make that mistake again. For now, he was stuck with Richardson and forced to sign him to a six-year rollover contract for a million dollars a year just before the next season began. Despite the big money, the tumultuous year had left Richardson cautious, angry, and resentful. His relationship with Broyles—America's most powerful athletics director—was now beyond repair.

Jim Haney, who authored the column that rattled Richardson, has directed the NABC for years. Although championing the cause of minority coaches is not part of the NABC's mission, Haney and his top aide Reggie Minton have helped initiate change, especially within the NCAA's own offices. Haney has witnessed a new emphasis. "In the 1970s there was a big issue as to whether you just had an African-American on your staff in football and basketball," he says.

Haney actually worries about what college basketball players think. "It would have benefited Arkansas and minorities both if there were contributing minority athletics directors at the school," he says. "In the college setting, if I'm an African-American player I might be thinking, 'What will I do, how can I stay involved in athletics?' But when it comes time to make decisions to see about the future, they think, 'I don't see anyone like me within the athletics department.'"

The new breed of young black coaches who were not politically inclined irked Richardson. Within the BCA, there was a fundamental disagreement about the group's purpose. Did the BCA exist to help young black assistant coaches? Or did it exist to use its influence in helping black kids get more scholarship opportunities?

Much of the debate likely stemmed from the background of the group's big three. Neither Richardson, nor John Thompson, nor John Chaney had ever been assistant coaches. The trio never used the BCA to secure job interviews or boost their own standing. Richardson and Chaney had taken the long road at unknown schools. Thompson, while a former Boston Celtic, had landed the Georgetown job when it was considered a graveyard for coaches. None of the three, when they were younger, had heard their names trumpeted on ESPN as deserving of a college job.

John Chaney asked the BCA to take his name off the group's letterhead. Richardson, Thompson, and George Raveling followed suit. Chaney said, "The organization has really deserted the kids as far as I'm concerned."

In February of 2000, sportswriter Orville Henry was hospitalized to have his gall bladder removed. Doctors found a malignant tumor on his pancreas. Richardson began checking on Henry every day. It was the most time he had spent around hospitals since Yvonne had passed away.

While Orville Henry was the godfather of sportswriters in Arkansas, some insiders criticize him, calling him a "mouthpiece" for Frank Broyles. Richardson never felt that way about Henry, though, and had great admiration for him.

Until his illness, Orville Henry sat in the middle of the Broyles-Richardson feud, keeping in touch with both men. Richardson claims that Henry told him Broyles had complained about the basketball coach's whopping salary. "That nigger is making too much money," is the way Richardson recalls Henry's account.

Regardless, Henry was another in a long line of older men on whom Richardson leaned for advice and friendship. This seems to dispel another theory heard from time to time in Arkansas, that Nolan Richardson was a racist who hated white people. What person who hated whites would hang around with crusty old guys like Don Haskins, Sid Simpson, Ed Beshara, and Orville Henry? The ways they became friends and the nature of the relationships were varied. They were Richardson's coach, boss, lunch buddy, and scribe.

Even the players noticed the pattern after a few years. Clint McDaniel, whose ball-hawking defense earned him a brief NBA career, says it's ridiculous to insinuate that Richardson is racist. "Nolan hardly had any black friends," he says. "The people who traveled with him and his genuine friends, they were mostly white."

"These are authentic friendships," longtime Arkansas judge Wendell Griffen says. "This notion that Nolan is racist, it's all part of the disinformation campaign. The tendency to believe what isn't true is easier," Griffen adds, "when you don't care what the truth is."

———

The new millennium brought harder times for Razorback basketball, at least by the standards that Nolan Richardson had set.

During the 2001 regular season, the Razorbacks lost their first three SEC games, but turned things around to finish 10-6 in league play. While they were waiting for the postseason SEC Tournament, a strange thing happened.

Richardson continued to enjoy his scenic ranch. The rolling hills and gorgeous views were a tonic for him and Rose, and he relied on the ranch the way other coaches depended on a drink. When the usual pressures of a college season piled up, Richardson resorted to finding solace there. "When I'm worried about things, I get on my horse and clear my brain," he says.

With the SEC Tournament looming that March, Richardson went for a walk. He noticed a path of blood. With sweat pooling in his palms, Richardson tiptoed along the trail until he came upon his beloved horse, Tulula, moaning in the grass. She had been shot with a high-powered rifle.

"Whoever did this knows who I am and where my farm is," Richardson said.

No arrests were ever made after Tulula's shooting. The horse survived, but the incident rattled Richardson, and he made comments to the effect that he would reevaluate his career at Arkansas.

Arkansas was awarded an NCAA bid in 2001, but again lost in the first round, this time in a shocker to Georgetown. The score was tied 63-63 when a Hoyas's substitute barely beat both buzzers—shot clock and game clock—to sink the winning shot. After officials watched replays, the basket was allowed. Arkansas ended the season 20-11. A few weeks later, Richardson's best player, sophomore Joe Johnson, announced he was leaving Arkansas early for the NBA.

A record of 20-11 is a fine season for most coaches, but Richardson was now seven years past his NCAA championship. Chancellor John

White noticed the change in Richardson's demeanor that season, and he met with Richardson privately.

"Nolan would make these statements," White recalls "that in northwest Arkansas there was nothing for black students to do." In an era where a prospective student's social-life options were increasingly important, Richardson's statements irritated the football coaches—and Frank Broyles—as well as the university administration. "I don't think he realized what a negative impact that was having on everybody's ability to try to recruit," White adds, "including our ability to recruit students."

In fact, according to White, football coach Houston Nutt went to Frank Broyles to complain about the statements. Broyles, in turn, discussed Richardson's comments with White. White then met with Richardson and asked him a single question: "What can I do to help you?"

Richardson cited general concerns on the challenges ahead, both for the basketball team and for the entire university.

Then Richardson asked White, "What can I do for you?"

The two men held each other's gaze for a moment. White, more than most administrators, could occasionally step away from his job and shed his suit and job title—the propriety of being an administrator sometimes seemed a burden to White. He leaned across the table, straining for Richardson, although the coach's hand was beyond reach.

"I need you to be *happy*," White said. "I need that to be obvious to the people you come in contact with. I don't think you realize that how you come across has far-reaching implications for what I am trying to accomplish here at the university."

Richardson assured White that he would try to be happy. "I came back and put it in a memo to him," White recalls.

NINETEEN

THINGS FALL APART

With **Joe Johnson** leaving for the NBA, the Razorbacks were bound to struggle throughout the 2001–02 season. Their schedule was rated the most difficult in the country by some experts, and included Wake Forest, Oklahoma, Illinois, Tulsa, Memphis— and Eddie Sutton's Oklahoma State team, which beat Arkansas just before Christmas.

As the season progressed, Richardson's frustration festered. In January of 2002, the Razorbacks lost four SEC games in a row for the first and only time in Richardson's tenure. Soon after, the coach was told by administrators that he had to control his comments on his own weekly television show. "Arkansas attempted to muzzle Richardson," *Sports Illustrated* wrote later, "prohibiting him from speaking out on matters of racial discrimination." The school wanted Richardson to sign a contract stressing that he would ". . . not directly or indirectly, disparage the Producer, the University of Arkansas, the [Razorback] Foundation, or any sponsor of the show for any reason." Such contracts and language are not uncommon, but Richardson took it as a direct attack. "It is this issue that seems to have pushed Richardson over the top," *Sports Illustrated* claimed.

On February 23, 2002, after a loss at Kentucky, Richardson was quoted nationally as saying, "If they go ahead and pay me my money, they can take the job tomorrow. I'm glad I don't have to answer to anyone but myself and my god upstairs. That's the only people I answer to, for real. I'll answer to the chancellor and the athletics director, but fans and things of that nature, I don't answer to those people."

The comments were interpreted by the media as several things— venting frustration, a challenge, a genuine offer to Arkansas administrators, and Richardson's interest in retiring.

Richardson's press conference in Kentucky happened to be the same weekend that the university was hosting the SEC track meet in Fayetteville. When Chancellor John White walked into the hospitality tent on Sunday, the press cornered him.

White said he was not yet aware of Richardson's comments. Newsmen relayed Richardson's claim: "If they go ahead and pay me my money, they can take the job tomorrow."

"It must have been just out of the frustration of the moment," White says, "and losing at Kentucky. I couldn't figure out what it was about. I left the track meet, went to the basketball arena where our women were playing, and saw the arena manager, Fred Vorsanger."

Vorsanger said, "There goes Nolan again. He said the same thing to me before he left for Kentucky."

"You're kidding," White said.

Vorsanger was not, although he himself had joked with Nolan to "take me with you. I'll carry the money."

White now concluded that Nolan's comments were premeditated and that he had not simply reacted in anger. "I had a lot of time to think about it," White says, "and what I came around to was this. If I had a dean or vice chancellor who made that statement, they wouldn't hold their position another week."

With two games to go in the SEC, the critical league tournament was just around the corner. White believed that he and Frank Broyles needed to meet with Richardson in a hurry—the coach was returning from Kentucky that very day—to find out the source of the trouble, and either allow Richardson to resign or get him pointed back in the right direction.

The meeting with Richardson that Sunday never took place. "Here's where I made a mistake," White says. "I said to Frank Broyles, okay, let's meet with Nolan tomorrow morning and tell him we're going to go ahead and do what he says, we're going to pay him his money and he can leave." Barring an all-out apology from Richardson, White says, they were going to accept his resignation.

Broyles told White, "I can't do it. I'm leaving early in the morning to Augusta to play golf."

Broyles was scheduled to return Wednesday night, the same night Richardson would be playing at Mississippi State. Richardson would be back Thursday. They agreed to delay meeting with Richardson until then.

"That was a huge mistake," White says of the missed opportunity for him and Broyles to meet with Richardson. The meeting that never took place, however, would have likely been for damage control. By the end of the evening on that Sunday, nearly all of the board of trustees had been notified. Frank Broyles, John White, and University of Arkansas system president Alan Sugg had decided to end Richardson's tenure. His contract had a clause that allowed the university to terminate Richardson "at the convenience of the University."

Pressure leads to bad decisions, Richardson had told his teams for years. The pressure of losing, his horse being shot, his deteriorated relationship with Frank Broyles, and simple exhaustion culminated in

Richardson's outburst. When Arkansas lost to Kentucky that week-end, they had lost nine of their last twelve games.

"I've earned the right to have the type of season I'm having," Richardson was often quoted as saying that month. Broyles must have disagreed.

Could John White have put out the fire if he had gotten Nolan Richardson alone? Perhaps he could have persuaded him to clarify his comments after the Kentucky game, or even apologize, to admit he was blowing off steam. At the very least, White believes he could have helped to avoid the disastrous press conference yet to come, on Monday.

White adds, "I think John Chaney and a civil rights attorney, lots of people got to Nolan and got him cranked up, frankly. Had we met on Monday, I think it would have been a much calmer kind of discussion and there would have been all kinds of movement on our part to try to negotiate something that Nolan would feel comfortable with." Instead, White huddled with university attorneys. "I just knew that if we didn't handle it well, we'd all be heading to court," he says.

With Broyles on a golf holiday at the historically all-white Augusta National Golf Club, things went from bad to worse.

"That's why I said I made a huge mistake," White says, a rare admission for a college administrator. "Frank [Broyles] had a number of major donors he was taking to Augusta for golf, so I thought, okay, let's just do it on Thursday. But as I look back, I just beat myself up over it. We should have done it on Monday. We should have had the discussion then. It was a contentious relationship all the time that I was here, between Frank and Nolan, and I kind of got tired of it. After a while you just say, my goodness, this obviously doesn't seem like it's going to work out."

Broyles had attempted to remove Richardson in 1987, then again in 2000, after White's arrival at the university—and those seasons went better for the Razorbacks than the 2002 season. As the losses mounted, Richardson knew Broyles would be pushing to fire him once again. The chancellor was a decent and caring man, but that would be of little consequence when it came to controlling Broyles.

On Monday, February 25, with no word from either the chancellor or the athletics director, Richardson hosted the rambling Monday press conference, and his comments were broadcast nationally, as he directed. The vast majority of viewers would have had no sense of Richardson's history, his battles to bust through a segregated profession, that his grandmother's parents had been slaves, or that his director of athletics preferred he fail. Without that perspective, it appeared that Richardson had simply lost his way.

Democrat-Gazette's sports editor Wally Hall wrote, "This season no one in the UA administration or on the board of trustees has been anything but supportive of Richardson." The ensuing trial during Richardson's lawsuit would prove Hall's claim to be spurious—depending on your sense of humor and what your idea of "supportive" was. Yet Hall also added, "Not long ago I wrote in this space that Richardson deserves this as a grace season. That sentiment still holds. If Nolan Richardson really still wants the job."

Wednesday, the Razorbacks played at Mississippi State, where they lost, 89-83. Afterward, Richardson's tone was much more sedate at the customary postgame press conference. He apologized to "99 percent of the fans" and some of the media for his statements on Monday. He admitted he was guilty of stereotyping in the same way he had been stereotyped for years. Richardson was quoted in the *Democrat-Gazette* as saying, ". . . Arkansas fans are the greatest fans in America. . . . If there's an apology, I give that. Because the fans and the people that I've lived around in Fayetteville are great, wonderful people . . ."

Even so, the coach would not retreat from his claim that he was regarded differently as the Arkansas coach because of his skin color. "I'm not treated differently from a fan standpoint," he said. "But everybody who follows college basketball or follows the Razorbacks or are being honest with themselves know that what I have said is a true fact. It's absolutely true. When you think about what I really said, you need to ask the question, is it true? Some will say, 'But he didn't have to say it.'"

Americans are notorious for lacking any sense of history, and white Americans are particularly forgetful—intentionally or not—about issues of race. Should Richardson have kept silent while his team struggled in 2002? While much of Arkansas white power-structure, both at the university and around the state, had heard enough over the years, most of that state's black population and a surprising number of closeted white progressives thought Richardson was both invigorating and important. Richardson could no more change his blunt honesty than he could begin ordering his teams to slow down and play more conservatively.

Would Richardson have been fired if he had been white? This simple question begs asking, but the answer is complicated. The kind of support and patience Richardson would have been given by Broyles, the media, and the fans in the state over the years would have been altered. How would his teams have performed if the coach could have focused his energies on winning, rather than believing that his boss preferred for him to fail? Defenders of Frank Broyles, ironically, like to point out that Broyles fired every football coach over the years—why should the basketball coach be any different?

After that Wednesday's Mississippi State game, Richardson told the press that he had addressed the Razorbacks on the subject of who would be their coach in the future. "I tell my players, don't fret for me, baby. If I get to leave the University of Arkansas, I graduated, and I did it my way."

He also said he believed his tenure at Tulsa and Arkansas "made it a better place for people to live and to have respect, because they know that I wasn't no Uncle Tom and I'm not politically going to tell you what you want to hear all the time." The coach was again both defiant and conciliatory. He mentioned having to answer to the school's president and to Frank Broyles. "I do apologize for things I've done wrong. . . . I'm not above that, and I've done that tonight."

Richardson was looking back, not looking forward. "If it comes to pass they're going to buy out my contract, I'm not going to be disappointed. Not at all," he said. "Because, see, the Good Lord brought me to Arkansas. When I was a kid growing up, I was afraid of Arkansas, Mississippi—where I am right now—and Alabama . . . I'm very proud of the fact that I started with five or six black coaches in the country, and now there's more than thirty-nine."

March 1, 2002. Less than a week had passed since the Kentucky game. Chancellor John White and Frank Broyles came to Richardson's office and gave him a choice. White suggested that Richardson could resign and coach the final home game against Vanderbilt, enjoy the adulation of the crowd one last time. Richardson was defiant. "You're going to have to fire my ass," he said.

White informed Richardson that the university would then be buying out his contract and paying him for six more years. After the meeting, White jotted down pages of notes, and his lengthy transcription was later published, wholly intact. The notes included Richardson saying that if he were fired, blacks would take the UA campus back to 1957—presumably to the Little Rock crisis—and that there would need to be tanks on campus because of picketing.

White denied that the meeting had been tape-recorded. "If you had been there in that meeting, you would have remembered it, too." White told the *Democrat-Gazette* that he didn't take any notes while the meeting was in progress.

White's transcription of the meeting would haunt Richardson

publicly and White privately. "For several days, when I would close my eyes and try to go to sleep at night, it was like it was a videotape, it would just start replaying that whole meeting," White said.

Richardson spent a lot of time during the ninety-minute meeting asking what would happen to longtime assistant coach Mike Anderson. The administrators promised Richardson that Anderson would be interviewed for the now-open job. Richardson knew that this meant a courtesy interview only.

When the meeting was nearly over, White said to Broyles, "Coach, would you mind if I had some time alone with Coach Richardson?"

Broyles complied, leaving the chancellor and the coach alone.

According to both White and Richardson, the chancellor reached out and put his hand on Richardson's. "Nolan," he asked, "would you pray with me?"

Richardson says, "I was surprised. I didn't know what to do." But he bowed his head. Richardson was cognizant of the historical implications of this gesture—the Bible had been used to sedate blacks in the Old South for centuries. And today, Richardson grudgingly admits that there is much to admire about John White. He's caring, smart, and sensitive.

What White was not, however, was more powerful than Broyles. Richardson knew it was difficult to hold that against White. By all accounts, White had attempted to wrestle control of the university away from Broyles, and he was rebuffed by the board of trustees.

As White finished his prayers, Richardson came to understand that White was genuine—he really was asking for help from a higher power. But the entity with higher power had already left the office, at White's request.

ESPN aired a program the same day Nolan Richardson was fired, an interview with the coach that had been prerecorded in January. The timing could not have been worse for him.

The ESPN interview included John White and Richardson discussing the just-published graduation rate of black players at Arkansas. The NCAA had released the study of black players at every Division I basketball program. The results, for black basketball players who entered as freshmen between 1990 and 1994, were based on a formula that evaluated whether a degree was received within six years of enrolling.

Richardson was the focus of the interview partly because the last year of the study was the season his Razorbacks won the NCAA title. ESPN compared the Razorbacks' rate to that of Duke, a private school that had a terrific percentage for graduation. Arkansas had not graduated a single black player during the specified time, 1990–94. Richardson said that the ultimate responsibility lay with each individual player, not the coach or administration.

The list of schools with a graduation rate of 0 percent included a lot more than Nolan Richardson's Razorbacks. Many of the schools were basketball powers with renowned coaches: Georgia Tech (Bobby Cremins), James Madison (Lefty Driesell), LSU (Dale Brown), Oregon State, Texas Tech, Cincinnati (Bob Huggins), Hawaii (Riley Wallace), Louisville (Denny Crum), Nevada, Pacific (Bob Thomason), Wyoming, Utah State, Virginia Commonwealth, Colorado, Long Beach State, Cal State–Sacramento, Cleveland State, Eastern Washington, Georgia Southern, Jacksonville State, McNeese State, Morehead State, Samford, SW Missouri (now Missouri State), Idaho, Memphis, Minnesota (Clem Haskins), UNLV, Oklahoma, UTEP (Don Haskins), Texas Pan-American, Toledo, and Wisconsin-Milwaukee.

The ESPN program did more to damage Richardson's reputation than any other single story and would be used repeatedly to justify his firing.

———

A few days later, *Democrat-Gazette* sports editor Wally Hall wrote a piece in response to all the media requests for the usually low-profile Arkansas press corps. He wrote that many of the inquirers wanted to know, "Has the media in Arkansas treated Nolan Richardson with kid gloves out of fear of being called racist?"

Hall wrote, "What everyone saw Monday night, Nolan Richardson's anger, was something the media in Arkansas has experienced dozens of times. We called it the real 'forty minutes of hell.' This time, though, he did it with cameras running and everyone got to see why he has been stroked and petted by the press for seventeen years. We've walked around on eggshells for years because of Richardson's anger."

The tension was clearly a two-way street between Hall and Richardson. When Little Rock civil rights attorney John Walker was asked by the same newspaper if he would be representing Richardson, he said, "Unless coach asks me to do something for him, then I'm not authorized to say one way or another, especially to the *Democrat.*"

There was still one more home game to play, and assistant coach Mike Anderson took the helm. Arkansas beat Vanderbilt, but the following week they lost to Tennessee in the first round of the SEC tourney. In both games, the Razorback players wrote the name of their deposed coach on their sneakers to honor him.

"I was shocked, totally shocked," Temple coach John Chaney recalls. "My president made it very clear that when I got ready to express my opinion, I could." While Chaney was disappointed in Arkansas's chancellor, he likes to remind people that John White was not the only higher-up who did not stand up for the coach. "Neither did [then-governor] Mike Huckabee, and he's an Evangelist! That's the house of righteousness? You can't dismiss the truth that was spoken by Nolan."

Huckabee did, in fact, weigh in. He told the Associated Press, "I think [Richardson is] one of the truly great people I've known, and I have appreciated that he has overcome more than most people. That's one of the things that a lot of people now don't fully comprehend. They haven't walked in his shoes. They haven't taken his journey. They may not fully understand some of the deep feelings that he carries inside. There's a wonderful success story in Nolan Richardson."

Richardson also received a letter of support from Huckabee, which read, in part, "Please don't let the critics and the media wear you down. I know from experience it's exasperating when those with small minds and big mouths seem to have all the answers. I face those types of people every day."

Chaney understands Richardson's refusal to sugarcoat statements during tough times. Before Temple played Xavier, Chaney had criticized the invasion of Iraq. "I made it very clear about Bush," Chaney says. "This man is guilty of treason and guilty of making a decision to kill our kids. In Ohio, they'd lost half a million jobs." Chaney found himself greeted by a hostile crowd, and got an escort to and from the bench by Ohio state troopers.

When Temple returned to Philadelphia, Chaney was pulled out of practice. It was ex-president Bill Clinton calling to thank Chaney for speaking up.

On March 9, the *St. Petersburg Times* ran a piece by Darrell Fry called "Don't Play the Race Card if You Can't Cover the Bet." Fry wrote, "These days the race card is tossed out like worthless lottery tickets." Then Darrell Fry brought out a card of his own, the one that would repeatedly be used to bury Richardson—the graduation-rate card. Zero percent from 1990 to 1994.

NABC director Jim Haney thinks that Richardson's graduation rate for that period is not entirely accurate. "Nolan had guys leaving to go to the NBA early," he says. "The way the graduation rate was determined then, it didn't count freshmen who transferred and graduated! Junior college kids didn't count and weren't factored in at all, and Nolan had lots of those guys. There's simply a high transfer rate among college players, and that can affect the way the percentages are calculated. You have to really study Nolan's circumstances. Now the APR [academic progress report, which factors in junior college players and transfers] gives you a more accurate rate." Corliss Williamson and Scotty Thurman, Haney points out, were the two most visible players, and they left school early for the professional ranks. Others would play pro ball in Europe.

Alex Dillard was the third-leading scorer on Arkansas's 1994 NCAA champs but wasn't as productive off the court, and he did not graduate with his class. Over a decade later, he is completing his degree requirements at home in Alabama. He takes the blame for his delay in graduation.

"Nolan didn't give a shit about us making it in basketball," he says. "He was more concerned about us succeeding in the real world. 'Your skills can only last this long,' he'd say. Now I truly understand what he meant. He was trying to prepare us for life. If we missed a day of class he would run our ass until we dropped."

The media's perception of Richardson's academics and the weak graduation numbers from 1990–94 exposed by the NCAA's study were not indicators of Richardson's priorities, Dillard claims. "Coach *said* it wasn't his job on TV, but that's all he cared about. School." Almost everyone close to the Razorbacks' basketball program—even players disgruntled about playing time—say that Richardson talked about education and opportunity constantly.

Scotty Thurman, whose three-pointer sealed the Razorbacks NCAA title in 1994, left Arkansas before his eligibility was up. The NBA didn't work out, but gigs in Greece and Italy paid nearly as well. When his long career in Europe was over, Thurman finished his degree in English at the historically black Philander Smith College in Little Rock. Today he works for a real estate company.

Thurman believes Richardson's policy of running his players as punishment for academic problems was a mistake, since running does not directly improve academic performance. "Looking back, I feel like there were some things that could have been done differently," Thurman says. "If a guy is coming to school for hoops, running only helps him get better on the basketball floor."

Thurman had both parents at home, and his father had played college ball at Grambling. "But a lot of the players didn't have both parents like I did. A lot didn't have a strong father figure, and they looked up to Coach Richardson." Thurman believes Richardson should have held players out of games for missing class, not just punished them by running. "If your son was coming to play for me," he says, "isn't it my responsibility to get him to go to class? Some of those guys came from tough situations."

Sometimes players were simply not interested in graduating. "Nolan had a player named Arlin Bowers," trainer Dave England recalls, "a great kid whose dream was to be a firefighter." Bowers would often insist that firefighters didn't need a college degree. Today, Bowers is a firefighter near Memphis. "It may surprise some people to learn that Nolan stressed academics all the time," England says.

In this respect, Richardson was a paradox—he stressed opportunity and education to his players daily but lashed out at critics who questioned his graduation rate, saying it wasn't his job to graduate players. Rather than admit to common academic shortcomings during his tenure—dozens of schools were on the same list—Richardson went on the attack. Rather than bragging (as he saw it) that he did indeed stress academic success, he confronted the very premise of their criticism.

TWENTY

MAKES ME WANNA HOLLER

The firing of Nolan Richardson left the black residents of Arkansas and black alumni bitter. After 2002, even moves the university made to diversify were viewed with suspicion. Old wounds opened, reminding the black community of Arkansas of the years of deception and delay at the university.

His dismissal spurred students, alumni, and faculty to consider reforms in the process of how UA recruited African-American students, as well as the manner in which the university hired and promoted minority faculty.

The African-American studies program at the University of Arkansas is part of the school's Fulbright College. J. William Fulbright, president of the University of Arkansas from 1939 until 1941, went on to be a U.S. senator for thirty years. He was one of the first senators to condemn the United States' invasion of Vietnam; before that, Fulbright stood up to the bullying and Communist witch hunts of Senator Joe McCarthy.

Charles Robinson, head of the African-American studies program, says the Fulbright name (and the seven-foot statue of him outside) reminds him of the daily complexities of living in the South. "Fulbright was an avowed racist. He's turning over in his grave right now, over the very existence of my program."

While Robinson admires Nolan Richardson, he was taken aback by the coach's comments after his graduation rate from 1990–94 was revealed, and was confused by Richardson's explanation on ESPN.

Robinson believes the Arkansas story is complicated. He is proud of the university, pointing out that it was the first major white university in the South to integrate. Yet the firing of Richardson left him shaking his head. "After all he's done, this man still can't control his own destiny. His time was up when his boss, the white athletics director, said it was up."

Arkansas did not take long to find a replacement for Nolan Richardson. With a lawsuit likely, the new hire was no surprise—African-American coach Stan Heath. Heath had just finished an incredible run in his first year as coach of Kent State, where they won thirty games and came within a single win of going to the NCAA Final Four.

Many felt the hiring of Heath was a deliberate move to avoid a lawsuit. "Absolutely, Heath was hired to keep the racial tension down," says Fayetteville *Morning News* sports editor Chip Souza. And most blacks in Arkansas believed that the hiring of Heath was cynical and cosmetic. "You can't fix the *Titanic* by changing out the deck chairs," Judge Wendell Griffen told the *Democrat-Gazette*.

In the spring of 2002, the enrollment of black students at UA was close to 6 percent, well below the 16 percent makeup of the state's population. Blacks also made up less than 4 percent of the UA faculty. Judge Griffen believed that the dismissal of Richardson would make things even worse. "Same song, different verse," Griffen said. "If the university didn't deal fairly with Nolan Richardson, then hiring a new [African-American] coach does nothing."

Professor Charles Robinson acknowledges that the bar was set high for Heath, who would have had to win *two* NCAA titles and earn four Final Four berths to surpass Richardson. "I feel the hiring was calculated, definitely," Robinson says. "I'm not saying Stan Heath wasn't a deserving coach, but as quickly as he was hired? And no interest in athletics about hiring other African-American coaches?"

Nobody in Arkansas's black community was surprised by Richardson's replacement. "Stan Heath was hired to appease the turmoil that was rising within the black alumni," says Lonnie Williams, who marched across campus to help Richardson challenge the issue of police dogs on campus in the 1980s.

Hiring a black coach to replace a fired black coach almost never happens, except at historically black colleges, and a small percentage of people viewed the hire as another bold move by Frank Broyles.

Lonnie Williams, who has since moved to Arkansas State University, doesn't buy that. He believes the hiring of Heath was premeditated to coincide with the threat of a lawsuit. "I told African-American staff members at the UA to ask for whatever they needed soon, because they [UA administration] are going to lean over backward to support diversity efforts. If there was a lawsuit that got settled, the well may quickly dry up."

Williams has seen enough to be certain that "America—especially Arkansas—is still afraid of a strong black man who can speak his mind. Nolan Richardson won't bite his tongue, he's still speaking up like a man. America can't handle that."

Stan Heath bristled at first. "I wasn't hired to help in the threat of a lawsuit," he stressed. "We'd won thirty games at Kent State." Yet Heath quickly points out that he knew he was walking into a hornet's nest in Hawg country. "My color was a plus at that particular job because it might calm some of the fire that was brewing because of Nolan's situation. My color helped in those terms, but we'd been to the Elite Eight at Kent State. Yes, the university in some ways was trying to use me to pacify a situation that was difficult. But I looked at it as an opportunity to continue the legacy of Eddie Sutton and Nolan. *Somebody* was going to take the job. All of us feel, as black coaches, we take jobs that are going to have big obstacles. They might not be the Duke or North Carolina job." Heath signed a five-year contract.

Chancellor John White would remain in his position until June of 2008, when he returned to teaching. When asked about the repercussions of the firing, and its effect on his attempts at diversity, he doesn't hesitate. "The difficulty has been, frankly, in getting past the continuing negative feelings within the state after Nolan Richardson's dismissal," he says. "It's still an uphill battle to get parents, particularly in the Delta, to have their kids come to northwest Arkansas and the university."

His remorse over what happened to Richardson seeps into his remarks about the controversy. "We were already there, doing well," White insists. "If anything, the firing set us back as far as the negative publicity associated with it, and as far as faculty and staff. In my eleven years here, we've had two women and two African-American student body presidents. It's hard to say that we're better off today, I wouldn't say that at all. I think it was just a sad chapter in the history of the University of Arkansas and Nolan Richardson, and I'm frankly not able to see what good has come from it. There are still people who have strong feelings on both sides of the issue and time has not ameliorated it the way I thought it would."

White does think there may be positives for Richardson on the heels of his own return to the classroom—as well as the departure of

Frank Broyles. "Maybe it will take Frank being off the scene and me being less visible for Nolan to feel comfortable," he says.

Lonnie Williams has sympathy for White's immense challenge of racial issues in Arkansas. Or some sympathy. "John White *wants* to do right on racial issues," Williams says, "but it's one step forward, two steps back. He can't control the underlying issues. He talks the talk, but when you bring in this many black staff and faculty, and have the same amount leaving? Diversity is always in the top five goals, but we never seem to get much better."

Williams feels perhaps John White's problems are coming from across campus. "John White wanted to move Broyles to a fund-raiser position away from athletics, according to newspaper reports, and some board of trustees members weighed in, then John White was rebuffed."

Broyles remained as athletics director. "That shows where the power is located. Athletics," Williams says.

Judge Wendell Griffen says, "The University of Arkansas is the Southern institution with the longest track record for having admitted blacks and the worst track record for treating them in this century."

Griffen says the number of blacks admitted, their inclusion in college life, the number of graduates, and the number of faculty employed and retained all reveal a deeper problem. "In Nolan Richardson, we have a stellar person, morally, professionally, and personally," Griffen says, "who literally was ousted because people were too unwilling to accept him as the person he is. That's *cultural incompetence* in its most glaring consequences. It is a classic example of what happens when incompetent people are in power and have to deal with cultural issues. The problem didn't lie with Nolan," Griffen insists, "the problem lay with Frank Broyles and John White and the institution that has historically been behind, when it had every reason and chance to be a leader."

While some people believe the firing of Richardson improved things for blacks on campus, that progress has been made, Griffen does not.

"I don't talk about the University of Arkansas and use the word 'progress,'" Griffen says. "I use the word 'movement.' If a student has an average of twenty points in a class, and later has an average of forty, that student has had movement but not progress. The University of Arkansas is still at the 'F' level, but seemingly determined to congratulate itself."

The state of Arkansas took a beating again in the national media—just as it had for decades—when Richardson was fired. "We've a feeling Arkansas won't come out looking too good," the *Democrat-Gazette* wrote in an editorial, and they were correct.

The editorial continued:

> Everybody else has taken sides in this case, so we'll break with our daily tradition and come down squarely in the mushy middle. We're not sure whether Nolan should have been fired, or bought out, or made to apologize, or just sent to his room without any supper. We just know that it was as disheartening to watch a grown man, head coach, and role model make a public ass of himself as it was to watch the consequences: a whole state in a shouting match over race. Again. The one thing Karl Marx was right about is that history happens twice—the first time as tragedy, the second as farce. And in this case all it took was about 50 years—from 1957 to now.
>
> Instead of a rousing debate about whether the struggling Razorbacks need a new coach after 17 years, too many of us got dragged into an argument over Nolan Richardson's skin color—just the way he wanted. Half a century ago, it was the

246 FORTY MINUTES OF HELL

white demagogues who could speak only of race; now it's the black ones. History has a way of being terribly just.

Their conclusion—"just move on"—was typical within the state, and indicative of the dominant mindset in Arkansas. Any bad news or ugly history, especially where race is concerned, needs to be put behind us as quickly as possible. Richardson's biggest sin might have been his refusal to let anyone forget.

Nearly every writer concurred with the decision to dump the coach. But a small few were sensitive to the dynamic of a black coach being covered by an all-white media. J. A. Adande, who is black, wrote in the *Los Angeles Times*, "I've read some tired columns that sarcastically lament poor Nolan Richardson and his $3 million buyout. These writers will never even have a chance of considering Richardson's perspective. They'll never write in a newsroom in which they're the minority."

William Rhoden of the *New York Times*, who lionized Richardson during his NCAA title run, was less supportive this time:

Upheavals and departures of coaching icons are rarely successful. Longtime coaches like Jerry Tarkanian, Bob Knight and Richardson often assume the stature of pope or ayatollah on their campuses. They often act as though they can trample on rules, behave in the most outrageous manner and make the most outrageous statements. In time, Tarkanian's rules violations, Knight's behavior and Richardson's angry statements became embarrassments that could not be offset by championships.

Other writers used the story to take yet another shot at the state of Arkansas.

Bernie Lincicome of the *Rocky Mountain News* wrote, "Nothing Richardson could have said would bring more discredit to Arkansas than its idiotic school cheer [known as "calling the hogs"], never mind all those reasonable and caring alumni wearing red hog snouts like hats."

Sid Simpson, who hired Richardson at Western Texas College, remains a staunch defender of the coach. But when pressed, Simpson will admit that Richardson has two flaws. Or rather, Simpson stresses, two strengths that can be seen as flaws.

"First, if you get Nolan trapped in a corner, he's going to fight his way out." This is apparent, Simpson says, from his response on ESPN's program about graduation rates. When challenged on the poor graduation rate of his championship team, Richardson could have said, "We always want to improve our graduation rates and we'll continue to stress higher education." Or he could have named several players who graduated before and after that time-specific study. Instead, Richardson insisted that it is not his job to graduate players—a direct contradiction to the way he actually dealt with his team over the years.

"Second," Simpson continues, "he responds from the heart, whether it's the right thing to say or not."

The question at his post-Kentucky press conference in 2002 was, "What were you and [Kentucky coach] Tubby Smith talking about after the game?"

"Hardly a question to make someone offer up a job that no one—let me repeat—no one has asked for," Wally Hall wrote.

Richardson could have said, "That's between Tubby and me," or "Just general stuff about our teams." Or even "No comment."

Instead, Richardson revealed that he and Smith talked about focusing on their paychecks during tough times, which led to Richardson's quote, "If they go ahead and pay me my money, they can take the job."

Richardson made an unusual decision for a fired coach that summer. He decided to stay in Arkansas, on his ranch outside Fayetteville. He'd return home to El Paso for visits, or fly to Birmingham, where Mike Anderson was quickly retooling the UAB program as their new head coach. His refusal to move away indirectly kept the controversy alive in Arkansas.

In March of 2002, black conservative talk-show host and pundit Armstrong Williams wrote his weekly column about the recently fired coach, titled "Nolan Richardson, Adios." The column ran nationally as well as at the Townhall.com Web site.

Armstrong Williams admitted in 2005 to being paid $240,000 by the George W. Bush administration to endorse its "No Child Left Behind" program. This was a foolish business decision on the Bush administration's part, since Williams has consistently championed conservative establishment causes without under-the-table cash. Any journalist who accepts such a payment damages his credibility.

Williams wrote that Richardson had ". . . gained admiration as the first prominent Southern college coach to recruit black athletes . . ." That wasn't even close to correct. Williams, predictably, hammered Richardson for his graduation rate from 1990 to 1994. He also challenged Richardson's claim of discrimination. "It is precisely this sort of culture of victimization that conditions blacks to regard themselves as inferior."

Williams defended the University of Arkansas's decision, writing that the coach's remarks ". . . were plainly racist . . . I mean, can you imagine the outrage that would occur if a white basketball coach calmly surveyed the reporters in attendance at his press conference, then demanded that the local newspapers hire more whites?" This was a strange comparison as there is nowhere in the country a room of all African-American media—TV, radio, newspapers—would be covering the team of a white coach.

Richardson's mindset is common, Williams says. About Richardson's complaints on dealing with an all-white media every day, Williams says, "If writers are fair and objective, and don't make judgments on race, it doesn't matter. Are people being denied the opportunity or are they choosing to do other things? If there is evidence to support that they [blacks] are applying for jobs, and they're denied, that's different. If people choose another profession, that's an issue of choice, not racism."

Williams believes there is a mentality that Richardson and others hold on to that has dragged him down. "[People from Richardson's era] can't relate to the progress we're making. They want to stay stuck in the past. It's difficult, because you become a prisoner of that period. There's some truth [to Richardson's charges], not everybody has clean and pure hands. We are talking about the South."

"There are older people," Williams says, "who feel that, because of racism, they were robbed of something they can never get back. Racism was vicious, it had an impact, and it was systemic. The wounds are still there. When they see Rodney King or Sean Bell, that reinforces things for them that not much has changed. It haunts them and that is their burden."

However, Williams says Richardson was being unreasonable. "Blacks feel they are held to a higher standard, but most of that is imagined."

The key to life for Armstrong Williams: "Forgive people, judge them as individuals, not as a group." He closed by saying, "I've never experienced racism, it has never impacted my life."

"Armstrong Williams is either a liar, a freak, or not intelligent enough to discern racism," former Air Force coach Reggie Minton says. "We study history for a reason. Nobody can take those experiences away from you. You learn from what you've seen and experienced. For anyone to say, 'Why can't he let go?' . . . Well, people can't let go for a reason."

Minton's time as a black man coaching at the ultraconservative Air Force Academy left him with very specific ideas about how the world changes. "I don't buy into the premise that racists are plotting this," Minton says, "but there needs to be somebody around who raises the level of awareness."

Once, before joining the administration at the NABC, Minton was having dinner with three generals from the Air Force.

"Is there anything we can do?" one of the generals asked Minton.

Minton mentioned a new aircraft trainer, the most recent model of plane. "Make the cockpit bigger."

"We could easily do that," one general said. "Nobody's ever brought that up."

"That's because everybody who is sitting at this table fits in the cockpit," Minton answered.

Minton says today, "If not everybody is aware of the problem, things won't change. America should know that only 3 percent of college administrators in athletics are minorities; that is where you start."

Even funerals seemed to be divided along the Broyles/Richardson line. Sportswriter Orville Henry died a few weeks after Richardson was fired, and Richardson delivered the eulogy at historic Central High School in Little Rock. Although Frank Broyles had been close to Henry as well, he was not asked to speak.

A month later, Richardson was back in Little Rock, but this time it wasn't for a funeral. St. Mark's Baptist Church in Little Rock hosted a tribute in support of Richardson, a celebration of his long career.

The list of speakers at St. Mark's included former NBA star Darrell Walker, who had played for Eddie Sutton. Walker was confident of Richardson's place in history. "Anytime you see a [black] coach getting hired whether it's Division I, II, III, think about Nolan Richardson," he said. But his remarks also illustrated the difference of opinions within the state about whether Richardson was out of line or right on. "I'm glad you did what you did," Walker said, looking at Richardson. Everyone in attendance—nearly all African-Americans—rose in a standing ovation.

Lonnie Williams was the only current University of Arkansas employee to speak. Williams said, "He showed us that there are still a few Davids in the world, ready to take on Goliath."

It was Wendell Griffen, an eloquent and charismatic speaker, whose brilliance colored the afternoon. Griffen credited Richardson for his "refusal to let himself be defined by the myths commonly applied to black men and black leaders. He may speak coarsely, but never deceitfully. It may not be the truth we want to hear, but it's always the truth we cannot deny. Thank you, coach, for refusing to sell out your principles and worship popularity at the price of integrity. Thank you for reminding our state that you will not ignore the business of social justice just because you are a basketball coach. Thank you for not allowing yourself to be put on a plantation, even if they do pay you a million dollars."

TWENTY-ONE

BATTLE ROYAL

In early December of 2002, Richardson went ahead with plans to file a lawsuit against the University of Arkansas, Frank Broyles, John White, and the fund-raising Razorback Foundation.

It was a trying time for Richardson and his family. Later that month, Richardson's son—Nolan "Notes" Richardson III—was terminated as the head coach of Tennessee State, where trailblazing coaches John McLendon and Harold Hunter had preceded him. Richardson III had been an Arkansas assistant for ten seasons.

Notes' problem stemmed from a disagreement with his Tennessee State assistant Hosea Lewis concerning practice times on Christmas evening, when many of the TSU players were no-shows. Notes Richardson told police that he went to his car and brought an unloaded gun into the school's Gentry Center in response to threats from Lewis, who, Notes says, had a chain. Although he disputes the circumstances of his firing, in the ensuing days he signed a statement with campus police acknowledging that he used the gun as a threat.

Bringing a gun onto campus in Tennessee is a felony, but the school did not attempt to prosecute Richardson III after he quickly resigned in early January of 2003. Tennessee State's president was quoted nationally as saying, "What he did is something that was beyond belief in terms of anyone in higher education doing something like that."

Richardson's lawsuit didn't go to trial until 2004. His arguments were centered upon allegations of racism and his own freedom of speech—speaking out on racism, which he claimed was a matter of public concern. The judge quickly tossed out everything directed at the Razorback Foundation.

If Richardson proved either racism or the stifling of his right to free speech, he would win. The trial lasted nearly a month, beginning on May 5, 2004, and included forty-four witnesses over eighteen days. Both parties waived the chance for a jury trial. Some legal experts felt that this was Richardson's best bet, since the coach would have had a difficult time finding a sympathetic jury because of the amount of money at stake.

Philip Kaplan, the lawyer representing the University of Arkansas, said in his opening statement that Richardson's lawsuit was based on his hatred of Frank Broyles. According to Broyles, at his February 28, 2002, meeting, Richardson told him, "I will destroy you. You will have no legacy."

UA football coach Houston Nutt testified at the trial, saying that Richardson told him that Broyles "may like you now, but wait until your ass goes 5-6, or 4-7 and see what happens."

Part of Richardson's claims focused on the treatment of Houston Nutt, who, Richardson felt, received favorable treatment. However, Judge William Wilson, who is white, couldn't find substantial difference, aside from the fact that assistant basketball coach Mike Anderson was underpaid.

Judge Wilson did point out that in a written memo Broyles recommended to Chancellor White that Richardson's six-year contract should not be "rolled over." Broyles also added that he thought all contracts should be limited to five years. The rollover, a powerful equivalent of a professor's tenure, was once popular, but the current trend among even the biggest contracts was moving away from them. "However," Wilson wrote, "Broyles failed to mention in his memo that he had recommended a ten-year contract for Nutt in October of 1999, which White approved. This evidence is disturbing . . ."

In his final ruling on the case, Judge William Wilson seemed to struggle for wiggle room, writing how difficult his decision was, and that ". . . some pieces will always be missing." Before going much further, he stressed that ". . . this case has been hard to decide. Judging, like coaching, often appears easier from the bleachers."

The university took the curious position that Frank Broyles was not responsible for Richardson's firing.

At the trial, Broyles claimed that he regretted using the word "nigger" to a table of media representatives. Judge Wilson, in his written summary, remained troubled by the "redneck = nigger" comparison that Broyles had hoped to see in print:

> It should ring out loudly and clearly—an African-American calling a Caucasian a "redneck" is nowise the same as a Caucasian person calling an African-American a "nigger."
>
> Although some may argue that there is no real difference, they are wrong, and I suspect they know it. . . . The fact is that terms like "nigger," "spic," "faggot," and "kike" evolve and reinforce entire cultural histories of oppression and subordination. They remind the target that his or her group has always been and remains unequal in status to the majority group.

Judge Wilson would continue chipping away at Broyles. In his argument about Broyles's comments at the banquet, he reasoned:

> Defendants have argued that Broyles's banquet comments two years before the firing are "too remote" and "stray" to support an inference that Broyles harbored racial hostility toward Richardson. They argue that his remarks are, therefore, insufficient to constitute direct evidence of discrimination because there was no causal link between the remark and the firing. . . .
>
> I disagree.
>
> In this instance, the issue is not Broyles's words themselves, but his apparent desire to use race in a publication, which would create conflict among fans and garner support for firing Richardson . . . Broyles solicited an article making the comparison and [I] can think of no other reason why he would do so . . . Broyles had already attempted to get support for firing Richardson as early as February 2000. This solicitation can hardly be seen as anything but a willingness to "stir the racial pot."
>
> . . . Broyles was animated when making the statement . . . he knew he was sitting between two news media persons, that there was no contention that their conversation was "off the record." [One media representative] testified that he asked Broyles if he wanted to be quoted as a source in the requested article, and Broyles responded with the equivalent of "perish the thought."
>
> These statements were made at a time when Broyles, a decision maker, was considering Richardson's termination. I find that this is direct evidence of discrimination and is sufficient to require a mixed-motive analysis of any employment decisions made by Broyles before October 2000. . . .

Frank Broyles testified that this was the only time in his entire life that he had uttered the word "nigger."

While it seems that it would make a difference whether Broyles was quoting the irate and anonymous fan, or stating his own opinion, Judge Wilson did not think so. The judge felt certain that it was Broyles's own feelings (redneck = nigger) that were being communicated, although Broyles insists he was quoting the all-important-yet-mysterious fan. In his summary, Wilson cited the conflicting testimony of two media representatives who were at the banquet: Paul Eels (who died later in a car wreck) and Mike Nail.

> Paul Eels . . . heard it as a direct statement, rather than as a quote . . . I do not think that it makes any difference whether it was a direct statement or a quote, but everyone interested in the case knew that the distinction was very important to Coach Broyles. Nail testified that, in a private conversation prior to trial, Eels told him that it was a quote. This means that either Nail or Eels lied about this specific point. I am satisfied that Eels told the truth.

Judge Wilson's findings determined that the University of Arkansas's decision to dump Richardson was made on Sunday, February 24, 2002. Wilson relied on the testimony of thirteen witnesses (including all but the lone African-American member of the board of trustees, who was told the following Thursday). This meant Richardson was effectively fired the day after his Kentucky press conference ("They can have this job if they just pay me my money"), but before Richardson's ramble on the following Monday—the televised, scattered lecture for which Richardson became nationally known.

In other words, Richardson's final press conference was meaningless, a moot point—although that fateful Monday was used by fans and media to justify what had already been decided.

Did Richardson know the ax was about to fall, instinctively sense his time was up? He knew he was in trouble, and that Broyles had wanted to fire him in 1987, then again in 2000. Richardson's romp through the 2000 SEC Tournament put out that fire. The coach understood he simply did not have the players to pull off another miracle that March—and save his job. In any case, a host of administrators and trustees knew Richardson was terminated on February 24; the school would wait until February 28 to actually inform Richardson. Judge Wilson wrote, ". . . the decision was not only unfair, but an administrative nightmare."

On February 24, Chancellor White told media representatives that in his view, Richardson was just frustrated after a tough loss, despite the feeling he had after talking to Bud Walton Arena manager Fred Vorsanger. The *Democrat-Gazette* even wrote a piece on February 25, 2002, under the headline, "Chancellor Expects Nolan to Complete Contract," despite the loss and comments at Kentucky. "He puts the most intense pressure on himself," White said. "I fully expect to see him complete his contract at the University of Arkansas."

Then on February 27, with Richardson's fate sealed, White told a local television station that he had no knowledge of a buyout planned for Richardson.

Both of these statements came up at the trial and were commented on by Judge Wilson in his summary, although throwing the media "off the scent" is a common tactic among administrators. Regardless, either John White misled the media, or he was not involved in Broyles's decision.

Richardson's attorney tried to catch Frank Broyles in a similar trap, pointing out that the athletics director had written complimentary evaluations of Richardson, as well as publicly said that Richardson would make a fine athletics director someday. Neither the evaluation nor the statement, he admitted under oath, was true, only intended to be "friendly."

Unless Richardson had miraculously swept through the SEC

Tournament again—and even if he had spoken the usual clichés after the Kentucky loss—he would have been fired. But since testimony indicated the decision to dump Richardson came on the same day that White made his comments, it appeared somebody else besides the chancellor was making the decisions at the University of Arkansas.

Perhaps as disturbing as Frank Broyles's attempts to rally racist comments from the media were the admissions under oath by university board of trustees members Gary George and Bill Clark that they occasionally told "nigger jokes." Gary George was the chairman at that time.

University officials using racist slang, and the implications of such language, disturbed Judge Wilson. He wrote:

> It seems to me . . . that when a person accepts an
> important position of trust with the entire University of
> Arkansas system, he would purge his vocabulary of such
> words—and work on his heart and mind in the same vein.
> Most troubling to me was that neither of these witnesses
> seemed abashed by their admissions.

Neither Clark nor George was asked to resign in the wake of those admissions.

The *Democrat-Gazette's* Wally Hall wrote, "Richardson's attorney, John Walker, was very successful at making Broyles look like an almost 80-year-old man with 50-year-old ideas and very outdated management skills. This suit revealed Broyles's mishandling of several coaches, fading the truth whenever he deemed necessary, his reference to the 'N word' and even how he answers to no one."

In the end, however, Judge Wilson wrote that the University of

Arkansas's claim—that Richardson was canned because of his statement after the Kentucky game ("If they go ahead and pay me my money, they can take the job tomorrow")—was both sufficient and accurate. This simple judgment settled things in the University of Arkansas's favor.

> This comment . . . showed a lost interest and lack of commitment to UAF, undermined public confidence and support for the program and had a negative impact on recruiting for all UAF sports. With these explanations, UAF has met its burden of articulating a legitimate reason for termination.

In fact, this was the only reason given by the university for dismissing Richardson. Judge Wilson also noted that according to numerous witnesses, Richardson had made those comments often, beginning in 1995. Yet Richardson was never challenged or questioned by university administrators about this apparently common statement. Anyone who has been around coaches—especially older coaches—knows that this "Why the hell do I do this for a living?" sentiment is as common as a 2-3 zone. Saying it into a microphone at a press conference at the University of Kentucky, however, is not.

Sid Simpson believes the *hiring* of Richardson was tinted with racism, because the coach's race was the only issue to Frank Broyles. However, he thinks race actually had less to do with Richardson's firing. "Broyles's ego got Nolan Richardson fired," he says. "Nolan would have gotten fired even if he were white. Broyles had been wanting to get rid of him for years. Nolan had become bigger than Broyles. He'd won a real national championship, not a fictional one," Simpson says, referring to Broyles's disputed 1964 title. "Then Nolan damn near won the NCAA championship again."

"The firing of Coach Richardson was not a black-or-white story," Arkansas sportswriter Chip Souza says. "But if you don't think race was involved, you're sadly mistaken."

Charles Prigmore, former Medical Center boss, says: "I don't think the race issue had anything to do with it. Nolan was grasping at straws when he sued the university. If he'd been Chinese or German I think he still would have been gone." Prigmore thinks the real problem was Richardson having a boss who thought he knew basketball. "I was the head football coach at three high schools, and I know you don't want a principal who used to be a head coach," he says. "Frank Broyles was an enemy of success, and Richardson had gotten too successful."

Carrol Williams (no relation to Lonnie Williams) was Black Alumni Society president at Arkansas when Nolan Richardson was fired in 2002. "There was great discussion at that time about what had happened to Nolan Richardson," Williams says, "especially when we heard about the testimony of the board of trustees."

Specifically, it was the use of the "N word" in jokes and the realization that Frank Broyles might sit quietly and listen to those jokes. "At one time, we were going to go ahead and recommend, as a group, our BSA, that Frank Broyles be fired. But then we thought, 'We have to get real, John White is not going to fire Frank Broyles.' So instead we asked Chancellor White to step up and make a commitment to the African-American faculty and staff."

Bill Clark and Gary George, the members of the board of trustees at UA who used the word "nigger," eventually left the board. Broyles remained as AD until his retirement in the spring of 2007. But the BSA was mortified that any board member would use that kind of language and not be instantly cut loose from the school.

———

Judge Wilson's final summary makes it clear that he admires Richardson, not just for his obvious accomplishments but also for the coach's against-all-odds journey. In the end, Wilson sided with the University of Arkansas, but not before admonishing the administration for their clumsy collective management styles.

> Richardson should have been counseled about his sometimes intemperate remarks, and UAF administrators should have made more timely and direct responses to his complaints . . . I am inclined to believe that the firing could have been avoided, or postponed considerably, if there had been more and better communication by his supervisors.

Judge Wilson was troubled regarding what he clearly saw to be a difficult decision, and his sympathy for Richardson's situation is obvious:

> Although I have found against him on those points, his belief was clearly not unreasonable. In other words, while I do not believe that evidence of racial bias or impingement of free speech preponderates in favor of Plaintiff, the record is a long way from devoid of incidents which could cause him to hold these beliefs.

When Richardson's career crashed, the media almost invariably backed the University of Arkansas. Nearly always, his poor graduation rate from 1990 to 1994 was trotted out. When *Sports Illustrated* interviewed *SI* basketball writer Seth Davis, the title of the article was "Richardson Brought It Upon Himself"—although in the piece, Davis did conclude, ". . . it's clear from his behavior there was someone who didn't want him around."

John Smallwood of the *Philadelphia Daily News* wrote, "The University of Arkansas, Razorbacks fans and even the media that cover the athletics program didn't deserve what Nolan Richardson did to them . . . he was wrong to transport the image of Arkansas back to that of the racially intolerant 1950s and 1960s."

Without understanding the context, the history of the state, the university, and Frank Broyles, by taking Richardson's comments from his confusing Monday press conference at face value, people like Smallwood might find Richardson an ungrateful millionaire.

The coach, who had spent his professional life in an often-lonely confrontation with college sports' racist past, primarily was blamed for *reminding* the public about racism. "Why can't Nolan just get over it?" was the typical take from college basketball insiders. Wasn't America beyond racism, the reasoning went, if a black man was making a million bucks a year?

Yet was racism "over in America," as Newt Gingrich declared in 1995, if the board of trustees at a state's major university could put their feet up and ask, "Did you hear the one about the three niggers who went fishing?" How much of this racism was communicated, however subtly, to John White or Frank Broyles? Broyles claimed that in the 1960s, the board of trustees was the reason he was one of the last coaches in America to find qualified black players for his football team, and it's no stretch to think that, at the very least, the board's backwoods racism could influence Broyles again.

TWENTY-TWO

YOUR BLUES AIN'T LIKE MINE

In October of 2004, Frank Broyles lost his wife, Barbara, to complications from Alzheimer's disease. The couple had been married for fifty-nine years. Broyles continued working tirelessly on fundraising for Alzheimer's research and began writing a book about the disease.

Even with the lawsuit over, Chancellor John White felt like the Sisyphus of college administrators. In 2004, UA instituted a program where employees—on a voluntary basis—might learn to be more accepting of diversity. The program was called "Our Campus: Building a More Inclusive University of Arkansas."

Cynics pointed out that his training program in tolerance was instituted around the same time Richardson's suit for racial discrimination was filed. Barbara Taylor told the *Democrat-Gazette*, "Chronologically, they certainly coincided. But before the Nolan Richardson controversy and conflict arose, the diversity task force had already made that recommendation."

The university's enrollment today is still only 5 percent African-American, while the overall population of the state remains 16 percent. The faculty at UA is only 3 percent African-American. Yet it's undeniable that the school has attempted to diversify.

In January of 2005, the University of Arkansas hired an African-American woman named Carmen Coustaut as their first associate vice chancellor for diversity and education. In the spring of 2006, the University of Arkansas hired an African-American woman, Cynthia Nance, to be dean of the law school. Several key black university administrators and 43 percent of black faculty members have arrived since John White was hired in 1997. Of course, the ways in which an African-American championship basketball coach would have influenced that statistic are impossible to measure.

White said, when Richardson's removal was announced, "I'm strongly committed and I'm very concerned that the African-American community within the state not think that this is in any way a step back with respect to our commitment to that agenda." If not progress, there has been movement at University of Arkansas, and it's movement in the right direction.

Val Gonzalez, who conducted the workshops for the National Conference for Community Justice, was much more direct. "Discrimination is a real problem, right here at the University of Arkansas. Some of what we learned is not very pretty."

Nolan Richardson lost his appeal in the Eighth U.S. Circuit Court during May of 2006, in St. Louis. Judge Arlen Beam wrote, "The record amply supports a conclusion that Richardson's statement had a detrimental impact on the effective functioning of the public employer's enterprise—namely, the university's total athletics program. This public interest clearly outweighs any First Amendment privilege Richardson may have allegedly had in the making of the comment."

———

In February of 2007, Congressman Bobby Rush (D-Illinois) hosted hearings involving the NCAA, Congress, and experts on the struggles faced by African-American coaches. Rush called Nolan Richardson back to the battle.

Other witnesses who participated were NCAA President Myles Brand, Jesse Jackson, new BCA boss Floyd Keith, and Richard Lapchick from the Institute for Ethics and Diversity in Sports.

Bobby Rush stressed that legislation to correct the shocking lack of black football coaches would be appropriate. But NCAA President Myles Brand begged off any direct responsibility, saying, "The colleges and universities will not cede to the NCAA the authority to dictate who to interview or hire in athletics."

Richard Lapchick, one of the nation's foremost authorities on race and college sports, favors the NCAA using a policy similar to the "Rooney Rule," which had been put in effect, to make certain that every NFL coaching search would include at least one candidate of color. In his written statement, Lapchick suggested that legislation and lawsuits should both be options. "It's pretty clear that embarrassment hasn't been enough," he wrote.

The problem, Brand pointed out, was with the results of the searches.

Richardson cited the good ol' boy club of boosters who would almost certainly favor white coaches. The influence of well-heeled boosters over athletics departments—and thus entire universities—is a given today. The head coaching jobs in college football may be the last place where boosters can cling to white leadership.

At the time, fewer than 3 percent of head football coaches at all NCAA institutions were black, although more than half of the athletes were. Men's basketball, where over 60 percent of the players are black, was better, since nearly 30 percent of its head coaches were black.

Frankie Allen, now the basketball coach at historically black Maryland–Eastern Shore, knows the biggest reason that college basketball is decades ahead of football. "Basketball coaches *organized* a lot sooner, with the BCA," Allen says. "The guys at the top of the profession were all doing great—Thompson, Chaney, and Richardson. We had big-name people behind us, and they weren't afraid to speak out."

TWENTY-THREE

BROTHERS AND KEEPERS

Arkansas fired Stan Heath in the spring of 2007, and the timing was obvious. With the conclusion of the Nolan Richardson lawsuit, Heath was expendable. His teams struggled his first three seasons, but in his fourth and fifth years, Arkansas finally qualified for the NCAA Tournament again. Heath's teams won over those five seasons, in order, nine, twelve, eighteen, twenty-two, then twenty-one games.

"Maybe I didn't do enough to protect myself," Heath says. "It was set up to be a pacifying situation after Nolan. [Frank Broyles said] ticket sales were down. But I can read. In 2006–07, we had more fans than the year before." Indeed, in 2006, the Razorbacks were twelfth in the nation—out of over three hundred schools—in overall attendance. In 2007, Heath's last season, they were ninth.

Arkansas would embarrass itself that spring by offering the job to a succession of five coaches—all white—who would consecutively turn down the job. Dana Altman left Creighton for a day before changing his mind and returning to Omaha. Finally, after the fifth rejection, Broyles found Arkansas their white coach in John Pelphrey, who had *not* led South Alabama to the NCAA Tournament. (Pelphrey quickly hired Rob Evans, Richardson's longtime friend.)

Heath noticed the parade of white coaches Arkansas fawned over that April. "I have no problems with the new coach, but if you just look at [Pelphrey's] résumé, the measuring stick had changed. I was an Elite Eight coach, and they hired a coach who had come from the NIT."

Unaware of the swirl of politics and maneuvering around him, Heath was focused on his quickly improving team. "I never felt that Dr. White was trying to manage the athletics department; I just thought he was a cheerleader. Dr. White's a nice guy, but it wasn't his decision [to fire Heath]. I can tell you, that is a fact."

Heath believes White made every effort to try to wrestle control of athletics from his supposed subordinate, Frank Broyles. "My second or third year," Heath says, "Dr. White wanted to make a change in the athletics director's job. What I remember came back to us—and this was a rumor—was this. If you try to change [Broyles's] job, you're going to lose yours. The lesson was that Broyles is going to run the athletics department."

Heath's point—the unchecked power of Broyles—echoes the feelings of many within the state: The University of Arkansas, in their decades of silence, condoned Broyles's behavior. "Even when a federal judge criticized him harshly for racially insensitive comments last summer, nobody from the university offered even the mildest censure," the *Chronicle of Higher Education* would write. "Not one peep of public reproach has been heard from any other state or university officials."

Heath is also quick to point out all Broyles has accomplished and his high regard in the world of college sports. Broyles, however, continued his pattern by meddling with Heath's basketball team. "He had opinions on the staff he wanted me to hire," Heath said.

That didn't bother Heath so much, since Broyles was admired for uncovering great assistants. Rather, it was his boss's basketball ideas and his management style. "Broyles never was a guy who told me to run this play or that play, but he certainly had his opinions on *style* of play. That was where he wanted to have some input. There were times when he had his opinion, but we had difficulty because he was almost like an overseer. We struggled with our communication."

Heath's timing in taking the job put him in an awkward place stylistically. He simply didn't play at the same pace as Richardson. "But Broyles was pushing us into a full-court press," he says. Heath thinks this was a matter of expedience for Broyles. "In the early part of his career, he wanted Nolan to play more Eddie Sutton's style. The fans were used to that. At the end of the day, Broyles wanted to make the fans in Arkansas happy. He wanted me to *replace* Nolan by playing Nolan's style."

Each year Heath's team improved, even getting to the championship game of SEC in his final season. By the conclusion of the 2007 season, Heath was itching with anticipation. His Razorbacks had consistently done better, and had no seniors.

Then the crimson rug was ripped from beneath his feet. "There are coaches going to the NIT, and they get raises. Bill Self lost in the first round of the NCAAs in 2007," Heath points out. Self's Kansas team won the national championship the following year.

Heath says there was one constant motivator for Broyles, which became apparent at the SEC conference meetings each spring. The league meetings involve university presidents, athletics directors, head coaches, and faculty representatives.

The young head coach and veteran AD, who was closing in on eighty years of age, would sit together. "During the basketball meeting, Broyles would sleep through the whole thing," Heath says. "People would be looking around, smiling at me."

Only one thing could awaken Broyles, Heath claims. One year the SEC bosses said they wanted Arkansas to give up a home game in basketball to play in something called "The SEC Challenge." Each home game was worth at least $300,000 to Arkansas. "He immediately woke up and snapped to attention," Heath says.

At certain times, though, money could be tossed around freely at Broyles's discretion. Both Nolan Richardson and football coach Houston Nutt were paid piles of money *not* to coach the Razorbacks. Richardson's payments finally ended in June of 2008.

Stan Heath handled his firing gracefully, and he bounced back within weeks, landing as the coach of the University of South Florida. In retrospect, he sees his time in Fayetteville differently. "Nolan made the job easier for me," he says. "People went out of their way to be kind to me." When things went badly for Heath, Richardson reached out and shared one of his favorite lines from Ol' Mama: "All sickness isn't death." Richardson also stuck up for the embattled Heath publicly.

"I wanted to sort of take the baton from Nolan," Heath says. The baton Heath would get came in the form of the same pink slip. "But it was only one person that led to my change," Heath says. "There was only one direction I was looking as to what happened to me."

"Frank Broyles fired everybody," one longtime Arkansas athletics department employee says. "Nolan Richardson lasted seventeen seasons, far longer than any football coach. [Football coaches] Lou Holtz, Ken Hatfield, Jack Crowe, Joe Kines, Danny Ford, and Houston Nutt were all either fired, forced out, or made to feel unwelcome by Broyles."

A common refrain heard around Fayetteville, Arkansas—athletics staff, faculty, waitresses, Wal-Mart execs among them—is how loved Nolan Richardson was during his tenure at the university.

Yet the criteria white people in Arkansas use to determine what constitutes racism is fuzzy. When Arkansans are presented with the obstacles Richardson had overcome in his career—reared in racist El Paso, "don't hire that nigger" sentiments at both Tulsa and Western Texas, dogs being brought in to black fraternity parties—these are dismissed with a shrug.

Frank Broyles—the face of the University of Arkansas since the early sixties—urging media representatives to use the word "nigger" in print? That was poor judgment. Board of trustees members telling nigger jokes? Well, it wasn't as though they'd lynched Nolan Richardson, or anyone else.

Hiring a black man to replace Richardson, keeping him in the post as long as the lawsuit was alive, then dumping him despite his team's dramatic improvement—that wasn't racist either, folks in Fayetteville said. That was the nature of college sports.

NABC director Jim Haney, whose column caused Richardson to reexamine his role as a "token" assistant athletics director, thinks obliviousness to Richardson's struggle indicates a poor sense of the past. "Just hiring an African-American to be a coach was at one time a huge step," Haney says. "Then there was that image of the recruiter who couldn't possibly understand the intricacies of the game. Next was, can we hire a black coach at a large state university? In Richardson, Thompson, and Tubby Smith, we've seen African-Americans lead teams to the NCAA title."

Haney also sees the firing of coaches of color as potentially a good thing. "At the end of the day, you want to be judged on the merits of what you do. Winning, fan base, academics, those things, just as a human being, not based on age or race. Guys like Nolan, John Thompson, Reggie Minton, they were trailblazers."

Despite the progress, today the Black Coaches Association is at a crossroads. Richardson, Chaney, and Thompson are no longer coaching. A lack of direction in the late 1990s—along with allegations by the BCA that its former executive director Rudy Washington had misused BCA funds—nearly led to the BCA's demise. The BCA itself sued Washington, seeking an accounting of funds, and there was an out-of-court settlement.

The BCA's influence has waned, but it may be on the rebound. They've changed their name to Black Coaches and Administrators. Their current director, Floyd Keith, has struggled to restore confidence and financial stability and has pushed the BCA coaches to get involved with at-risk kids.

The BCA was also the force behind the Football Hiring Report Card, which rates each college that hires a new football coach and evaluates their interest in considering candidates of color.

No matter how many basketball games Clarence Gaines, John McClendon, Dave Whitney at Alcorn State, or Don Corbett at North Carolina A&T won, nobody within the white power structure moved to offer them a job. Head coaches at historically black colleges today likely earn one-tenth of what their counterparts are paid at mostly white state universities.

Perhaps the most disturbing example of this is football legend Eddie Robinson, who coached at Grambling State University in Louisiana, only twenty-five miles from the Arkansas border. Robinson served at Grambling, a historically black college, for fifty-six years, lasting through eleven United States presidents. He could boast more football wins than any other coach and sent more than two hundred players to the NFL. He had a graduation rate of 80 percent (when football graduation rates were around 50 percent nationally). For his first fifty seasons, Robinson never had a player get in trouble with the law.

Despite being the winningest football coach of all time, Eddie Robinson was never even offered an *interview* for a major university head coaching job. Robinson, of course, is not the only man to be overlooked. To this day, in the history of major college football, there have been fewer than thirty black head coaches.

Some schools have been surprisingly progressive in their hiring.

The University of Mississippi has had two black basketball coaches. Texas schools like SMU, Texas A&M, Rice, and Houston have as well. Texas basketball, though, is still behind the curve. Don Haskins's historic team remains the only Texas school that has ever won the NCAA basketball championship.

"Integration in sports—as opposed to integration at the ballot box or in public conveyances—was a winning proposition for the whites who controlled the sports-industrial complex," wrote William Rhoden in his book, *Forty Million Dollar Slaves*. "They could move to exploit black muscle and talent, thus sucking the life out of black institutions, while at the same time give themselves credit for being humanitarians."

Rhoden laments that while the integration of sports often benefited the black athlete, the historically black colleges received a major blow as their talent pool thinned. The same was true of the Negro Leagues once Jackie Robinson opened those floodgates. Integration was ultimately not seen as a challenge to white coaches and administrators.

Nolan Richardson eclipsed Frank Broyles in popularity, and that may have been seen as a threat to the director of athletics' power within the state and school. Whenever black men were put in positions of power—as head coaches, for example—it meant a drastic difference from simply having black athletes on the court.

Haskins's 1966 championship returned to the national mindset with the release of the movie *Glory Road*. Stories appeared across the country, and retro Texas Western jerseys became popular. The *Nation*'s David Zirin called the 1966 game "the Selma Bridge of sports."

The Texas Western Miners' season was a coincidence of events that writers dream of discovering. The acerbic and crusty Haskins was the accidental hero and fine literary and artistic material. Instead of using the real Haskins, though, Disney coated him in cliché. It's hard to figure why the film's director encased its celluloid Haskins in plastic, when the real one was so much more interesting.

Glory Road is filled with deliberate inaccuracies, which was unfortunate, since the true story was more compelling. The movie even missed Haskins's real innovation, aside from his being color-blind—getting inner-city playground players to play slower offensively. Texas Western slowed down the run-and-gun Kentucky Wildcats, contrary to the movie's portrayal.

Haskins likely could never have considered starting five blacks at any other major school in Texas, and some credit would have to go to the Hispanic-majority El Paso that abolished its Jim Crow laws in 1962—after Nolan Richardson and Bert Williams were refused service in a popular restaurant.

Glory Road is nonetheless a finely constructed film. The banter and camaraderie between the players is perfect in this happily-ever-after story. But it all felt a little too feel-good.

UTEP, now a school with a Hispanic majority, had countless black athletes who have, like the 1966 Miners, brought fame and money to the school. Yet by 2005, UTEP had not had a black coach in any major sport. (Only women's basketball had a black head coach—they could claim Wayne Thornton, who coached for fifty dollars a month during a single season in 1978–79.) UTEP's road ran one way. Black athletes were welcome. Black leaders were not.

Since that glorious 1966 game, Richardson's alma mater has had seven athletics directors, eleven football coaches, four men's track coaches, and three other basketball coaches. (Don Haskins finally retired in 1999.) That's *twenty-five positions of leadership* for some deserving coach.

Every single one of those twenty-five jobs was filled by a white male. Obviously, Don Haskins was not doing the hiring. Three white coaches—all assistants with no wins on the major college level—followed Haskins. On two of those hires, UTEP even passed over Nolan Richardson.

Richardson pushed his teams to play at a furious pace.
(*Copyright © Aynsley Floyd*)

Colorblind coach Don Haskins began an avalanche of desegregation.
(*Courtesy of UTEP*)

Rose Richardson, 1885–1968. "Ol' Mama" was Richardson's de facto mother. (*Courtesy of Nolan Richardson*)

Richardson's scoring average at Texas Western College plummeted under Haskins's slowdown system. (*Courtesy of UTEP*)

New York Nirvana: Tulsa's 1981 NIT championship put Richardson in the national spotlight. (*Courtesy of University of Tulsa Sports Information*)

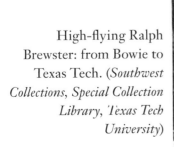

High-flying Ralph Brewster: from Bowie to Texas Tech. (*Southwest Collections, Special Collection Library, Texas Tech University*)

Yvonne Richardson (*left*), Rosario Richardson (*middle*), Nolan Richardson.
(*Courtesy of Nolan Richardson*)

Leading the faithful:
Frank Broyles, University
of Arkansas football
coach and director of
athletics for fifty years.
(*Wesley Hitt/Getty Images*)

"He could have had a
PhD in psychology":
Nolan Richardson and
three-point ace Pat
Bradley. (*Jonathon
Daniel/Getty Images
Sport/Getty Images*)

Nolan Richardson and his
wife, Rosario, celebrate
after beating Duke for the
1994 NCAA title.
(*Damian Strohmeyer/
Sports Illustrated/Getty
Images*)

Throwing the book away:
Razorback substitute Ken
Biley climbs to the top.
(*Hawgs Illustrated*)

"A whole lot of courage":
Arkansas football walk-on Darrell Brown.
(*Courtesy of Darrell Brown*)

Unofficial Arkansas high school
touchdown leader Bob Walters
(*above*); nephew Danny Walters
(*right*) became one of the
greatest Razorbacks ever.
(*Courtesy of the Walters family*)

"We can recruit, motivate, and teach, but can we coach? I never hear that": Nolan Richardson and TV analyst Billy Packer. (*Hawgs Illustrated*)

"He seems to make a system out of anger": Richardson in the late 1990s. (*Brian Bahr/Getty Images Sport/Getty images*)

Vamanos! Richardson returned to the border to coach the Mexican National Team. (*El Paso Times/ Victor Calzada*)

The most important African-American coach in history: a pensive
Richardson before the championship team reunion in 2009.
(*Eric Howerton, Now Creative Inc.*)

One allegation that the University of Arkansas made at the trial was that Richardson was not really trying to find another job. They mentioned those two openings at UTEP since Richardson's termination. While Richardson may have been happy at times to collect his $500,000 a year from Arkansas (which would end if he accepted a coaching spot elsewhere), he was, in fact, interested in the UTEP job in 2006. But Richardson claims that the interest was not reciprocated.

"They brought Nolan in for an interview," Haskins said, "and they told him they were going to hire a black coach, but the athletics director didn't want Nolan."

UTEP finally did hire a black man in 2006, when Tony Barbee, an assistant coach from the University of Memphis, was named basketball coach. Forty years had elapsed since Haskins's historic win.

Firing coaches is part of college basketball. A study of what happens to coaches—both white and black—after they have been terminated is instructive.

New BCA boss Floyd Keith claims this is where racism still prevails. "Classic example. Here's Nolan Richardson," Keith told Skip Myslenski in a widely syndicated column. "He proved himself. He had no violations. Then I look around, I'm not going to name names, but here's a coach that, at Iowa State, hugged and kissed coeds, got drunk, and he's working again. There's something wrong here."

Keith was referring to Larry Eustachy, whose demise became a national story when photos of him at Big Twelve parties surfaced on the Internet. Eustachy resigned and acknowledged his addiction to alcohol. He was hired at the University of Southern Mississippi within a year of leaving ISU.

Young black coaches like Randy Ayers and Wade Houston got very brief chances, then never resurfaced, despite the fact that college sports is a business that possesses a limitless ability to recycle white coaches. Eustachy, Tom Penders, Bob Huggins, Eddie Sutton, and Bob Knight were all rocked by controversy.

Eddie Sutton, who represented the good old days to the good old boys of Arkansas, left Fayetteville for Kentucky. Things went terribly wrong at Kentucky, and Sutton resigned amid accusations of cash payments made to a top recruit. Sutton's career was renewed at Oklahoma State, and he led his alma mater to a couple Final Fours. His time at Oklahoma State would come to an end with a bizarre DWI. Campus cops hoisted the drunken coach—whose blood alcohol level was three times the legal limit—into his car at the Gallagher-Iba Arena. Minutes later, he swerved across four lanes of traffic, slammed into the rear of another vehicle, then crashed into a tree. Sutton was able to find work again, resurfacing for most of a season as the head coach at the University of San Francisco.

The well-documented case of Bob Knight is interesting as well. Knight and Richardson are nearly the same age, and both men played for coaches who won NCAA titles—Knight for Fred Taylor at Ohio State. Although Richardson was not a member of Haskins's 1966 team, he was certainly the better player. By the time Knight was only twenty-four, he was the army's head coach at West Point. With not a single black man coaching a major college team, Knight simply would not have been given the chance if he had been black. Richardson, of course, toiled at an obscure high school and junior college for over a decade, at a time when Knight was landing a plum Big Ten job.

Both Knight and Richardson won NCAA titles, although Knight won three. Knight's controversies at Indiana were reported nationally. He was dumped by Indiana in September 2000, but despite the negative publicity, Knight quickly resurfaced at Texas Tech. A group of alumni and fans—not Knight—sued IU soon after he was fired. Knight waited until he was hired and secure at Texas Tech, and then finally filed suit in November 2002, after negotiations for a settlement collapsed.

One of Richardson's former assistants, Wayne Stehlik, admitted to ESPN.com that part of the reason Richardson was untouchable was that he had sued Broyles. "Athletics directors and chancellors or presidents are probably a little bit nervous," Stehlik said, "because of how it turned out there at Arkansas."

The firing of Nolan Richardson remained a source of controversy in Arkansas when Razorback football coach Houston Nutt was let go. Nutt became the head football coach at Arkansas in 1998. His 2006 team was 7-1 in SEC play, and 10-4 overall. Going into the 2007 season—his tenth—Nutt had plenty to be proud of, although he hadn't approached the success that Richardson had in basketball.

Then a Freedom of Information Act request revealed that Nutt, who is married with children, sent close to a thousand text messages to an attractive TV anchorwoman. Arkansas was 3-4 then in the SEC, going into the last game in 2007, and five SEC teams had better records. Yet Chancellor John White and Frank Broyles stood by him, at least publicly.

During that tumultuous autumn, Stanley Reed, the new chairman of the board of trustees at UA, claimed the public had lost confidence in Coach Nutt. The fickle fans were ready for a change, and the "lost confidence" excuse clearly echoed the removal of Richardson, but Reed insisted Arkansas did not want to fire Houston Nutt. "It would look bad," he said.

What happened next would look worse. In a dramatic season finale, Arkansas beat the #1-ranked LSU Tigers in Baton Rouge. It appeared as though all might be forgiven and Nutt would remain a Razorback. But behind the scenes, boosters started the ball rolling on removing Nutt. A monstrous $3-million buyout was assembled through the Razorback Foundation. And they wouldn't have to fire the football coach. Houston Nutt resigned.

Chancellor John White stated at the ensuing press conference that UA wished to remove the "golden handcuffs" that were so invasive in Nutt's life. Since Nutt was resigning, the university should have been free of any financial obligation to him, but clearly there had been an agreement. White publicly encouraged the Razorback Foundation to shell out over $3 million to Nutt.

Stanley Reed was then quoted as saying, "It gets to the point of fairness and equity. We did not want to fire Houston Nutt. He had done a great job . . ."

Nutt had a conference record of 42-40. He never won an overall conference championship and, of course, no national championship, or the equivalent of a basketball Final Four. A day later, Nutt took a lucrative job at the University of Mississippi. Nutt wouldn't have to return any of the $3 million—he was free to coach at another school.

Richardson had been terminated in Fayetteville for essentially *suggesting* the same thing that the UA would later *do* for Houston Nutt: "If they go ahead and pay me my money, they can take the job tomorrow." Yet Richardson's buyout included a strict provision—he would lose any subsequent money if he took another job.

Richardson's overall winning percentage—70 percent—was far better than Nutt's overall percentage, not to mention the conference titles, Final Fours, and the 1994 NCAA title. When the University of Arkansas decided to dump Richardson, there was no talk of "fairness and equity" and whether firings would "look bad." Richardson seems to only have ground his heel into the sense of decorum that made it possible for Nutt to walk away with enough money to fill a Wal-Mart truck.

John White points out that Richardson was given the opportunity to resign in 2002. "Houston Nutt didn't come out and say that 'If they pay me my money I'm gone tomorrow.' We actually treated Houston the same way as Nolan, but there was no way from a public relations perspective that, nationally, people would understand why would Arkansas fire Nutt after the seasons he's just had. We couldn't fire him if we wanted to recruit another coach. There was an IRS rule change that meant Nutt couldn't afford to leave."

Whenever Richardson's firing resurfaced, his graduation rate from 1990–1994 was always mentioned as justification. That argument should have changed dramatically on October 4, 2007.

The Northwest Arkansas *Morning News* ran their usual "Briefly" column on page two of the sports section. The first three short pieces were these important issues in Arkansas:

- Tony Parker was taking time off from the French Olympic team to concentrate on his spot with the San Antonio Spurs.
- Knicks coach Isiah Thomas focused his mind on basketball during his sexual harassment trial.
- Lakers center Kwame Brown was charged with disorderly conduct.

The last section of the column was titled "Graduation Rates Increase Slightly." Most of the brief story on the NCAA's latest study—from 1997 until 2002 this time—discussed how overall graduation rates for all athletes were on the rise.

Then, this single sentence: "Arkansas' football team had a graduation rate of 53 percent, and the men's basketball team was at 50 percent."

Richardson's name was not even mentioned, although those were his final years coaching.

Why wouldn't Arkansas—which was embarrassed by his published graduation rates from 1990 to 1994—be shouting about this great academic improvement at the end of Richardson's tenure?

There had to be a big story the next day, when everyone at the

UA athletics department had a chance to plan a press conference to get their story out. *UA basketball had a respectable graduation rate in Richardson's last five years!* But the next day, there was nothing.

For most of Richardson's tenure, *Morning News* sports editor Chip Souza was an hour away, in Fort Smith. He had no excuse as to why the "new and improved" graduation rate was not a front-page piece. And he wonders why Richardson was constantly hammered for his older graduation rate after he was fired. "Nobody mentioned it when he was winning the national championship," Souza says. "It was just never an issue, until he lost and then had that press conference."

The story line about the new graduation rate was so small that almost nobody noticed, even in Arkansas.

Judge Wendell Griffen knows why the new study has never been publicized. "Frank Broyles and John White *wanted* to get rid of Nolan," Griffen says. "White was on the 'Graduation Rate Bandwagon,' thinking that graduation rates are somehow indicative of how people are doing their jobs. But athletics' function is to win games, not produce Nobel scientists. If Nolan had graduated every player and won half of his games, he would have been fired a long time ago."

Still, why not publicize the latest study, which exonerated the basketball program and shed a good light on then-embattled football coach Houston Nutt? "It would be an admission they were wrong," former UA administrator Lonnie Williams says. "You don't pick someone up that you've been kicking."

Griffen thinks that in many ways, the NCAA even speaking about graduation rates is hypocritical. "The coach of the basketball team does not have an obligation to graduate anybody, and there's not a performance feature in most contracts. The fact is that not even the dean of a college or a department head has an obligation to graduate people at a certain percentage. For the NCAA to suggest that coaches have to do what nobody else is required to do is a kind of lunacy. But that's what you get from this good old boy network, when everybody knows [college sports] is about dollars."

Forty years after the passage of the Civil Rights Act, which prohibited racial discrimination in hiring, the Southeast Conference hired its first African-American football coach. Sylvester Croom was named the Mississippi State coach in 2004.

College basketball remains far more progressive. One of the last college leagues to desegregate their teams was the glamorous Atlantic Coast Conference. Today, the ACC sets the national standard for black basketball coaches.

With twelve members in its fold, the ACC—perhaps the best league in the country—had seven black head coaches in the 2008–09 season: Boston College (Al Skinner), Georgia Tech (Paul Hewitt), Florida State (Leonard Hamilton), Clemson (Oliver Purnell), Miami (Frank Haith), Virginia (Dave Leitao), and North Carolina State (Sidney Lowe).

Not a single black head coach was employed in the ACC when Richardson won his NCAA title in 1994 (although Bob Wade had been the Maryland coach in the late 1980s).

Perhaps what lifted Nolan Richardson to greatness—his unwavering us-against-the-world attitude—might have contributed to his downfall. But Judge Wendell Griffen points out that Richardson had an important task at hand. "A brain surgeon doesn't have a chip on his shoulder," he says, "he simply uses a scalpel and is insistent on helping patients." What happened to Richardson left Griffen miffed. "We talk about opportunity," he says, "but we denigrate people who challenge the barriers."

"Nolan has the irony of being uncommonly good and universally misunderstood," Griffen says. "Nolan's battle has been in the cause of inclusion and equality but because he's a black man of action and courage—without apology or timidity—he's misunderstood as being angry or having a chip on his shoulder."

Stan Heath thinks each African-American coach needs to be taken on his own merits and politics, regardless of age. "You can't put us in the same box. Those guys [Chaney, Thompson, and Richardson] I have tremendous respect for. They voiced concerns and broke barriers in those early years and were instrumental in my development. For any coach, though, you don't become politically involved until you have success. Then you have a microphone in front of you. Were they as vocal their first years?"

Todd Day, Arkansas's all-time leading scorer, says, "When Nolan was young, he believed everything was against him. If you didn't agree with him, then you were against him, too. As he got older, he kept that edge, but that's what made him an incredibly successful coach."

Many are perplexed that Nolan Richardson could still feel disrespected or insecure when he was making so much money. Frank Broyles could be said to equate dollars and respect, but for Richardson respect had little to do with income.

Former UTEP All-American Fred Reynolds tells a story that would resonate with Richardson. Reynolds had a long pro career in Europe, returned to El Paso, and used his degree in criminal justice to become a highway patrolman. He also married a successful doctor.

For the last few years, he's bought season tickets for UTEP basketball. In 2007, an athletics department employee phoned to inform Reynolds of a new plan for season-ticket holders. Reynolds would not only have to pay for his seats, but was now required to make a donation to UTEP athletics. Although he didn't mind buying tickets, Reynolds said his career on the court was enough of a donation.

"I know your wife is a doctor," he says the UTEP employee told him. Meaning, of course, that the couple had plenty of money.

When Reynolds complained about this to the UTEP athletics director a week later, he got a similar response. "It's not like you're poor, Fred," he says he was told.

Reynolds believes his wife's status and their jobs were irrelevant. He gave great years on the court at a crucial time in UTEP basketball history. To the white people asking him, he believes, this contribution meant too little. Asking him to contribute money, even though he could well afford it, was a form of disrespect.

The long history of racism affected black athletes and coaches to varying degrees. Bob Walters was just one of countless black athletes in Arkansas whose career was stolen.

Negro schools didn't count, so his ninety-six career touchdowns were never listed as the state record. Instead, the Arkansas Activities Association for years listed a player from Osceola who scored eighty-eight touchdowns.

Walters was first diagnosed with cancer in the late 1970s, when Danny Walters was in high school. He had three brutal bouts. First, colon cancer. Then it spread, necessitating the removal of one lung in 1984. The cancer finally metastasized to his brain and kidneys. Walters never complained about the cancer that slowly ate him alive—or the racism that ruined his playing career.

"That was just Bob," his widow, Sheryl, says. "He didn't harbor bitterness."

While Walters was being devastated by the disease, though, he became keen on having his star guard Tim Hardaway join Don Haskins. "Bob liked the man," Sheryl says, "and he felt Haskins was someone who would see a person as a person, and an athlete as an athlete. Tim wound up in El Paso because Bob had both an admiration for, and trust in, Don Haskins."

Walters—who'd steered his nephew to Arkansas to play football—pushed Hardaway to sign early rather than wait until the later signing period, when there would no doubt have been a long line. "Bob liked the idea of people recognizing skills," Sheryl says, "rather than the whole black-white bit. He saw that in Haskins, I guess. There were so many places Bob went where he felt he didn't get a good shake because he was black."

Walters was able to both forgive Arkansas through his nephew and honor his own battles with segregation by sending Hardaway to Haskins.

"Bob Walters understood history," Tim Hardaway adds. "That's why he was happy to see me with Don Haskins."

Walters passed away in 1985 at the age of forty-three.

The challenges for the new generation of African-American coaches pose a different set of problems. "There are struggles that are common to the human condition," Judge Wendell Griffen says, "but it's a special experience for coaches of color. Coaches of the Stan Heath era are dealing with different facts, but they're still dealing with the issues of inclusion that Nolan had. One of the privileges of being white is that you never have to worry about boosters not supporting you, or the trustees of the institution wondering if you are white enough to head the program."

Griffen provides a simple analogy of what it has been like for blacks to navigate through American society. "I'm right-handed, but I never wake up and think about it. When I sit down at one of those preformed desks in a college lecture hall, I can fit." To those right-handers who are comfortable, everything seems fine. "Only left-handed people are aware of the fact that these desks are set up differently," Griffen says.

In May 2008, Griffen lost his reelection campaign. An ordained Baptist minister, he had been an appeals court judge in Little Rock for over a decade. During his tenure he had to appear before an ethics panel, where he was successful in fighting for his right to free speech. Griffen was highly critical of more than the way the University of Arkansas had treated minorities and Nolan Richardson. Griffen had pointedly criticized President Bush and also endorsed an increase in minimum wage in Arkansas.

Although his successor, Judge Rita Gruber, did not bring up Griffen's comments during the campaign, she told the Associated Press, "I think it's fair to say there were a lot of people in the community who were disappointed with the statements he's made over the years."

Even in defeat, Griffen was defiant. "I would much rather have maintained my integrity," he said, "and experienced these results than sacrificed my integrity for political expediency."

Ed Beshara died in Tulsa in the spring of 2007 at the age of ninety-one. The son of immigrants, Beshara often felt the strain of being an outsider. While Beshara and Richardson looked comically different standing side by side, Richardson believed he and Beshara were two of a kind. Beshara's background provided him with empathy for the underdog, something Richardson always found endearing. For twenty years, hardly a week would pass without Beshara and Richardson talking.

The month before Beshara's death, Richardson drove from Arkansas daily—four hours round-trip—to spend time with his friend. Beshara would hold Richardson's thick hand and call him "my adopted son," while a stream of nurses and doctors came and went. It was the first time Richardson made the trek to Tulsa on a regular basis since Yvonne had been sick.

"They were friends until the end," says Ed Beshara Jr., who took over his father's business. "My dad loved Nolan a great deal. Nolan is extremely loyal and will remember you forever if you try to help him."

Richardson's eulogy in tribute to Beshara brought the mourners to their feet, applauding through their tears. "I'd never seen people cheer at a funeral," Beshara Jr. says, "but they did that day."

TWENTY-FOUR

ANOTHER COUNTRY

Panama convinced Nolan Richardson to coach its national team in 2005. Richardson was thrilled to lead a national team where his fluency in Spanish would be useful, even if it meant coaching in obscurity. Panama posted its best finish in twenty-six years, but the news was hardly mentioned in the States.

Richardson's next crack at leading a Spanish-speaking squad was a homecoming of sorts. He was named the Mexican National Coach in the spring of 2007. The Mexicans, who had hopes of an Olympic bid, set up training camp across the Rio Grande from El Paso in Juárez, Mexico.

Today's Texas-Mexico border is radically different from the one Nolan Richardson grew up on. Juárez is now home to somewhere around two million people and a vast sprawl of poverty. The bridges that connect El Paso to Juárez are teeming with window-washers, accordion players, and trinket salesmen hustling like walk-ons at varsity tryouts. NAFTA's "free trade" has damaged the already-troubled Mexican economy—half-built concrete structures sit uncompleted all over town. Post-9/11 security measures and a rash of violence have discouraged tourism, one of the few steady sources of cash. Hundreds of women have been murdered in Juárez during the last decade and the crimes remain unsolved. If there was ever a city that should have "Us Against the World" as its motto, it's Juárez.

The Mexican team accepted Richardson without hesitation, as though he had simply been stuck in traffic on the bridge for a few decades. Richardson's squad featured players with both NCAA credentials and Mexican passports.

The players who did *not* participate for Mexico, however, devastated the team before Richardson ever coached a game. Eduardo Najera had an impressive run during his nine years in the NBA, but Najera claimed he would not represent Mexico under the current leadership of the Olympic committee. Earl Watson, whose mother was born in Mexico, may have made a bigger impact for Richardson. Watson was a solid NBA point guard, and Richardson's scrambling-and-trapping style would have been the perfect showcase for him. While Watson never officially declined, he didn't join the team either.

Nolan Richardson remains surprisingly fit for a man in his late sixties. He has a trim waist, muscular shoulders, and he's thirty pounds lighter than when he prowled the sidelines at Arkansas. His hair has gone gray, and he's let it grow out, along with a mustache that has evolved into a goatee. He leans forward when he walks, the way a young Mike Tyson did when he answered the bell.

Richardson appeared to reverse the aging process at practice in Juárez, morphing into a younger man. He hopped out of the way to avoid a collision. Grabbing the ball, he demonstrated the correct way to jump-stop. He was quick to halt play and hammer home a point. Occasionally he laughed along with his team, sometimes even at mistakes, as if they all shared the same secret—it's great to be back on the basketball court.

The most impressive aspect of his coaching comeback was how Richardson ran his practice with his fluent border Spanish—and Spanglish. He switched back and forth as easily as he had traversed the border as a boy. It didn't take him long to recall the words for "trap" and "fast break."

His "Forty Minutes of Hell" depended on a brutally fast pace. During the first week of training, nearly every player was bent over, hands to knees, and gasping for breath. *"Qué pasa, hórale, muévanse!"* Richardson said, but they couldn't move at the pace he was demanding.

Even after surrendering a layup, the Mexicans were required to racehorse the ball back down the court. "If you want to take the other team's heart, *no hay nada como hechar una canasta enseguida de la de ellos*," Richardson says. Scoring quickly after his own teams' defensive breakdowns. Attacking the attacker. A Richardson trademark.

The Mexican National Team would take the floor the last day of May 2007.

It wasn't at Bud Walton Arena. Instead, it was a meaningless exhibition game in a dank Juárez gym. Meaningless with one exception— it was Mexico's first game with Nolan Richardson as coach. Ninety minutes before the match was to begin, the gym was jammed and the atmosphere was festive. Musicians, busking for pesos, set up outside the entrance. Inside, dozens of autograph-seekers and cell-phone-wielding photographers formed a queue, but the target wasn't the players.

A few minutes later, in a decaying locker room deep in the bowels of the building, Richardson gathered the red-white-and-green-clad players. "*Vamos a empezar* a half-court defense," Richardson said, but as the game progressed, he'd turn up the pressure with his "*Cuarenta minutos de infierno.*"

After a few brief reminders, the players rose to their feet.

"*Vámanos,*" Richardson hollered, and the team gathered around him in a tight circle, every hand reaching forward. "This is a new beginning for us," Richardson said, and the coach indeed looked new in his all-white attire. Clean, fresh, and young. Then he led the chant—"*Uno, dos, tres . . . México!*"

With the reborn Richardson guiding them, the undermanned Mexican team put on a valiant showing in Las Vegas in the summer of 2007, hoping to qualify for the Olympics for the first time in decades. They opened with an upset over bronze winner Puerto Rico, and it appeared as though Richardson might have to recall the Spanish expression for "Hollywood ending."

The Mexicans beat Venezuela later, but stumbled in games against Canada, Argentina, Uruguay, and Panama. In the end, Mexico did not win enough to qualify for the Beijing Olympics. Despite these disappointments, the Mexican team earned a measure of respect against the overstocked Americans—a monstrous team good enough for a Wheaties box, a team that had been winning by an average of 47 points. In his pregame talk, USA (and Duke) coach Mike Krzyzewski lectured his young squad on the historical importance of Nolan Richardson.

Mexico converted time and again off fast breaks, often after made baskets, and in the third quarter Mexico pulled within a dozen. Richardson's team would run 100 points on the Americans, the most the USA team allowed the entire tournament. That wasn't nearly enough. In the end Mexico lost by 27 points.

"**Nolan Richardson was one** of the best five coaches in the nation," Don Haskins said shortly after the Mexican team was eliminated. "It's terrible that he's not coaching in college. I don't even care about that black coach stuff," he added. "All I know is he was one hell of a coach."

Don Haskins died in September of 2008. The funeral services were held at the Methodist church near downtown El Paso, where Richardson had hustled parking cars on Sundays during his college days. Within a week of Haskins's death, Richardson's first wife, Helen, who had been on dialysis for years, passed away as well.

A few months later, Nolan Richardson was inducted into the College Basketball Hall of Fame in Kansas City. Other inductees included Charles Barkley, Danny Manning, and television commentators Dick Vitale and Billy Packer.

Richardson and his wife, Rosario, arrived early, and were quickly surrounded by a crew of Razorback supporters and ex-players. Just then, there seemed to be some sort of disturbance; the Arkansas group turned back toward the street, with big eyes.

Frank Broyles was getting out of an SUV.

Broyles looks more like a basketball man than a football coach. He's well over six feet, long-armed, and moves gracefully. For a man in his eighties, he looks fantastic. Broyles had no official responsibility to be at Richardson's Hall of Fame night; he had retired from the university nearly a year earlier.

Richardson helped Rose remove her red leather coat. She said something to him about the surprise guest. Richardson didn't seem too worried, though. "Let's just enjoy ourselves," he told her.

Several of Richardson's players were there. Ken Biley. Scotty Thurman. Corliss Williamson. Clint McDaniel. So was his attorney in the lawsuit, John Walker. Former assistant coach Wayne Stehlik and longtime basketball secretary Terri Mercer were there, as was his old boss from the junior college, Sid Simpson, and Arkansas's new AD, Jeff Long.

The press conference was jammed, with close to five hundred fans and media in attendance. Each inductee was given five minutes to speak.

Richardson is still a powerful public speaker and has an incredible sense of drama. His voice didn't crescendo with the power of a storefront preacher this time. Instead, he sounded reflective. Richardson mentioned Ol' Mama, Sid Simpson, and Don Haskins. His public talks often refer to his inevitable reckoning some day with Saint Peter at the Pearly Gates. This time he brought up somebody else.

"I noticed Frank Broyles is here," Richardson said, "and I appreciate him coming."

The Arkansas faithful in attendance saw it as a profound moment—Broyles took a small step; Richardson took one as well.

Scotty Thurman was surprised but not shocked. "They both know they could have handled it differently," he says. "People who have a lot of power play those battles. Deep down they don't really like each other, but they respect each other."

When all the inductees had spoken, master of ceremonies Reggie Minton invited anyone who wanted to interview or congratulate the inductees to come forward. Lines quickly formed in front of each honoree. Frank Broyles, who was sitting at the very back, got in line to shake hands with Nolan Richardson.

The next morning at breakfast, Richardson talked about his mixed emotions after both receiving a great honor and seeing Broyles. Richardson's tone had mellowed again. He admitted that he had noticed Broyles waiting patiently at the back of the line and said that Broyles was complimentary and congratulatory when he finally got his turn.

In February 2009, the school finally honored the 1994 NCAA title team—and coach. It marked the fifteenth anniversary of their championship and would be Richardson's first time on campus since he was fired. The ten-year anniversary had come and gone without mention because of the ongoing lawsuit. Frank Broyles had retired a year earlier and been replaced by Jeff Long, who seemed genuinely interested in bringing Richardson back into the Razorback family.

Northwest Arkansas had been rocked earlier in the month by vicious ice storms. Trees were torn out at their roots, buildings damaged, and power lines were dead all over the Ozarks. The lack of power had hit Madison County, just south of Fayetteville, especially hard. With no phone service or electricity functioning in this mountainous part of the state, a hundred workers were sent from Pennsylvania to assist the local electric cooperative in restoring power. Nearly a third of the conscripted workers from the North were African-American.

Madison County is virtually all-white, and the ice storm exposed an archaic mindset that still lives on in Arkansas, only minutes from the state's university.

The Pennsylvania workers were harassed by gangs of white men driving around them, hollering racial epithets, waving Confederate flags and guns. The imported workers figured they'd better call the sheriff's office—not in Madison County, though. They phoned nearby Washington County instead.

Madison County was in the national news after Barack Obama was elected in November, as well. In Huntsville, the day after the election, the owners of the Faubus Motel removed the Stars and Stripes and raised the Confederate flag. American voters, the owners claimed, had turned their backs on the principles of our founding fathers. The motel was at one time owned by the former governor but no longer had any connection to the Faubus family.

Even after the phone and power lines had been repaired, the

mangled trees and busted branches remained all over northwest Arkansas.

The Razorback basketball team had won just a single SEC game going into this final home contest. It was their worst season since joining the SEC.

Ken Biley would have walked to the reunion from Kansas City, where he works for H&R Block. "I've had all kinds of excitement in my life," says the surprise starter of the 1994 champs. "I've witnessed my wife giving birth to our kids. But my starting in that championship game, that honor did more for me than anyone could imagine."

Today, Biley still needs a few more classes for his college diploma. He's continued to watch sports in the fifteen years since Arkansas won it all, especially championship games, looking for a story that would mirror his own. He has uncovered nothing even close. "This wasn't a fourth down gamble in football," Biley says. "This was the NCAA championship on national TV. What would the critics say about Nolan if we had lost the game?"

The reunion weekend began with a Richardson staple—the team, along with wives, family, and friends, were invited to his home for a colossal barbecue. The players went out on the town afterward, but managed to be up the next day by nine a.m. for another typical Richardson event, a free basketball clinic at the Yvonne Richardson Community Center. The center, situated in Fayetteville's tiny traditional black neighborhood south of downtown, was opened in Yvonne's honor a few years after her death.

The players from the 1994 team were the guest coaches, but for the first few minutes of the clinic, they sloughed about and yawned, arms crossed and shirts untucked. Former Razorback assistant Wayne Stehlik tried to bring the kids and coaches to life with a warm-up drill, a simple relay race for the youngsters. Even that couldn't motivate the former NCAA champs, who were no longer subject to curfews to ensure a good night's sleep.

When the relay was just a minute old, Richardson appeared at the entrance. The parents noticed, then some of the campers—none of whom were born yet when Richardson led the Razorbacks to the title. A couple of his former players noticed, too.

Corliss Williamson leaped into a basketball stance. "Hey, I want to win this!" he shouted to his team, pacing up and down his line, bending at the waist to attempt a chest bump with one kid.

Clint McDaniel took Williamson's cue and began pushing his young campers, too. "We're not going to let them beat us!" McDaniel said. Then Ken Biley and the rest of the Razorbacks jumped in the kids' faces, high-fiving, fist-bumping, and taunting the nearest competitors. When it was over, the winning line jumped up and down and exchanged hugs, as though they were champions as well. The clinic had undergone an astonishing transformation. Richardson hadn't said a word.

College basketball is a business—that's a refrain repeated any time a coach is fired. If it is indeed true, then firing Nolan Richardson was a bad business decision. The Razorbacks have never been the same. Seven years after Richardson's removal, it's nearly impossible to conclude that Broyles's judgment was correct, since the Razorbacks have never come close to approaching his success.

With the current Arkansas team struggling, Nolan nostalgia gripped the state, and the reunion of the 1994 champs allowed Razorback fans a brief glimpse of their past glory—and an opportunity to reconsider what had transpired with their iconic coach.

"It was a sad day for the University of Arkansas," former chancellor John White says, in retrospect. "Nolan Richardson is just an absolute icon. He's not only an asset for the University of Arkansas, he's an asset for this nation. I just hated that it came to that kind of conclusion." White wasn't alone in his sentiments, and the weekend festivities would go a long way toward building trust between Richardson and the school.

There's also the "What if?" factor. Richardson's infamous press conference in 2002 began with the sports information director reading an encouraging letter from the parents of a recruit. The recruit was Andre Iguodala, who never enrolled at Arkansas because of Richardson's removal. Iguodala went to Arizona instead, then was the ninth pick in the NBA draft, made the All-Rookie team, and became an NBA All-Star. Joe Johnson was the only player of Richardson's ever to rise to that status in the NBA. Razorback fans could only speculate how good they might have been with Richardson coaching Iguodala.

The reunion banquet had the glitz and glamour of the Grammy Awards. The posh hall was packed with a crowd of nearly a thousand people who'd paid a hundred dollars each. Full-size color photos decorated the walls. Souvenirs from the title run were being hawked at the door. If Arkansas had at one time been viewed as backward, you wouldn't have known it this night. The expenditures would have made a Wall Street CEO blush.

Each player was given a minute to speak. Richardson was last, and praised some of the most obscure players effusively. Just before he was finished, he said, "I'm the only coach in America who was fired and still stayed in town." It was his way of saying both that he still loved Arkansas and that his firing was unjust.

One of the first things anyone entering Bud Walton Arena sees in the main lobby is a seven-foot cutout of Nolan Richardson, in a trophy case with a plaque that reads, "Arguably the most popular coach in any sport in Razorback history."

Two entire trophy cases commemorate "The Nolan Richardson Era." Another one is devoted to the 1994 NCAA title team. Just to the side is a miniature theater, where you can push a button and learn about the Razorbacks. Above the entrance, a sign proclaims: THE NOLAN RICHARDSON THEATER. On the side is a plaque dedicating the theater to Yvonne Richardson. All of these displays were built before Richardson was dumped in 2002, and all of them have remained, even through the contentious lawsuit.

Ralph Brewster, Richardson's first great player from Bowie, has little remorse about his own career. Brewster's impulse—to go along with what was best for his coach, instead of what might have been best for himself—is an indicator of the charisma of his coach, he says. Today he is proud of his role in Richardson's life. "Nolan will stand the test of history," Brewster says. "A lot of changes in the view of Nolan are going to come with time. He is an original who spoke the truth and stood on righteousness."

The leading scorer in Arkansas history, Todd Day, concurs about the test of time. "Nolan Richardson is the greatest African-American coach in history," he said days before Richardson came back to campus.

The 2009 SEC season had been a disaster for second-year coach John Pelphrey. The only league game Arkansas won leading up to the reunion was the day after Richardson had privately addressed Pelphrey's Razorbacks.

The Georgia game was a return to the best days and a chance for the fans to remember. Richardson addressed the crowd of 19,724 at halftime, and their reaction was deafening. "If a Phantom fighter jet had flown through Bud Walton [Arena] right then," Wally Hall wrote, "it would not have been seen or heard." There was still plenty of history that Richardson could invoke that made Razorback fans happy.

The overflowing emotion found its way into the current team. Arkansas won, 89-67, a rare win for the 2009 team that would finish 2-14 in the SEC—dead-last place.

TWENTY-FIVE

GO TELL IT ON THE MOUNTAIN

Nolan Richardson began his career determined to be different from his college coach. Nobody could have predicted all the ways he'd wind up like Don Haskins.

Haskins and Richardson won historically important NCAA championships, and it's difficult to invoke the name of either man without an ensuing discussion of race. Both were attacked for their graduation rates of black players on those title teams. In the end, both men did better in this regard than originally perceived.

Richardson even drove a pickup truck, although he surely had his choice of any car in town. The Razorbacks innocently began referring to Richardson as "The Bear" in the 1990s.

Haskins remained at UTEP for nearly forty years and may have been the last of that breed of coach. Richardson never applied for another job while coaching the Razorbacks.

"Nolan fell in love with Arkansas," longtime athletics trainer

Dave England says. "I know it hurt him those times when it seemed like Arkansas didn't love him back."

Richardson has done more than win championships to earn that love. He has been involved in over thirty charities during his time in Fayetteville. Sometimes Richardson used his name in hosting fund-raisers; sometimes he put up his own money. His annual golf tournament in El Paso honors his daughter while raising thousands of dollars for leukemia research. After Yvonne's death, his empathetic antenna for the downtrodden became even more sensitive; he'd hand out large sums of cash like Halloween candy if sick children were involved. Sid Simpson says, "That's the direction Nolan seems to be going. He'd pick up a load of crippled kids and take them to a game, but he'd never tell anyone." Shortly after Yvonne died, Richardson learned there was a child in Paragould, Arkansas, who had cancer. "He wrote out a check for fifteen thousand, and had it delivered to the family," Simpson says.

Yet another aspect of Richardson's life that mirrors Don Haskins is his selective memory. Even as detailed evidence of his humanitarian giving mounted, he claimed to have no recollection of specific stories of generosity. He either has terrible recall, is too humble, or he's helped so many people he really has lost track.

Arkansas was the punch line of jokes and a source of national embarrassment at one time. Today, despite the recent raising of the Confederate flag and intimidation of the black repairmen after the ice storm, race relations are improved.

Elizabeth Jacoway, the author of two books about race and Arkansas, was born there in the 1940s. "My sense is that Arkansas has changed dramatically," Jacoway says. "People who lived through the Civil Rights movement understand the very slow nature in which change can come about."

Are Americans and Arkansans better off being reminded of that great distance and remembering that slow nature of change? Does discussing the racist history of the nation help us move forward or keep us stuck in the past? Does Richardson's outspokenness open wounds or help close them?

Anyone taking a close look at Nolan Richardson's life should understand how both memory and his sense of justice have haunted him. The austere woman who raised Richardson had an archive of stories about her own parents' enslavement. The poorest Mexican-Americans in segregated Texas could sit at lunch counters, splash in swimming pools, and lean back in air-conditioned movie theaters. He could not.

Standing toe-to-toe with American racism became unavoidable for Richardson.

By simply asking for a Coke, he had an inadvertent hand in ending Jim Crow laws in El Paso. At the time he began his career, there was not a single black man coaching major college basketball. Powerful people thought of him as the "nigger coach" upon his arrival in Snyder and Tulsa. In Arkansas he toiled at a campus where police dogs bared their teeth at black fraternity brothers and sisters. The most powerful man at the school spent a decade as the proud front man of segregation in Arkansas athletics, and later tried to prod a table full of journalists into using the word "nigger" in print. Being the first black at every outpost rubbed Richardson raw, especially in Arkansas, a state where sundown towns thrived, George Wallace triumphed, and, even into the new millennium, the state university board of trustees felt that "nigger jokes" were funny.

His refusal to keep quiet makes a lot more sense in that context; the long arc of his life puts that fateful 2002 press conference in perspective.

Richardson understood that Broyles wanted to fire him for years. Today, if the entire text of that 2002 news media gathering is read aloud, a few things become apparent. One, it's clear that Richardson was mostly talking to and about Frank Broyles—although he allowed that he has to "answer to" Broyles and the UA administration. Knowing Broyles preferred that he fail in order to facilitate his firing became an unbearable strain. Also apparent is that Richardson, under the extreme pressure of coaching a fledgling college basketball team, reverted to his own history and memory by quoting Ol' Mama.

After winning the NCAA title in 1994, Richardson's cause and his passion changed, and he obsessed about equality for black coaches, himself included. He continued to talk about race because racism was not over. In the world of college sports, one has only to count the number of black athletics directors and head football coaches to deduce that something is still wrong. Richardson's error was to think that trotting the elephant of racism out in front of a room full of white reporters and television crews during a mediocre season was a good idea.

Did he always comport himself in the best manner for his cause during the five decades that he coached? Of course not. But if the world was going to change, somebody had to follow Ol' Mama's advice. Nolan Richardson kicked down the damn door.

Richardson's ranch is a ten-minute drive west of Fayetteville, among the rolling hills that rest on the edge of northwest Arkansas. The town blends first into suburbs, then to farms. Just before the road turns to gravel, the land unfolds into a scenic panorama, calm and peaceful in every direction. At the end of the road there is an iron gate that reads RICHARDSON RANCH. The house is simple, understated, and rustic. It's much more a cabin than a castle.

The kitchen is also the dining room and the epicenter of all activity at the Richardson ranch. On any given weekend, and not just championship team reunions, their home is filled with ex-players, family, neighbors, and friends. His wife, Rosario, will be cooking; maybe green chile caldillo. Richardson will man the taco station expertly, folding in diced tomatoes and shredded cheese.

And there are kids, kids everywhere. School groups and church groups. Nieces and nephews and grandkids. And especially the children of former players.

One recent Fourth of July weekend, the five kids there just happened to be young girls, between two and ten years of age. The ex-Razorbacks at the ranch that holiday weren't very good players or even on great teams. That didn't matter to Richardson, who waited on them as if they were All-Americans.

While the adults were still feasting, the girls invented a game. They would run in a loop about the size of the center-jump circle. Then the lead one, the oldest, would turn a dramatic dance move into a split or somersault. The younger girls would imitate the first, then they'd all fall down, dissolving in laughter. Occasionally, they'd return to the table to trade bites and share bowls.

A hero of the Irish Civil Rights movement once said, "Our revenge will be the laughter of our children." This is the philosophy of the Richardson ranch, where the sound of young kids' laughing resonates.

Rose Richardson moved to the couch to watch the dance routine digress into silliness. Nothing makes the Richardsons happier than having children around, and during the girls' chaotic tumbles a palpable happiness descended on everyone. Rose was having as much fun as they were, although she courteously declined to try the cartwheels and flips.

When the dishes were done, Richardson roared, "Who wants to see the animals?" and the girls erupted into pandemonium. They formed a line behind Richardson, who led them outside.

Richardson roams his ranch these days with his giant Great Dane, Billy, at his hip. One of the girls walked up to Billy and reached to scratch his belly. The barn was nearby, but most of the horses were out in the pasture. So were the llamas. The youngest girl clung to Richardson's leg, and he hoisted her up. Then the coach bellowed, and his horses came running. She hugged his neck and hooted with joy.

The Horse Whisperer has nothing on Nolan Richardson. His thoroughbreds, Tennessee walkers, and quarter horses respond to anything he shouts. The kids were enthralled, shadowing Richardson as he directed the animals. Across the rolling hills, goats, lambs, and some pot-bellied pigs lazed about.

The animals have been a big part of Nolan and Rose Richardson's life since losing Yvonne in 1987. "Some people need someone or something to depend on them and she is one of those people," Richardson told the *Tulsa World* about his wife, but he could have been talking about himself as well.

A wide wooden porch surrounds most of the house and affords the best view. As sunset approaches, the ranch becomes bathed in a light that a religious person might call heavenly. Around the "U" of the porch on the north side of the house is a garden about the size of half a basketball court. The garden is filled with statues of kids jumping in puddles, running, skipping rope. Laughing. It's as if the Richardsons have tried to distill and freeze childhood—and memory—to protect and preserve it after losing Yvonne.

Something became clear that holiday weekend. Richardson *did* love Arkansas too much. He should have packed his boxes and loaded up the moving vans soon after carving his place in history in 1994. But even outsiders eventually need a place to rest, a home. Something else became clear, too. Nobody could remind people of where they came from, cross borders, or inspire players to believe in a cause like Nolan Richardson. Those were his gifts; his career a type of bridge.

Richardson has let his Afro grow gray and long, and he really does look like a historical figure—like Frederick Douglass with a goatee. Maybe that's fitting. Richardson attended a school named after the former slave who kept reminding America of its sins.

John McLendon never got the shot he'd earned at a big university. Neither did countless other black coaches. Other coaches of color of his era had terrific teams, but what distinguishes Nolan Richardson is the nature of his trailblazing career, as the first black coach to go into the old Confederacy—and the embers of racism—and have astonishing success. Richardson—outspoken, passionate, and righteous—is the most important African-American coach America has known.

Despite his garden full of statues of children at play, he could not freeze time. Memory, though. Memory endures, because Nolan Richardson, as relentless as forty minutes of hell's full-court pressure, won't let us forget. He has begun to fulfill his former chancellor's request to be happy, even if he's still an outsider, on the wrong side of the fence at the university where he won the championship. The basketball court where he finally returned belongs to him—although you won't find his name on it. Regardless, Richardson's shadow and history remind, admonish, and exhort Arkansas.

ACKNOWLEDGMENTS

Robert Boswell and Antonya Nelson have provided advice, books, friendship, beer, gourmet meals, and parenting tips for the last fourteen years. They are the best friends a writer could hope for.

Barry Pearce is a loyal and unselfish friend, as well as a fine writer.

Several people gave me great suggestions on the manuscript: Carol Capitani, Tom Spieczny, Josh Wheeler, Barry Pearce, Jeff Vance, Connie Voisine, Robert Boswell, Sheila Black, Tracy Sherrod, and Candice Morrow.

Thanks to: Geoffery Stark at University of Arkansas Special Collection.

Thanks to American sports heroes David Meggyesy, Dave Zirin, Doug Harris, Michael James, Steve and Tracey Yellen, and Ben Jobe.

Thanks also to John Conroy, Dennis Daily, Henry Thomas, Ken Olsen, Garrett Hongo, Austin Hoover, Keith French, Mike Thomas, and Modzel "Bud" Greer.

For help steering me around the UA campus, thanks to: Jim Harris, Donita Ritchie, Terri Mercer, Findlay Edwards, Robbie Edwards, and Wayne Stehlik.

Thanks also to Rosie Dixon and Frank Fellone at the *Democrat-*

Gazette, Glen Guthrie, John Podesta, David Shields, Dagoberto Gilb, Jennifer Grotz, Sharon Ord-Warner, Michael Collier, and Chris Engskov.

Big thanks to New Mexico State's Lou Henson, Duncan Hayse, Tama Garski, Chris Burnham, Harriet Linkin, Monica Torres, Pam Jansma, Bill Conroy, and Dr. Waded Cruzado.

Interviews were conducted with the following people: Ballard Shapleigh, Jimmie Tramel, Darren Ivy, Marc Spears, Wally Hall, Bob Holt, Chip Souza, David Hargiss, Steve Narisi, Joe Neal, Charles Robinson, Carrol Williams, Bob Carver, Fred Vorsanger, Dave England, Dr. John White, Rudy Keeling, Dick Versace, Tony Barone, Steve Green, Kelly Green, Pat Foster, Lanny Van Eman, Sid Simpson, Bob O'Day, Kenny John, Alvis Glidewell, Manny Placillas, Dwight Williams, Andy Stoglin, Mike Anderson, Earnest Starks, Phillip Trapp, Lyell Thompson, Otto "Bud" Zinke, Reggie Minton, Judge Thomas Spieczny, Don Haskins, Eddie Mullens, Lou Henson, Jim Haney, Almer Lee, Scotty Thurman, Alex Dillard, Clint McDaniel, Pat Bradley, Ben Daggett, Jeremy Rose, Ralph Brewster, Melvin Patridge, Tim Hardaway, Larry Gipson, Ed Beshara Jr., Alan Mantooth, Norris Stevenson, Charles Prigmore, John Phillips, Frankie Allen, Thomas Trotter, Jay Jennings, John Chaney, Stan Heath, Charles Martin, Richard Pennington, Lonnie Williams, Wendell Griffen, Darrell Brown, Sheryl Walters, Shelton Walters, Danny Walters, Irv Cross, Milton Katz, Bert Williams, Madalyn Richardson, Rosario Richardson, and Nolan Richardson.

Nearly a dozen people were interviewed who insisted that their names not appear. Thanks to them, as well.

Frank Broyles turned down repeated requests to be interviewed.

Thanks to the *Democrat-Gazette* for allowing me access to their archives.

Lonnie Williams gave me sage advice. Both Wendell Griffen and Darrell Brown not only made themselves constantly available, but were inspiring. Just as inspiring was the Walters family, whose stories of Bob Walters still resonate. Meeting Bert Williams was an honor.

The research and suggestions of Charles Martin, Richard Pennington, and Milton Katz were invaluable. All three have authored important works on race and college sports. Richard Lapchick's research was also helpful.

Ben Osborne at *SLAM* magazine first published my piece on Nolan Richardson, and his encouragement was vital. Thanks also to Khalid Salaam and Susan Price at *SLAM*.

Special thanks to Christina Morgan, who championed this project initially.

Bobbito Garcia and Jesse Washington at *Bounce* magazine gave me encouragement, as did Alexander Wolff of *Sports Illustrated*. Dan McGrath and Barry Temkin of the *Chicago Tribune* were also supportive.

Thanks to Don Johnson, Scott Peterson, and everyone in the Sports Literature Association.

Glory Road, Dan Wetzel's book about the 1966 Texas Western team and Don Haskins, was terrific help. So was Frank Fitzpatrick's book *The Walls Came Tumbling Down*. Barry Jacob's book *Across the Line: Profiles in Basketball Courage* was a wonderful resource.

The quote "Our revenge will be the laughter of our children" is from the Irish Republican hero Bobby Sands.

UTEP, Tulsa University, Western Texas College, Eastern Arizona Junior College, Bowie High School, the *Democrat-Gazette*, and the University of Arkansas all provided information, photos, or media guides.

Eric Howerton at Now Creative Inc. and *Hawgs Illustrated* provided great help with photos.

Big thanks to Nolan Richardson and his family. Nolan was always available and willing to talk.

What I miss most about college basketball is the sense of optimism sometimes lacking in the book business. My amazing agent, Andrew Blauner, is an exception, and he has been a fantastic help. Thanks, Bird!

Thanks to editor extraordinaire Dawn Davis, Maya Ziv, Van Luu, and everyone at HarperCollins and Amistad.

Finally, thanks to my incredible wife, Connie Voisine, and to our daughter, Alma Bradburd, for their love and patience.

WHO'S WHO IN
NOLAN RICHARDSON'S STORY

Mike Anderson: Longtime assistant to Richardson, he also played point guard for him at Tulsa. Now the coach at University of Missouri.

Jim "Bad News" Barnes: Born in Arkansas, Barnes was probably the best player in Texas Western (later UTEP) history. Richardson helped recruit him to TWC.

Ed Beshara: Tulsa clothier and close friend of Richardson. Beshara died in 2007.

Ken Biley: Benchwarmer; a surprise starter in the NCAA title game of 1994.

Jim Bowden: Former UTEP director of athletics who encouraged Richardson to apply at Tulsa University.

Pat Bradley: Best three-point shooter in Arkansas history.

Ralph Brewster: Richardson's best player at Bowie High School in El Paso. Went to Texas Tech in exchange for their recommendation of Richardson for a junior college job.

Charlie Brown: First black player at Texas Western College (later UTEP).

Darrell Brown: First black football player to attempt to play for Frank

Broyles's segregated teams at the University of Arkansas in the mid-1960s.

Frank Broyles: Icon of Arkansas sports; his association with UA as football coach and director of athletics lasted fifty years. He hired and fired Richardson.

James Cash: First black basketball player in the Southwest Conference at TCU.

John Chaney: Outspoken African-American basketball coach at Temple.

Bill Clark: University of Arkansas Board of Trustees member who admitted using the word "nigger" in conversation and jokes.

Bill Connors: Iconic Tulsa sportswriter who covered Richardson's time at Tulsa.

Rosario "Rose" Davila: Richardson's longtime wife; mother of the late Yvonne Richardson.

Harold Davis: Richardson's coach for his first season at Texas Western College.

Todd Day: Leading scorer in Arkansas history, helped lead team to their first Final Four.

Alex Dillard: Hot-shooting sub who scored in bunches for Richardson's 1994 team.

Evans Dunne: Wealthy Tulsa booster who was originally opposed to hiring Richardson.

Rob Evans: Texas Tech assistant in the 1970s and 1980s, who recruited Ralph Brewster in 1977. Later the head coach at Mississippi; now an assistant at Arkansas.

Orval Faubus: Governor of Arkansas during the Little Rock Central crisis.

Hayden Fry: Former Arkansas assistant coach under Frank Broyles, then head coach at SMU who brought the first black player (Jerry LeVias) to the Southwest Conference.

Clarence "Big House" Gaines: Highly successful coach at historically black Winston-Salem State.

Rocky Galarza: El Paso icon and Bowie High School star whose three-sport heroics predated Richardson's by a decade.

Gary George: University of Arkansas Board of Trustees member who admitted using the word "nigger" in conversation and jokes.

Alvis Glidewell: Longtime El Paso high school basketball coach after whom Richardson modeled his first pressure defenses.

Judge Wendell Griffen: University of Arkansas double graduate, civil rights and justice advocate, friend of Richardson.

Wally Hall: Longtime sportswriter for the Arkansas *Democrat-Gazette*.

Jim Haney: Head of the National Association of Basketball Coaches (NABC); his articles on the lack of black administrators enlightened and infuriated Richardson.

Tim Hardaway: Star guard at UTEP for Don Haskins in the 1980s; his high school coach, Bob Walters, was from Arkansas.

David Hargiss: Former Arkansas football player in the mid-1960s who defended and befriended black walk-on Darrell Brown.

Don Haskins: Richardson's college coach, he was the first man to start five blacks and win an NCAA basketball title in 1966.

Stan Heath: African-American coach who replaced Richardson at Arkansas in 2002; now at the University of South Florida.

Orville Henry: Iconic Arkansas sportswriter and close friend of Richardson.

Nemo Herrera: Longtime Bowie High School coach who mentored Richardson.

Darren Ivy: Penned most of the articles in *Untold Stories*, the collection of articles about black athletes in Arkansas during the time of segregation.

Ben Jobe: Politically conscious college coach who led historically black Southern University to the NCAA tournament.

Kenny John: Richardson's workout partner at Fort Bliss, played at UTEP, outstanding high school coach in El Paso.

Jimmy King: Tulsa basketball coach whose firing opened the way for Richardson.

Almer Lee: First black basketball player to letter at Arkansas.

Jerry LeVias: First black football star in the Southwest Conference, recruited by Hayden Fry, former assistant to Frank Broyles.

Charles Martin: UTEP professor; one of America's top scholars on the integration of college sports.

Wilson Matthews: Former Little Rock Central football coach; joined Frank Broyles's first staff at Arkansas.

Lee Mayberry: Star guard on Richardson's first Final Four team at Arkansas.

Terri Mercer: Longtime Arkansas basketball secretary.

Clint McDaniel: Defensive star of Richardson's NCAA champs in 1994.

John McLendon: Legendary black coach; won three consecutive national titles at Tennessee State; the godfather of black coaches and fast break basketball.

Oliver Miller: Center on Richardson's first Final Four team at Arkansas.

Reggie Minton: Groundbreaking black basketball coach at Air Force; now codirects the NABC.

Gordon Morgan: First black professor at University of Arkansas.

Steve Narisi: Arkansas native and TV journalist who has studied the desegregation of the Southwest Conference.

Joe Neal: Leader of progressive movements in Arkansas.

Melvin Patridge: Bowie High School basketball star on Richardson's final teams there.

Paul Pressey: Richardson's best player at Tulsa; went on to a long NBA career.

Helen Richardson: Richardson's high school sweetheart and first wife; mother of Madalyn, Notes, and Bradley.

Jon Richardson: First black scholarship football player at Arkansas, no relation to Nolan.

Madalyn Richardson: Richardson's first child.

Nolan "Notes" Richardson III: Richardson's son and former assistant coach.

Yvonne Richardson: Richardson's daughter; died of leukemia in 1987.

Will Robinson: the first black coach in Division I at Illinois State.

Sid Simpson: Richardson's athletics director at Western Texas College in Snyder.

Andy Stoglin: Teammate of Richardson at UTEP, assistant at Tulsa and Arkansas, later the head coach at Jackson State.

Eddie Sutton: Arkansas coach whose departure opened the door for Richardson in 1985.

John Thompson: First black coach to win NCAA title in Division I, at Georgetown.

Lyell Thompson: Professor at Arkansas for decades who pushed for desegregation.

Scotty Thurman: He made the decisive "3" to beat Duke for NCAA title in 1994.

Phillip Trapp: Longtime UA psychology professor who pushed Frank Broyles to desegregate.

Ken Trickey: Oral Roberts University coach in the 1970s whose fast-breaking teams had great success.

Lanny Van Eman: Arkansas basketball coach in the early 1970s, before Eddie Sutton.

Fred Vorsanger: Former Fayetteville mayor and manager of Bud Walton Arena at UA.

Duddy Waller: Arkansas basketball coach who signed the first black players at Arkansas in the late 1960s.

Bob Walters: Scored ninety-six touchdowns in high school in Arkansas but was ignored by the segregated teams of the South. Later was Tim Hardaway's high school basketball coach.

Bert Williams: Former El Paso city alderman (later mayor) who wrote the anti–Jim Crow legislation in El Paso after being denied service at a restaurant with Richardson.

Carrol Williams: Head of University of Arkansas black alumni group.

Dwight Williams: Key guard on Richardson's first junior college teams; transferred to Texas Tech.

Lonnie Williams: Longtime Arkansas administrator; now at Arkansas State.

Corliss Williamson: Center on Richardson's 1994 champs.

Judge William Wilson: Presiding judge in Richardson's court case.

Otto "Bud" Zinke: Senate Council member at UA, antiwar activist, quiet leader of desegregation movements on campus.

BIBLIOGRAPHY

Allen, James, Jon Lewis, Leon Litwack, and Hilton Als. *Without Sanctuary: Lynching Photographs in America*. New York: Twin Palms Publishers, 2000.

Brodie, Ralph, and Marvin Schwartz. *Central in Our Lives: Voices from Little Rock Central High School, 1957–1959*. Little Rock: The Butler Center for Arkansas Studies, 2007.

Broyles, J. Frank. *Hog Wild: The Autobiography of Frank Broyles*. Memphis: Memphis State University Press, 1979.

Dailey Jr., Maceo and Kristine Navarro, eds. *Wherever My People Chance to Dwell: Oral Interviews with African-American Women of El Paso*. Inprint Edition, 2000.

Dowling, William. *Confessions of a Spoilsport*. Harrisburg: Penn State University Press, 2007.

Edwards, Harry. *The Revolt of the Black Athlete*. New York: Free Press, 1969.

Ellsworth, Scott. *Death in a Promised Land: The Tulsa Race Riots of 1921*. Baton Rouge: LSU Press, 1992.

Encyclopedia of Arkansas History and Culture, encyclopediaofarkansas.net.

Fitzpatrick, Frank. *The Walls Came Tumbling Down*. Lincoln: University of Nebraska Press, 2000.

Frei, Terry. *Horns, Hogs, and Nixon Coming*. New York: Simon & Schuster, 2002.

Graves, John William. *Town and Country: Race Relations in an Urban Rural Context, Arkansas, 1865–1905*. Fayetteville: University of Arkansas Press, 1990.

Halberstam, David. *The Fifties*. New York: Villard Books, 1993.

Ivy, Darren. *Untold Stories: Black Sports Heroes Before Integration*. Little Rock: Wehco Publishers, 2002.

Jacobs, Barry. *Across the Line: Profiles in Basketball Courage*. Guilford, CT: Lyons Press, 2007.

Jacoway, Elizabeth. *Turn Away Thy Son*. Fayetteville: University of Arkansas Press, 2008.

Jacoway, Elizabeth, and C. Fred Williams. *Understanding the Little Rock Crisis*. Fayetteville: University of Arkansas Press, 1999.

Jennings, Jay. *Carrying the Rock*. Emmaus, PA: Rodale Press, 2010.

Katz, Milton. *Breaking Through: John B. McLendon, Basketball Legend and Civil Rights Pioneer*. Fayetteville: University of Arkansas Press, 2007.

Kenan, Randall. *The Fire This Time*. New York: Melville House, 2007.

Kriegel, Mark. *Pistol: The Life of Pete Maravich*. New York: Free Press, 2008.

Madigan, Tim. *The Burning: Massacre, Destruction, and the Tulsa Race Riot of 1921*. New York: St. Martin's Griffin, 2003.

Maraniss, David. *Clemente: The Passion and Grace of Baseball's Last Hero*. New York: Simon & Schuster, 2007.

Meggyesy, David. *Out of Their League*. Lincoln: University of Nebraska Press, 2006.

Morgan, Gordon. "The Firing of Nolan Richardson." Unpublished.

Morgan, Gordon, and Izola Preston. *The Edge of Campus: A Journal of the Black Experience at the University of Arkansas*. Fayetteville: University of Arkansas Press, 1990.

Onoda, Hiroo. *No Surrender: My Thirty-Year War*. Annapolis: U.S. Naval Institute Press, 1999.

Pennington, Richard. *Breaking the Ice: The Racial Integration of Southwest Conference Football*. Jefferson, NC: McFarland Publishers, 1987.

Powers, Elia. "Mulling Ways to Add Minority Coaches." Inside Higher Education, March 1, 2007.

Reed, Roy. *Faubus: The Life and Times of an American Prodigal.* Fayetteville: University of Arkansas Press, 1997.

Remnick, David. *King of the World: Muhammad Ali and the Rise of an American Hero.* New York: Vintage, 1999.

Rhoden, William. *Forty Million Dollar Slaves: The Rise, Fall, and Redemption of the Black Athlete.* New York: Three Rivers Press, 2007.

_____. "Sports of the Times; For Black Coaches, New Direction Needed." New York Times, February 19, 1995.

Riffel, Brent. "The Body Count: Lynching in Arkansas." Historymatters. gmu.edu.

Romo, David. *Ringside Seat to a Revolution.* El Paso: Cinco Puntos Press, 2005.

Roy, Elizabeth. *Bitters in the Honey: Tales of Hope and Disappointment Across Divides of Race and Time.* Fayetteville: University of Arkansas Press, 1999.

Shields, David. *Black Planet: Facing Race During an NBA Season.* Lincoln, NE: Bison Books, 2006.

Wetzel, Dan, with Don Haskins. *Glory Road.* New York: Hyperion, 2005.

Zirin, David. *What's My Name, Fool? Sports and Resistance in the United States.* Chicago: Haymarket Books, 2005.

_____. *Welcome to the Terrordome: The Pain, Politics, and Promise of Sports.* Chicago: Haymarket Books, 2007.

_____. *A People's History of Sports in the United States.* New York: New Press, 2008.

FILM, MEDIA, AND PERIODICALS

Black Magic, directed by Don Klores, ESPN Films, 2008.

UTEP, University of Arkansas, and Tulsa University all provided media guides for basketball and football.

The following magazines and newspapers were helpful: *Arkansas Times, Democrat-Gazette, Morning News, Chronicle of Higher Education, Sporting News, Sports Illustrated, USA Today.*

ABOUT THE AUTHOR

Rus Bradburd is the author of the acclaimed *Paddy on the Hardwood: A Journey in Irish Hoops*. A college basketball coach for fourteen seasons, he teaches writing classes at New Mexico State University and lives in Las Cruces, New Mexico, with his wife, the poet Connie Voisine, and their daughter. Visit rusbradburd.com.